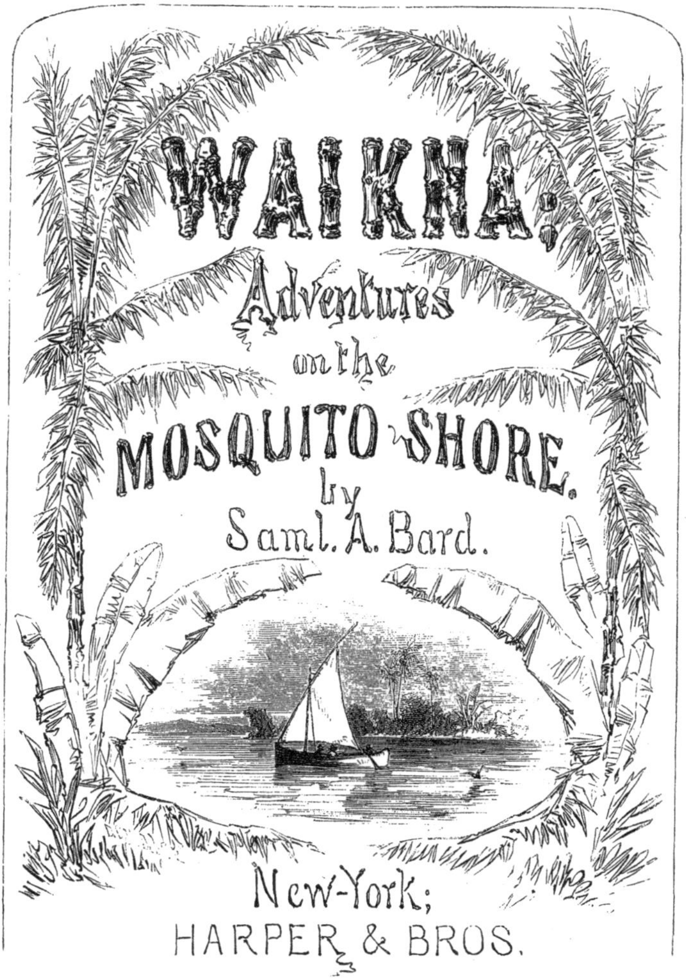

WAIKNA;

Adventures on the MOSQUITO SHORE.

by
Saml. A. Bard.

New-York;
HARPER & BROS.

WAIKNA;

OR,

ADVENTURES

ON THE

MOSQUITO SHORE.

BY SAMUEL A. BARD.

"Whatever sweets salute the northern sky,
With vernal lives, that blossom but to die;
These here disporting, own the kindred soil,
Nor ask luxuriance from the planter's toil;
While sea-born gales their gelid wings expand,
To winnow fragrance round the smiling land."
GOLDSMITH.

WITH SIXTY ILLUSTRATIONS.

NEW YORK:
HARPER & BROTHERS,
329 & 331 PEARL STREET.
1855.

PREFACE.

SCENE.—*A lonely shore.*

Enter YANKEE *and* MOSQUITO MAN.

Well, my dark friend, who are you?

"*Waikna!*" A man!

And what is your nation?

"*Waikna!*" A nation of men!

Pretty good for you, my dark friend! There was once a great nation—a few old bricks are about all that remains of it now—whose people were proud to call themselves —— but then what do you know about the Romans?

"Him good for drink—him grog?"

Bah! No!

"Den no good! bah, too!"

Exeunt ambo.

Now such a dialogue took place, or might have taken place, on the Mosquito Shore. For all artistic purposes it did take place ; and, as my book is chiefly devoted to the Mosquito man and his country, it shall be called WAIKNA—a word that, in the Mosquito tongue, means simply MAN, but which is proudly claimed as the generic designation of the people of the entire coast.

CONTENTS.

CHAPTER I.

CHAPTER II.

CHAPTER III.

CHAPTER IV.

CHAPTER V.

CHAPTER VI.

CHAPTER VII.

CHAPTER VIII.

CHAPTER IX.

CHAPTER X.

CHAPTER XI.

CHAPTER XII.

CHAPTER XIII.

CHAPTER XIV.

CHAPTER XV.

CHAPTER XVI.

APPENDIX.

ILLUSTRATIONS.

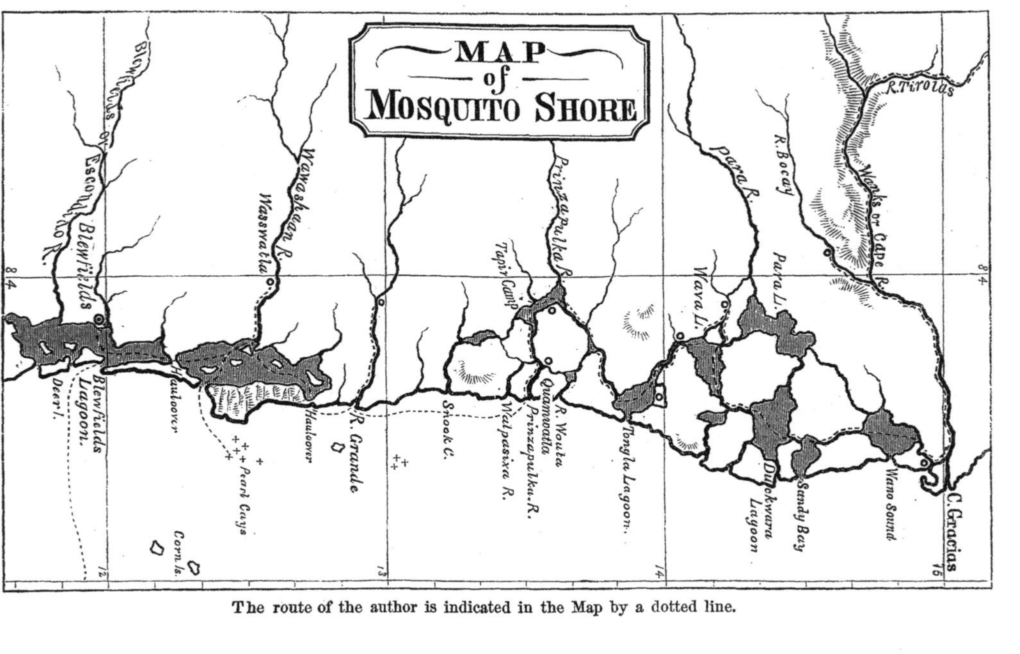

The route of the author is indicated in the Map by a dotted line.

THE

MOSQUITO SHORE.

A MONTH in Jamaica is enough for any sinner's punishment, let alone that of a tolerably good Christian. At any rate, a week had given me a surfeit of Kingston, with its sinister, tropical Jews, and variegated inhabitants, one-half black, one-third brown, and the balance as fair as could be expected, considering the abominable, unintelligible Congo-English which they spoke. Besides, the cholera which seems to be domesticated in Kingston, and to have become one of its local institutions, had begun to spread from the stews, and to invade the more civilized parts of the town. All the inhabitants, therefore, whom the emancipation had left rich enough to do so, were flying to the mountains, with the pestilence following, like a sleuth-hound, at their heels. Kingston was palpably no place for a stranger, and that stranger a poor-devil artist.

The cholera had cheated me of a customer. I was moody, and therefore swung myself in a hammock, lit a cigar, and held a grand inquisition on myself, as the poets are wont to do on their souls. It ran after this wise, with a very little noise but much smoke :—

"Life is pleasant at twenty-six. Do you like life ?"

Rather.

"Then you can't like the cholera ?"

No !—with a hurried pull at the cigar.

"But you'll have it here !"

Then I'll be off !

"Where ?"

Any where !

"Good, but the exchequer, my boy, how about that ? You can't get away without money."

There was a long pause, a great cloud of smoke, and much swinging in the hammock, and a final echo—

Money! Yes, I *must* have money !

So I got up, spasmodically opened my portmanteau, dived deep amongst collars, pencils and foul linen, took out my purse, turned its contents on the table, and began to count.

Forty-three and a half, forty-four, forty-five, and this handful of small silver and copper. Call it fifty in all.

"Only fifty dollars!" ejaculated my mental interrogator.

Only fifty! responded I.

"'T won't do!"

I lit another cigar. It was clear enough, it would n't do; and I got into the hammock again. Commend me to a hammock, (a *pita* hammock, none of your canvas abominations,) and a cigar, as valuable aids to meditation and self-communion of all kinds. There was a long silence, but the inquisition went on, until the cigar was finished. Finally "I'll do it!" I exclaimed, in the voice of a man determined on some great deed, not agreeable but necessary, and I tossed the cigar stump out of the window. But what I determined to do, may seem no great thing after all; it was only to paint the portrait of my landlady.

"Yes, I'll paint the old wench!"

Now, I am an artist, not an author, and have got the cart before the horse, inasmuch as my narrative does not preserve the "harmonies," as every well-considered composition should do. It has just occurred to me that I should first have told who I am, and how I came to be in Jamaica, and especially in that filthy place, Kingston. It is n't a long story, and if it is not too late, I will tell it now.

As all the world knows, there are people who sell rancid whale oil, and deal in soap, and affect a great contempt for artists. They look down grandly on the quiet, pale men who paint their broad red faces on canvas, and seem to think that the few greasy dollars which they grudgingly pay for their flaming immortality, should be received with meek confusion and blushing thanks, as a rare exhibition of condescension and patronage. I never liked such patronage, and therefore would paint no red faces. But there is a great difference between red, bulbous faces, and rosy faces. There was that sweet girl at the boarding-school in L—— Place, the Baltimore girl, with the dark eyes and tresses of the South, and the fair cheek and elastic step of the North! Of course, I painted her portrait, a dozen times at least, I should say. I could paint it now; and I fear it is more than painted on my heart, or it would n't rise smiling here, to distract my thoughts, make me sigh, and stop my story.

An artist who would n't paint portraits and had a soul above patronage—what was there for him to do in New York? Two compositions a year in the Art Union, got in through Mr. Sly, the manager, and a friend of mine, were not an adequate support for the most moderate man. I 'll paint grand historical paintings, thought I one day, and straightway purchased a large canvas. I had selected my subject, Balboa, the discoverer of the Pacific, bearing aloft the flag of Spain, rushing breast-deep in its waves, and claiming its boundless shores and numberless islands for the crown of Castile and Leon. I had begun to sketch in the plumed Indians, gazing in mute surprise upon this startling scene, when it occurred to me—for I have patches of common sense scattered amongst the flowery fields of my fancy—to count over the amount of my patrimonial portion. Grand historical paintings require years of study and labor, and I found I had but two hundred dollars, owed for a month's lodging, and had an unsettled tailor's account. It was clear that historical painting was a luxury, for the present at least, beyond my reach. It was then some evil spirit, (I strongly suspect it was the ——,) taking the cue doubtless from my projected picture, suggested :—

"Try landscape, my boy ; you have a rare hand for landscapes—good flaming landscapes, full of yellow and vermillion, you know !"

Although there was no one in the room, I can swear to a distinct slap on the back, after the emphatic "you know" of the tempter. It was a true diabolical suggestion, the yellow and vermillion, but not so sulphurous as what followed :—

"Go to the tropics boy, the glorious tropics, where the sun is supreme, and never shares his dominion with blue-nosed, leaden-colored, rheumy-eyed frost-gods ; go there, and catch the matchless tints of the skies, the living emerald of the forests, and the light-giving azure of the waters ; go where the birds are rainbow-hued, and the very fish are golden ; where—"

But I had heard enough ; I was blinded by the dazzling panorama which Fancy swept past my vision, and cried, with enthusiastic energy,

" Hold ; I 'll go to the glorious tropics !"

And I went—more 's the pity—in a little dirty schooner, full of pork and flour ; and that is the way I came to be in Jamaica, dear reader, if you want to know. I had been there a month or more, and had wandered all over the really magnificent interior, and filled my portfolio with sketches. But that did not satisfy me ; there were other tropical lands, where Nature had grander aspects, where there were broad lakes and high and snow-crowned volcanoes, which waved their plumes of smoke in mid-heaven, defiantly, in the very face of the sun ; lands through whose ever-leaved forests Cortez, Balboa, and Alvarado, and Cordova had led their mailed followers, and in whose depths frowned the strange gods of aboriginal superstition, beside the deserted altars and unmarked graves of a departed and mysterious people. Jamaica was beautiful certainly, but I longed for what the transcendentalists call the sublimely-beautiful, or, in plain English, the combined sublime and beautiful—for, in short, an equatorial Switzerland. And, although Jamaica was fine in scenery, its dilapidated plantations, and filthy, lazy negroes, already more than half relapsed into native and congenial barbarism, were repugnant to my Amerieean notions and tastes. They grinned around me, those negroes, when I ate, and scratched their heads over my paper when I drew. They followed me every where, like black jackals, and jabbered their incomprehensive lingo in my ears until they deafened me. And then their odor under tropical heats! Faugh! "'Twas rank, and smelt to heaven!"

I had, therefore, come down from the interior to set up my easel in Kingston, paint a few views, and thereby raise the wind for a trip to the mainland. Of course, I did not fly from painting red-faced portraits in the United States, to paint ebony ones in Jamaica. My scruples, however, did not apply to customers. There was a "*brown man*," which is genteel Jamaican for mulatto, who was an Assembly-man, or something of the kind, and wanted a view of the edifice at Spanish-town, wherein he legislated for the "emancipated island." I had agreed to paint it for the liberal compensation of twenty pounds. But one hot, murky morning, my brown lawgiver took the cholera, and before noon was not only dead, but buried—and my picture only half-finished! *Mem.* As people have a practice of dying, always get your pay beforehand.

Voltaire, I believe, has said, that if a toad were asked his ideal of beauty, he would, most likely, describe himself, and dwell complacently on a cold, clammy, yellow belly, a brown, warty, corrugated back, and become ecstatic on the subject of goggle eyes. And, I verily believe, that if my landlady had been asked the same question, she would have coquettishly patted up her woolly curls over each oleaginous cheek, and glanced toward the mirror, by way of reply. Black, glossy black, and *fat*, marvelously fat, yet she was possessed, even she, of her full share of feminine vanity. There was no mistaking, from the first day of my arrival, that her head was running on a portrait of herself. She was fond of money and penurious, and careful, therefore, not to venture upon a proposition until she had got some kind of a clew as to what her immortality would be likely to cost. I had, however, diplomatically evaded all of her approaches, up to the unfortunate day when my Assembly-man died. She brought me the news herself, and saw that it annoyed rather than shocked me, and that I stopped painting with the air of a man abandoning a bad job. She evidently thought the time favorable for a *coup de main* ; there was a gleam of cunning in her little, round, half-buried eyes, and the very ebony of her cheek lightened palpably, as she said :

" So your picture will be no good for nothing ?"

No !

" You have not got the —— ?"

And she significantly rubbed the fore-finger of one hand in the palm of the other.

No !

There was a pause, and then she resumed :

" I want a picture !"

Eh ?

"A picture, you know!"

And now she complacently stroked down her broad face, and exhibited a wide, vermilion chasm, with a formidable phalanx of ivories, by way of a suggestive smile.

No, I never paint portraits!

"Not for ten pounds?"

No; nor for a hundred,—go!

And my landlady rolled herself out of the room with a motion which, had she weighed less than two hundred, might have passed for a toss.

It was on the evening of this day, and after this conversation, one half of the Assembly-house at Spanish-town staring redly from the canvas in the corner, that I lay in my hammock and soliloquized as aforesaid. It was thus and then, that I resolved to paint my landlady.

And having now, by means of this long parenthesis, restored the harmonies of my story, and got my horse and cart in correct relative positions, I am ready to go ahead.

I not only resolved to paint my landlady, but I did it, right over the half-finished Assembly-house. It was the first, and, by the blessing of Heaven, so long as there are good potatoes to be dug at the rate of six cents the bushel, it shall be my last portrait. I can not help laughing, even now, at that fat, glistening face, looking for all the world as if it had been newly varnished, surmounted by a gaudy red scarf, wound round the head in the form of a peaked turban; and two fat arms, rolling down like elephants' trunks against a white robe for a background, which concealed a bust that passeth description. That portrait—"long may it wave!" as the man said, at the Kossuth dinner, when he toasted "The day we celebrate!"

MY LANDLADY.

My landlady was satisfied, and generous withal, for she not only paid me the ten pounds, and gave me my two weeks board and lodging in the bargain, but introduced me to a colored gentleman, a friend of hers, who sailed a little schooner twice a year to the Mosquito Shore, on the coast of Central America, where he traded off refuse rum and gaudy cottons for turtle-shells and sarsaparilla. There was a steamer from Kingston, once a month, to Carthagena, Chagres, San Juan, Belize, and "along shore ;" but, for obvious reasons, I could not go in a steamer. So I struck up a bargain with the fragrant skipper, by the terms of which he bound himself to land me, bag and baggage, at Bluefields, the seat of Mosquito royalty, for the sum of three pounds, "currency."

Why Captain Ponto (for so I shall call my landlady's friend, the colored skipper) named his little schooner the "Prince Albert," I can not imagine, unless he thought thereby to do honor to the Queen-Consort ; for the aforesaid schooner had evidently got old, and been condemned, long before that lucky Dutchman woke the echoes of Gotha with his baby cries. The "Prince Albert" was of about seventy tons burden, built something on the model of the "Jung-frau," the first vessel of the Netherlands that rolled itself into New York bay, like some unwieldy porpoise, after a rapid passage of about six months from the Hague. The wise men of the Historical Society have satisfactorily shown, after long and diligent research, that the "Jung-frau" measured sixty feet keel, sixty feet beam, and sixty feet hold, and was modeled after one of Rubens' Venuses. The dimensions of the "Prince Albert" were every way the same, only twenty feet less. The sails were patched and the cordage spliced, and she did not leak so badly as to require more than six hours' steady pumping out of the twenty-four. The crew was composed of Captain Ponto, Thomas, his mate, one seaman, and an Indian boy from Yucatan, whose business it was to cook and do the pumping. As may be supposed, the Indian boy did not rust for want of occupation.

It was a clear morning, toward the close of December, that Captain Ponto's wife, a white woman, with a hopeful family of six children, the three eldest with shirts, and the three youngest without, came down to the schooner to see us off. I watched the parting over the after-bulwarks, and observed the tears roll down Mrs. Ponto's cheeks as she bade her sable spouse good-by. I wondered if she really could have any attachment for her husband, and if custom and association had utterly worn away the natural and instinctive repugnance which exists between the superior and inferior races of mankind? I thought of the condition of Jamaica itself, and mentally inquired if it were not due to a grand, practical misconception of the laws of Nature, and the inevitable result of their reversal? It can not be denied that where the superior and inferior races are brought in contact, and amalgamate, there we uniformly find a hybrid stock springing up, with most, if not all of the vices, and few, if any of the virtues of the originals. And it will hardly be questioned, by those experimentally acquainted with the subject, that the manifest lack of public morality and private virtue, in the Spanish-American States, has followed from the fatal facility with which the Spanish colonists have intermixed with the negroes and Indians. The rigid and inexorable exclusion, in respect to the inferior races, of the dominant blood of North America, flowing through different channels perhaps, yet from the same great Teutonic source, is one grand secret of its vitality, and the best safeguard of its permanent ascendency.

Mrs. Ponto wept ; and as we slowly worked our way outside of Port Royal, I could see her waving her apron, for she was innocent of a more classical signal, in fond adieus. We finally got out from under the lee of the land, and caught in our sails the full trade-wind, blowing steadily in the desired direction. I sat long on deck, watching the receding island sinking slowly in the bright sea, until Captain Ponto signified to me, in the *patois* of Jamaica, which the deluded people flatter themselves is English, that dinner was ready, and led the way into what he called the cabin. This cabin was a little den, seven feet by nine at the utmost, low, dark and dirty, with no light or air except what entered through the narrow hatchway, and, consequently, hot as an oven. Two lockers, one on each side, answered for seats by day, and, covered with suspicious mattresses, for beds by night. The cabin was sacred to Captain Ponto and myself, the mate having been displaced to make room for the gentleman who had paid three pounds for his passage ! I question if the "Prince Albert" had ever before been honored with a passenger ; certainly not since she had come into the hands of Captain Ponto, who therefore put his best foot forward, with a full consciousness of the importance of the incident.

2

Ponto had been a slave once, and was consequently imperious and tyrannical now, toward all people in a subordinate relation to himself. Yet, as he had evidently been owned by a man of consequence, he had not entirely lost his early deference for the white man, and sometimes forgot Ponto the captain in Ponto the chattel. It was in the latter character only, that he was perfectly natural; and, although I derived no little amusement from his attempts to enact a loftier part, I shall not trouble the reader with an episode on Captain Ponto. He was a very worthy darkey, with a strong aversion to water, both exteriorly and internally. The mate, and the man who constituted the crew, were ordinary negroes of no possible account.

But Antonio, the Indian boy, who cooked and pumped, and then pumped and cooked—I fear he never slept, for when there was not a "sizzling" in the little black caboose, there was sure to be a screeching of the rickety pump—Antonio attracted my interest from the first; and it was increased when I found that he spoke a little English, was perfect in Spanish, and withal could read in both languages. There was something mysterious in finding him among these uncouth negroes, with his relatively fair skin, intelligent eyes, and long, well-ordered, black hair. He was like a lithe panther among lumbering bears; and he did his work in a way which accorded with his Indian character, without murmur, and with a kind of silent doggedness, that implied but little respect for his present masters. He seldom replied to their orders in words, and then only in monosyllables. I asked Captain Ponto about him, but he knew nothing, except that he was from Yucatan, and had presented himself on board only the day previously, and offered to work his passage to the main land. And Captain Ponto indistinctly intimated that he had taken the boy solely on my account, which, of course, led to the inference on my part, that the captain ordinarily did his own cooking. He also ventured a patronizing remark about the Indians generally, to the effect that they made very good servants, "if they were kept under;" which, coming from an ex-slave, I thought rather good.

All this only served to interest me the more in Antonio; and, although I succeeded in engaging him in ordinary conversation, yet I utterly failed in drawing him out, as the saying is, in respect to his past history, or future purposes. Whenever I approached these subjects he became silent and impassible, and his eyes assumed an expression of cold inquiry, not unmingled with latent suspicion, which half inclined me to believe that he was a fugitive from justice. Yet he did not look the felon or knave; and when the personal inquiries dropped, his face resumed its usual pleasant although sad expression, and I became ashamed that I had suspected him. There was certainly something singular about Antonio; but, as I could imagine no very profound mystery attaching to a cook, on board of the "Prince Albert," after the first day, I made no attempts to penetrate his secrets, but sought rather to attach him to me, as a prospectively useful companion in the country to which I was bound. So I relieved him occasionally at the pump, although he protested against it; and

ANTONIO.

finally, to the horror of Captain Ponto, and the palpable high disdain of the mate, I became so intimate with him as to show him my portfolio of drawings. His admiration, I found to my surprise, was always judiciously bestowed, and his appreciation of outline and coloring showed that he had the spirit of an artist. Several times, in glancing over the drawings, he stopped short, looked up, his face full of intelligence, as if about to speak, and I paused to listen. Each time, however, the smile vanished, the flexible muscles ceased their play and became rigid, and a cold, filmy mist settled over the clear eyes which had looked into mine. Whatever was Antonio's secret, great or small, it was evidently one that he half-wished, half-feared to reveal. I was puzzled to think that there could exist any relation between it and my paintings; but Antonio was only a cook, and so I dismissed all reflection on the subject.

On our third day out, the weather, which up to that time had been clear and beautiful, began to change, and night settled black and threatening around us. The wind had increased, but it was loaded with sultry vapors—the hot breath of the storm which was pressing on our track. Captain Ponto was not a scientific sailor, and kept no other than what is called "dead reckoning." He had made the voyage very often, and was confidant of his course. Upon that point, therefore, I gave myself no uneasiness; not so much from faith in Captain Ponto, as because there was nothing in the world to be done, except to follow his opinion. Nevertheless the captain was serious, and consulted an antediluvian chart which he kept in his cabin. It was a Rembrandtish picture, that negro tracing his forefinger slowly over the chart, by the light of a candle, which only half revealed the little cabin, while it brought out his grizzly head and anxious face in strong relief against the darkness. What Captain Ponto learned from all this study is more than I can tell; but when he came on deck, he ordered a reef to be made in the sails, and a variation of several points in our course, for the wind not only freshened, but veered to the north-east. The hot blasts or puffs of air became more and more frequent, and occasional sheets of lightning gleamed along the horizon. The sea, too, was full of phosphorescent light; fiery monsters seemed to leap around us and wreath and twine their livid volumes in our wake. I could hear the hiss of their forked tongues where the waters closed under our stern. I stood, leaning over the bulwarks, gazing on the gleaming waves, and thinking of home—for the voyager on the great deep always thinks of home, when darkness envelops him, and the storm threatens—when Antonio silently approached, so silently that I did not hear him, and took his place at my side. I was somewhat startled, therefore, when, changing my position a little, I saw, by the dim, reflected light of the sea, his eyes fixed earnestly on mine. "Ah, Antonio," I said, "is that you?" and I placed my hand familiarly on his shoulder. He shrank beneath it, as if it had been fire. "What's the matter?" I exclaimed, reproachfully; "have I hurt you?"

"Pardon me!" he ejaculated, rather than spoke, in a voice deep and tremulous; "I know now that it is not you who will die to-night!"

"What do you mean? You are not afraid, Antonio? Who thinks of dying?" I replied, in a light tone.

"No! it is not myself. I was afraid it might be you; for, sir," and he laid a hand cold and clammy as that of a corpse on mine; "for, sir, there is death on board this vessel!"

This was said in a voice so awed and earnest that I was impressed deeply, in spite of myself, and for some moments made no reply. "You talk wildly, Antonio," I finally said; "we are going on bravely, and shall all be in Bluefields together in a day or two."

"All of us, never," he replied, "never! The Lord, who never lies, has told me so!" and, pressing near me, he drew from his bosom something resembling a small, round plate of crystal, except that it seemed to be slightly luminous, and veined or clouded with green. "See, see!" he exclaimed, rapidly, and held the object close to my eyes. I instinctively obeyed, and gazed intently upon it. As I gazed, the clouds of green seemed to concentrate and assume a regular form, as the moisture of one's breath passes away from a mirror, until I distinctly saw, in the center, the miniature of a human head, of composed and dignified aspect, but the eyes were closed, and all the lineaments had the rigidity of death.

"Do you see?"

"I do!"

"It is *Kucimen*, the Lord who never lies!" and Antonio thrust his talisman in his bosom again, and slowly moved away. There was no mistake in what I had seen, and although I am not superstitious, yet the feeling that some catastrophe was impending gathered at my heart. It was in vain that I tried to smile at the Indian trick; the earnest voice of the Indian boy still sounded in my ears, "All of us, never!" What reason should he have for attempting to practice his Indian *diablerie* on any one, least of all on me? I rejected the thought, and endeavored to banish the subject from my mind.

Meanwhile the wind had gathered strength, and Captain Ponto had taken in sail, so that we had no more standing than was necessary to keep the vessel steady before the wind. The waves now began to rise, the gloom deepened, the hot puffs of air became more and more frequent, and the broad lightning-sheets rose from the horizon to the very zenith. The thunder, too, came rolling on, every peal more distinctly, and occasional heavy drops of rain fell with an ominous sound on the deck. The storm was evidently close at hand; and I left the side of the vessel, and approached the little cabin to procure my *poncho*, for I preferred the open deck and the storm to the suffocation below. The hatchway was nearly closed, but there was a light within. I stooped to remove the slide, and in doing so obtained a full view of the interior. The spectacle which presented itself was so extraordinary that I stopped short, and looked on in mute surprise. The candle was standing on the locker, and kneeling beside it was the captain. He was stripped to the waist, and held in one hand what appeared to be the horn of some animal, in which he caught the blood which dripped from a large gash in the fleshy part of his left arm, just above the elbow, while he muttered rapidly some rude and strangely-sounding words, unlike any I had ever before heard. My first impression was that Antonio had tried to fulfill his own prediction, by attempting the life of the captain; but I soon saw that he was performing some religious rite, a sacrifice or propitiation, such as the *Obi* men still teach in Jamaica and Santo Domingo, and which are stealthily observed, even by the negroes professing Christianity and having a nominal connection with the church. I recognized in the horn the mysterious *gre-gre* of the Gold Coast, where the lowest form of *fetish* worship prevails, and where human blood is regarded as the most acceptable of sacrifices. Respecting too rigidly all ceremonies and rites, which may contribute to the peace of mind of others, to think of disturbing them, I silently withdrew from the hatchway, and left the captain to finish his debasing devotions. In a short time he appeared on deck, and gave some orders in a calm voice, as one reässured and confident.

I was occupied below for only a few minutes, yet when I got on deck again the storm was upon us. The waves were not high, but the water seemed to be caught up by the wind, and to be drifted along, like snow, in blinding, drenching sheets. I was nearly driven off my feet by its force, and would have been carried overboard had I not become entangled in the rigging. The howling of the wind and the hissing of the water would have drowned the loudest voice, and I was so blinded by the spray that I could not see. Yet I could feel that we were driving before the hurricane with fearful rapidity. The very deck seemed to bend, as if ready to break, beneath our feet. I finally sufficiently recovered myself to be able, in the pauses of the wind, and when the lightning fell, to catch glimpses around me. Our sails were torn in tatters, the yards were gone, in fact every thing was swept from the deck except three dark figures, like myself, clinging convulsively to the ropes. On, on, half-buried in the sea, we drifted with inconceivable rapidity.

Little did we think that we were rushing on a danger more terrible than the ocean. The storm had buffeted us for more than an hour, and it seemed as if it had exhausted its wrath, and had begun to subside, when a sound, hoarse and steady, but louder even than that of the wind, broke on our ears. It was evident that we were approaching it, for every instant it became more distinct and ominous. I gazed ahead into the hopeless darkness, when suddenly a broad sheet of lightning revealed immediately before us, and not a cable's length distant, what, under the lurid gleam, appeared to be a wall of white spray, dashing literally a hundred feet in the air—a hell of waters, from which there was no escape. "*El Roncador!*" shrieked the captain, in a voice of utter despair, that even then thrilled like a knife in my heart. The fearful moment of death had come, and I had barely time to draw a full breath of preparation for the struggle, when we were literally whelmed in the raging waters. I felt a shock, a sharp jerk, and the hiss and gurgle of the sea, a sensation of immense pressure, followed by a blow like that of a heavy fall. Again I was lifted up, and again struck down, but this time with less force. I had just

THE SHIPWRECK.

enough consciousness left to know that I was striking on the sand, and I made an involuntary effort to rise and escape from the waves. Before I could gain my feet I was again struck down, again and again, until, nearer dead than alive, I at last succeeded in crawling to a spot where the water did not reach me. I strove to rise now, but could not; and, as that is the last thing I remember distinctly of that terrible night, I suppose I must have fallen into a swoon.

HOW long I remained insensible I know not, but when my consciousness returned, which it did slowly, like the lifting of a curtain, I felt that I was severely hurt; and, before opening my eyes, tried to drive away my terrible recollections, as one rousing from a troubled dream tries to banish its features from his mind. It was in vain; and, with a sensation of despair, I opened my eyes! The morning sun was shining with blinding brilliancy, and I was obliged to close them again. Soon, however, I was able to bear the blaze, and, painfully lifting myself on my elbow, looked around me. The sea was thundering with awful force, not on the sandy shore where I was lying, but over a reef two hundred yards distant, within which the water was calm, or only disturbed by the combing waves, as they broke over the outer barrier. Here the first and only object which attracted my attention was our schooner, lying on her beam ends, high on the sands. The sea, the vessel, the blinding sun and glowing sand, and a bursting pain in my head, were too palpable evidences of my misfortune to be mistaken. It was no dream, but stern and severe reality, and for the moment I comprehended the truth. But, when younger, I had read of shipwrecks, and listened, with the interest of childhood, and a feeling half of envy, to the tales of old sailors who had been cast away on desert shores. And now, the first shock over, it was almost with a sensation of satisfaction, and something of exultation, that I exclaimed to myself, "shipwrecked at last!" Robinson Crusoe, and Reilly and his companions, recurred to my mind, and my impulse was to leap up and commence an emulative career. But the attempt was a failure, and brought me back to stern reality, in an instant. My limbs were torn and scarified, and my face swollen and stiff. The utmost I could do was to sit erect.

I now, for the first time, thought of my companions, and despairingly turned my eyes to look for them. Close by, and nearly behind me, sat Antonio, resting his head on his hands. His clothes were hanging around him in shreds, his hair was matted with sand, and his face was black with dried blood. He attempted to smile, but the grim muscles could not obey, and he looked at me in silence. I was the first to speak:

Are you much hurt, Antonio?

"The Lord of Mitnal never lies!" was his only response; and he pointed to the talisman on his swarthy breast, gleaming like polished silver in the sun. I remembered the scene of the previous night, and asked;—

Are they all dead?

He shook his head, in sign of ignorance.

Where are we, Antonio?

"This is El Roncador!"

And so it proved. We were on one of the numerous coral keys or cays which stud the sea of the Antilles, and which are the terror of the mariners who navigate it. They are usually mere banks of sand, elevated a few feet above the water, occasionally supporting a few bushes, or a scrubby, tempest-twisted palm or two, and only frequented by the sea-birds for rest and incubation, and by turtles for laying their eggs. Around them there is always a reef of coral, built up from the bottom of the sea by those wonderful architects, the coral insects. This reef surrounds the cay, at a greater or less distance, like a ring, leaving between it and the island proper a belt of water, of variable depth, and of the loveliest blue. The reef, which is sometimes scarcely visible above the sea, effectually breaks the force of the waves; and if, as it sometimes happens, it be interrupted so as to leave an opening for the admission of vessels, the inner belt of water forms a safe harbor. Except a few of the larger ones, none of these cays are inhabited, nor are they ever frequented, except by the turtle fishers.

It was to the peculiar conformation of these islands that our safety was owing. Our little vessel had been driven, or lifted by the waves, completely over the outer reef. The shock had torn us from our hold on the ropes, and we had drifted upon the comparatively protected sands. The vessel too, had been carried upon them, and the waves there not being sufficiently strong to break her in pieces, she was left high and dry when they subsided. There was, nevertheless, a broad break in her keel, caused probably by striking on the reef.

Two of the five human beings who had been on board of her, the captain and his mate, were drowned. We found their bodies ;—but I am anticipating my story. When we had recovered ourselves sufficiently to walk, Antonio and myself took a survey of our condition. "El Roncador," *the Snorer*, is a small cay, three quarters of a mile long, and at its widest part not more than four hundred yards broad,—a mere bank of white sand. At the eastern end is an acre or more of scrubby bushes, and near them three or four low and distorted palm-trees. Fortunately for us, as will be seen in the sequel, "El Roncador" is famous for the number of its turtles, and is frequented, at the turtle season, by turtle-fishers from Old Providence, and sometimes from the main land. Among the palm-trees, to which I have referred, these fishermen had erected a rude hut of poles, boards, and palm-branches, which was literally withed and anchored to the trees, to keep it from being blown away by the high winds. It was with a heart full of joy that I saw even this rude evidence of human intelligence, and, accompanied by Antonio, hastened to it as rapidly as my bruised limbs would enable me. We discovered no trace of recent occupation as we approached, except a kind of furrow in the sand, like that which some sea-monster, dragging itself along, might occasion. It led directly to the hut, and I followed it, with a feeling half of wonder, half of apprehension. As we came near, however, I saw, through the open front, a black human figure crouching within, motionless as a piece of bronze. Before it, stretched at length, was the dead body of Captain Ponto. The man was Frank, of whom I have spoken, as constituting the crew of the Prince Albert. It was a fearful sight! The body of the captain was swollen, the limbs were stiff and spread apart, the mouth and eyes open, and conveying an expression of terror and utter despair, which makes me shudder, even now, when I think of it. Upon his breast, fastened by a strong cord, drawn close at the throat, was the mysterious *gre-gre* horn, and the gash in his arm, from which the poor wretch had drawn the blood for his unavailing sacrifice, had opened wide its white edges, as if in mute appeal against his fate.

The negro sailor had drawn the body of the captain to the hut, and the trail in the sand was that which it had made. I spoke to him, but he neither replied nor looked up. His eyes were fixed, as if by some fascination, on the corpse. Antonio exhibited no emotion, but advancing close to the body lifted the *gre-gre* horn, eyed it curiously for a moment, then tossed it contemptuously aside, exclaiming :—

"It could not save him : it is not good !"

The words were scarcely uttered, when the crouching negro leaped, like a wild beast, at the Indian's throat; but Antonio was agile, and evaded his grasp. The next instant the poor wretch had returned to his seat beside the dead. The negro could not endure a sneer at the potency of the *gre-gre*. Such is the hold of superstition on the human mind !

I tried to induce the negro to remove the body, and bury it in the sand ; but he remained silent and impassible as a stone. So I returned with Antonio to the vessel, for the instincts of life had come back. We found, although the little schooner had been completely filled, that the water had escaped, and left the cargo damaged, but entire. Some of the provisions had been destroyed, and the remainder was much injured. Nevertheless they could be used, and for the time being, at least, we were safe from starvation. My spirits rose with the discovery, and I almost forgot my injuries in the joy of the moment. But Antonio betrayed no signs of interest. He lifted boxes and barrels, and placed them on the sands, as deliberately as if unloading the vessel at Kingston. I knew that it was not probable the wrecked schooner would suffer further damage from the sea, protected as it was by the outer reef, yet I sought to make assurance doubly sure, by removing what remained of the provisions to the hut by the palm-trees. Antonio suggested nothing, but implicitly followed my directions.

We had got out most of the stores, and carried them above the reach of the waters on the sands, when I went back to the hut, with the determination, by at once assuming a tone of authority, to have the negro remove and bury the body of the captain. I was surprised to find the hut empty, and a trail, like that which had attracted my notice in the morning, leading off in the direction of the bushes, at some distance from the hut. I followed it; and, in the centre of the clump, discovered the negro filling in the sand above the corpse. He mumbled constantly strange guttural words, and made many mysterious signs on the sand, as he proceeded. When the hole was entirely filled, he laid himself at length above it. I waited some minutes, but as he remained motionless, returned to the hut. We now commenced carrying to it, such articles of use as could be easily removed. But we had not accomplished much when Frank, the negro, presented himself; and, approaching me, inquired meekly what he should do. He was least injured of the three, and proved most serviceable in clearing the wreck of all of its useful and moveable contents.

By night I had bandaged my own wounds and those of my companions, and over a simple but profuse meal, forgot the horrors of the shipwreck, and gave myself up, with real zest, to the pleasures of a cast-away! I cannot well describe the sensation of mingled novelty and satisfaction, with which I looked out from the open hut upon the turbulent waters, whence we had so narrowly escaped. The sea still heaved from the effects of the storm, but the storm itself had passed, and the full tropical moon looked down calmly upon our island, which seemed silvery and fairy-like beneath its rays.

At first, all these things were quieting in their influences, but as the night advanced I must have become feverish, for notwithstanding the toils of the day, and the exhaustion of the previous night, I could not sleep. My thoughts were never so active. All that I had ever seen, heard, or done, flashed back upon my mind with the vividness of reality. But, owing to some curious psychical condition, my mind was only retrospectively active; I tried in vain to bring it to a contemplation of the present or the future. Incidents long forgotten jostled through my brain; the grave mingling strangely with the gay. Now I laughed outright over some freak of childhood, which came back with primitive freshness; and, next moment, wept again beside the bed of death, or found myself singing some hitherto unremembered nursery rhyme. I struggled against these thronging memories, and tried to ask myself if they might not be premonitions of delirium. I felt my own pulse, it beat rapidly; my own forehead, and it seemed to burn. In the vague hope of averting whatever this strange mental activity might portend, I rose and walked down to the edge of the water. I remember distinctly that the shore seemed black with turtles, and that I thought them creations of a disordered fancy, and became almost mad under the mere apprehension that the madness was upon me.

I might, and undoubtedly would, have become mad, had it not been for Antonio. He had missed me from the hut; and, in alarm, had come to seek me. I felt greatly relieved when he told me that there were real turtles on the shore, and not monsters of the imagination; and that it was now the season for laying their eggs, and therefore it could not be long before the fishers would come for their annual supply of shells. So I suffered him to lead me back to the hut. When I laid down he took my head between his hands, and pressed it steadily, but apparently with all his force. The effect was soothing, for in less than half an hour my ideas had recovered their equilibrium, and I fell into a slumber, and slept soundly until noon of the following day.

When I awoke, Antonio was sitting close by me, and intently watching every movement. He smiled when my eyes met his, and pointing to his forehead said significantly—

"It is all right now!"

And it was all right, but I felt weak and feverish still. A sound constitution, however, resisted all attacks, and it was not many days before I was able to move around our sandy prison, and join Antonio and Frank in catching turtles; for, with more foresight than I had supposed to belong to the Indian and negro character, they were laying in a stock of shells, against the time when we should find an opportunity of escape. Upon the side of our island, to which I have alluded as covered with bushes, the water was comparatively shoal, and the bottom overgrown with a species of sea-grass, which is a principal article of turtle-food. The surface of the water, also, was covered with a variety of small blubber fish, which Antonio called by the Spanish name of *dedales*, or thimbles—a name not inappropriate, since they closely resembled a lady's thimble both in shape and size. These, at the spawning or egg-laying period of the year, constitute another article of turtle-food. During the night-time the turtles crawled up on the shore, and the females dug holes in the sand, each about two feet deep, in which they deposited from sixty to eighty eggs. These they contrived to cover so neatly, as to defy the curiosity of one unacquainted with their habits. Both Antonio and Frank, however, were familiar with turtle-craft, and got as many eggs as we desired. When roasted, they are really delicious. The Indians and people of the coasts never destroy them, being careful to promote the increase of this valuable shell-fish. But on the main land, wild animals, such for instance as the cougar, frequently come down to the shore, and dig them from their resting places. Occasionally they capture the turtles themselves, and dragging them into the forest, kill and devour them, in spite of their shelly armor.

It was during the night, therefore, that Antonio and Frank, who kept themselves concealed in the bushes, rushed out upon the turtles, and with iron hooks turned them on their backs, when they became powerless and incapable of moving. The day following, they dragged them to the most distant part of the island, where they "shelled" them;—a

"SHELLING" TURTLES.

cruel process, which it made my flesh creep to witness. Before describing it, however, I must explain that, although the habits of all varieties of the turtle are much the same, yet their uses are very different. The large, green turtle is best known; it frequently reaches our markets, and its flesh is esteemed, by epicures, as a great delicacy.

The flesh of the smaller or hawk-bill variety is not so good, but its shell is most valuable, being both thicker and better-colored. What is called tortoise-shell is not, as is generally supposed, the bony covering or shield of the turtle, but only the scales which cover it. These are thirteen in number, eight of them flat, and five a little curved. Of the flat ones four are large, being sometimes a foot long and seven inches broad, semi-transparent, elegantly variegated with white, red, yellow, and dark brown clouds, which are fully brought out, when the shell is prepared and polished. These laminæ, as I have said, constitute the external coating of the solid or bony part of the shell; and a large turtle affords about eight pounds of them, the plates varying from an eighth to a quarter of an inch in thickness.

The fishers do not kill the turtles; did they do so, they would in a few years exterminate them. When the turtle is caught, they fasten him, and cover his back with dry leaves or grass, to which they set fire. The heat causes the plates to separate at their joints. A large knife is then carefully inserted horizontally beneath them, and the laminæ lifted from the back, care being taken not to injure the shell by too much heat, nor to force it off, until the heat has fully prepared it for separation. Many turtles die under this cruel operation, but instances are numerous in which they have been caught a second time, with the outer coating reproduced; but, in these cases, instead of thirteen pieces, it is a single piece. As I have already said, I could never bring myself to witness this cruelty more than once, and was glad that the process of "scaling" was carried on out of sight of the hut. Had the poor turtles the power of shrieking, they would have made that barren island a very hell, with their cries of torture.

We had been nearly two weeks on the island, when we were one morning surprised by a sail on the edge of the horizon. We watched it eagerly, and as it grew more and more distinct, our spirits rose in proportion. Its approach was slow, but at noon Frank declared that it was a turtle schooner, from the island of Cata-

A SAIL! A SAIL!

rina or Providence, and that it was making for "El Roncador." And the event proved that he was right; for, about the middle of the afternoon, she had passed an opening through the reef, and anchored in the still water inside. She had a crew of five men, in whom it was difficult to say if white, negro, or Indian blood predominated. They spoke a kind of *patois*, in which Spanish was the leading element. And although we were unqualifiedly glad to see them, yet they were clearly not pleased to see us. The *patrón*, or captain, no sooner put his foot on shore, than affecting to regard us as intruders, he demanded why we were there? and if we did not know that this island was the property of the people of Catarina? We replied by pointing to our shattered schooner, when the whole party started for it, and unceremoniously began to strip it of whatever article of use or value they could find, leaving us to the pleasant reflections which such conduct was likely to suggest.

While this was going on, I returned to the hut, and found that Antonio and Frank had already removed the shells which they had procured, as also some other valuables which we had recovered from the wreck, and had buried them in the sand—a prudent precaution, which no doubt saved us much trouble. A little before sundown, our new friends, having apparently exhausted the plunder, came trooping back to the hut, and without ceremony ordered us out. I thought, although the physical force was against us, that a little determination might make up for the odds, and firmly replied that they might have a part of it, if they wished, but that we were there, and intended to remain. The patron hereupon fell into a great passion, and told his men to bring up the *machétes*—ugly instruments, half knife, half cleaver. "He would see," he said, in his mongrel tongue, "if this white villain would refuse to obey him." Two of the men started to fulfill his order, while he stood scowling in the doorway. When they had got off a little distance, I unrolled a blanket in which I had wrapped our pistols, and giving one to Frank, and another to Antonio, I took my own revolver, and passed outside of the hut. The patron fell back, in evident alarm.

"Now, amigo," said I, "if you want a fight, you shall have it; but you shall die first!" And I took deliberate aim at his breast, at a distance of less than five yards. "Mother of Mercy!" he exclaimed, and glanced round, as if for support, to his followers. But they had taken to their legs, without waiting for further proceedings. The patron attempted to follow, but I caught him by the arm, and pressed the cold muzzle of the pistol to his head. He trembled like an aspen, and sunk upon the ground, crying in most abject tones for mercy. I released him, but he did not attempt to stir. The circumstances were favorable for negotiation, and in a few minutes it was arranged that we should continue to occupy the hut, and that he should remain with us, while his crew should stay on board the vessel, when not engaged in catching turtles. He did not like the exception in his favor; but, fearing that he might pull up anchor and leave us to our fate, I insisted that I could not forego the pleasure of his company.

The reader may be sure that I had a vigilant eye on our patron, and at night either Antonio or Frank kept watch, that he should not give us the slip. He made one or two attempts, but finding us prepared, at the end of a couple of days, resigned himself to his fate. Contenting ourselves with our previous spoil, we allowed the new comers to pursue the fishery alone. At the end of a week I discovered, by various indications, that the season was nearly over, and, accordingly, making a careless display of my revolver, told the captain that I thought it would be more agreeable for us to go on board his schooner, than to remain on shore. I could see that the proposition was not acceptable, and therefore repeated it, in such a way that there was no alternative but assent left. He was a good deal surprised when he discovered the amount of shells which we had obtained ; and when I told him that he should have half of it, for carrying us to Providence, and the whole if he took us to Bluefields, his good nature returned. He asked pardon for his rudeness, and, slapping his breast, proclaimed himself "*un hombre bueno*," who would take us to the world's end, if I would only put up my horrible pistol. That pistol, from the very first day, had had a kind of deadly fascination for the patron, who watched it, as if momentarily expecting it to discharge itself at his head. And even now, when he alluded to it, a perceptible shudder ran through his frame.

Two days after I had taken up my quarters on board of the little schooner, which, in age and accumulated filth, might have been twin-brother of the Prince Albert, we set sail from "El Roncador." As it receded in the distance, it looked very beautiful—an opal in the sea—and I could hardly realize that it was nothing more than a reef-girt heap of desert sands.

Although friendly relations had been restored with the patron, for the crew seemed nearly passive, I kept myself constantly on my guard against foul play. Antonio was sleeplessly vigilant. But the patron, so far from having evil designs, appeared really to have taken a liking to me, and expatiated

"EL RONCADOR."

upon the delights of Providence, where he represented himself as being a great man, with much uncouth eloquence. He promised that I should be well received, and that he would himself get up a dance—which he seemed to think the height of civility—in my honor.

About noon, on our third day from "El Roncador," the patron pointed out to me two light blue mounds, one sharp and conical, and the other round and broad, upon the edge of the horizon. They were the highlands of Providence. Before night, we had doubled the rocky headland of Santa Catarina, crowned with the ruins of some old Spanish fortifications, and in half an hour were at anchor, alongside a large New Granadian schooner, in the small but snug harbor of the island.

This island is almost unknown to the world ; it has, indeed, very little to commend it to notice. Although accounted a single island, it is, in fact, two islands ; one is six or eight miles long, and four or five broad, and but moderately elevated ; while the second, which is a rocky headland, called Catarina, is separated from the main body by a narrow but deep channel. The whole belongs to New Granada, and has about three hundred inhabitants, extremely variegated in color, but with a decided tendency to black. This island was a famous resort of the pirates, during their predominance in these parts, who expelled the Spaniards, and built defences, by means of which they several times repelled their assailants.

The productions consist chiefly of fruits and vegetables ; a little cotton is also raised, which, with the turtle-shells collected by the inhabitants, constitutes about the only export of the island. Vessels coming northward sometimes stop there, for a cargo of cocoa-nuts and yucas.

As can readily be imagined, the people are very primitive in their habits, living chiefly in rude, thatched huts, and leading an indolent, tropical life, swinging in their hammocks and smoking by day, and dancing, to the twanging of guitars, by night. My patron, whom I had suspected of being something of a braggart, was in reality a very considerable personage in Providence, and I was received with great favor by the people, to whom he introduced me as his own "very special friend." I thought of our first interview on "El Roncador," but suppressed my inclination to laugh, as well as I was able. True to his promise, the second night after our arrival was dedicated to a dance. The only preparation for it consisted in the production of a number of large wax candles, resembling torches in size, and the concoction of several big vessels of drink, in which Jamaica rum, some fresh juice of the sugar-cane, and a quantity of powdered peppers were the chief ingredients. The music consisted of a violin, two guitars and a queer Indian instrument, resembling a bow, the string of which, if the critic will pardon the bull, was a brass wire drawn tight by means of a perforated gourd, and beaten with a stick, held by the performer, between his thumb and forefinger.

I cannot attempt to describe the dance, which, not over delicate at the outset, became outrageous as the calabashes of liquor began to circulate. Both sexes drank and danced, until most could neither drink nor dance ; and then, it seemed to me, they all got into a general quarrel, in which the musicians broke their respective instruments over each other's heads, then cried, embraced, and were friends again. I did not wait for the end of the debauch, which soon ceased to be amusing ; but, with Antonio, stole away, and paddled off to the little schooner, where the last sounds that rung in my ears were the shouts and discordant songs of the revelers.

Providence, it can easily be understood, offered few attractions to an artist *minus* the materials for pursuing his vocation; and I was delighted when I learned that the New Granadian schooner was on the eve of her departure for San Juan de Nicaragua. Her captain readily consented to land me at Bluefields, and our patron magnificently waived all claims to the tortoise-shells which we had obtained at "El Roncador." I had no difficulty in selling them to the captain of "El General Bolivar" for the unexpected sum of three hundred dollars. Fifty dollars of these I gave to the negro Frank, who was quite at home in Providence. I offered to divide the rest with Antonio, but he refused to receive any portion of it, and insisted on accompanying me without recompense. "You are my brother," said he, "and I will not leave you." And here I may add that, in all my wanderings, he was my constant companion and firm and faithful friend. His history, a wild and wonderful tale, I shall some day lay before the world: for Antonio was of regal stock, the son and lieutenant of Chichen Pat, one of the last and bravest of the chiefs of Yucatan, who lost his life, under the very walls of Merida, in the last unsuccessful rising of the aborigines; and I blush to add that the fatal bullet, which slew the hope of the Indians, was sped from the rifle of an American mercenary!

Chapter III.

THE approach to the coast, near Bluefields, holds out no delusions. The shore is flat, and in all respects tame and uninteresting. A white line of sand, a green belt of trees, with no relief except here and there a solitary palm, and a few blue hills in the distance, are the only objects which are offered to the expectant eyes of the voyager. A nearer approach reveals a large lagoon, protected by a narrow belt of sand, covered, on the inner side, with a dense mass of mangrove trees; and this is the harbor of Bluefields. The entrance is narrow, but not difficult, at the foot of a high, rocky bluff, which completely commands the passage.

The town, or rather the collection of huts called by that name, lies nearly nine miles from the entrance. After much tacking, and backing, and filling, to avoid the innumerable banks and shallows in the lagoon, we finally arrived at the anchorage. We had hardly got our anchor down, before we were boarded by a very pompous black man, dressed in a shirt of red check, pantaloons of white cotton cloth, and a glazed straw hat, with feet innocent of shoes, whose office nobody knew, further than that he was called "Admiral Rodney," and was an important functionary in the "Mosquito Kingdom." He bustled about, in an extraordinary way, but his final purpose seemed narrowed down to getting a dram, and pocketing a couple of dollars, slily slipped into his hand by the captain, just before he got over the side. When he had left, we were told that we could go on shore.

Bluefields is an imperial city, the residence of the court of the Mosquito Kingdom, and therefore merits a particular description. As I have said, it is a collection of the rudest possible thatched huts. Among them are two or three framed buildings, one of which is the residence of a Mr. Bell, an Englishman, with whom, as I afterwards learned, resided that world-renowned monarch, "George William Clarence, King of all the Mosquitos." The site of the huts is picturesque, being upon comparatively high ground, at a point where a considerable stream from the interior enters the lagoon. There are two villages; the principal one, or Bluefields proper, which is much the largest, containing perhaps five hundred people; and "Carlsruhe," a kind of dependency, so named by a colony of Prussians who had attempted to establish themselves here, but whose colony, at the time of my visit, had utterly failed. Out of more than a hundred of the poor people, who had been induced to come here, but three or four were left, existing in a state of great debility and distress. Most of their companions had died, but a few had escaped to the interior, where they bear convincing witness to the wickedness of attempting to found colonies, from northern climates, on low, pestiferous shores, under the tropics.

Among the huts were many palm and plantain trees, with detached stalks of the papaya, laden with its large golden fruit. The shore was lined with canoes, *pitpans* and *dories*, hollowed from the trunks of trees, all sharp, trim, and graceful in shape. The natives propel them, with great rapidity, by single broad-bladed paddles, struck vertically in the water, first on one side, and then on the other.*

There was a large assemblage on the beach, when we landed, but I was amazed to find that, with few exceptions, they were all unmitigated negros, or Sambos (*i. e.* mixed negro and Indian). I had heard of the Mosquito shore as occupied by the Mosquito Indians, but soon found that there were

* The *dory* is usually hollowed from a solid piece of mahogany or cedar, and is from twenty-five to fifty feet in length. This kind of vessel is found so buoyant and safe, that persons, accustomed to the management of it, often fearlessly venture out to sea, in weather when it might be unsafe to trust to vessels of a larger kind.

The *pitpan* is another variety of canoe, excelling the *dory* in point of speed. It is of the same material, differing only in being flat-bottomed.

few, if any, pure Indians on the entire coast. The miserable people who go by that name are, in reality, Sambos, having a considerable intermixture of trader blood from Jamaica, with which island the coast has its principal relations. The arrival of the traders on the shore is the signal for unrestrained debauchery, always preluded by the traders baptizing, in a manner not remarkable for its delicacy or gravity, all children born since their last visit, in whom there is any decided indication of white blood. The names given on these occasions are as fantastic as the ceremony, and great liberties are taken with the cognomens of all notabilities, living and dead, from " Pompey" down to " Wellington."

Our first concern in Bluefields was to get a roof to shelter us, which we finally succeeded in doing, through the intervention of the captain of the " Bolivar." That is to say, a dilapidated negro from Jamaica, hearing that I had just left that delectable island, claimed me as his countryman, and gave me a little deserted thatched hut, the walls of which were composed of a kind of wicker work of upright canes, interwoven with palm leaves. This structure had served him, in the days of his prosperity, as a kitchen. It was not more than ten feet square, but would admit a hammock, hung diagonally from one corner to the other. To this abbreviated establishment, I moved my few damaged effects, and in the course of the day, completely domesticated myself. Antonio exhibited the greatest aptness and industry in making our quarters comfortable, and evinced an elasticity and cheerfulness of manner unknown before. In the evening, he responded to the latent inquiry of my looks, by saying, that his heart had become lighter since he had reached the continent, and that his Lord gave promise of better days.

"Look!" he exclaimed, as he held up his talisman before my eyes. It emitted a pale light, which seemed to come from it in pulsations, or radiating circles. It may have been fancy, but if so, I am not prepared to say that all which we deem real is not a dream and a delusion!

My host was a man of more pretensions than Captain Ponto, but otherwise very much of the same order of African architecture. From his cautious silence, on the subject of his arrival on the coast, I inferred that he had been brought out as a slave, some thirty-five or forty years ago, when several planters from Jamaica attempted to establish themselves here. However that may have been, he now called himself a "merchant," and appeared proud of a little collection of "osnaburgs," a few red bandanna handkerchiefs, flanked by a dingy cask of what the Yankees would call "the rale critter," which occupied one corner of his house or rather hut. He brooded over these with unremitting care, although I believe I was his only customer, (to the extent of a few fish hooks), during my stay in Bluefields. He called himself Hodgson, (the name, as I afterwards learned, of one of the old British superintendents,) and based his hopes of family immortality upon a son, whom he respectfully called *Mister* James Hodgson, and who was, he said, principal counselor to the king. This information, communicated to me within two hours after my arrival, led me to believe myself in the line of favorable presentation at court. But I found out afterwards, that this promising scion of the house of Hodgson was "under a cloud," and had lost the sunshine of imperial favor, in consequence of having made some most indiscreet confessions, when taken a prisoner, a few years before, by the Nicaraguans. However, I was not destined to pine away my days in devising plans to obtain an introduction to his Mosquito Majesty. For, rising early on the morning subsequent to my arrival, I started out to see the sights of Bluefields. Following a broad path, leading to a grove of cocoa-nut trees, which shadowed over the river, tall and trim, I met a white man, of thin and serious visage, who eyed me curiously for a moment, bowed slightly, and passed on in silence. The distant air of an Englishman, on meeting an American, is generally reciprocated by equally frigid formality. So I stared coldly, bowed stiffly, and also passed on. I smiled to think what a deal of affectation had been wasted on both sides, for it would have been unnatural if two white men were not glad to see each others' faces in a land of ebony like this. So I involuntarily turned half round, just in time to witness a similar evolution on the part of my thin friend. It was evident that his thoughts were but reflections of my own, and being the younger of the two, I retraced my steps, and approached him with a laughing "Good morning!" He responded to my salutation with an equally pregnant "Good morning," at the same time raising his hand to his ear, in token of being hard of hearing. Conversation opened, and I at once found I was in the presence of a man of superior education, large experience, and altogether out of place in the Mosquito metropolis. After a long walk, in which we passed a rough board structure, surmounted by a stumpy pole, supporting a small flag—a sort of hybrid between the Union Jack and the "Stars and Stripes"—called by Mr. Bell the "House of Justice," I accepted his invitation to accompany him home to coffee.

His house was a plain building of rough boards, with several small rooms, all opening into the principal apartment, in which I was invited to sit down. A sleepy-looking black girl, with an enormous shock of frizzled hair, was sweeping the floor, in a languid, mechanical way, calculated to superinduce yawning, even after a brisk morning walk. The partitions were hung with many prints, in which "Her Most Gracious Majesty" appeared in all the multiform glory of steel, lithograph, and chromotint. A gun or two, a table in the corner, supporting a confused collection of books and papers, with some ropes, boots, and iron grapnels beneath, a few chairs, a Yankee clock, and a table, completed the furniture and decoration of the room. I am thus particular in this inventory, for reasons which will afterward appear.

At a word from Mr. Bell, the torpid black girl disappeared for a few moments, and then came back with some cups and a pot of coffee. I observed that there were three cups, and that my host filled them all, which I thought a little singular, since there were but two of us. A faint, momentary suspicion crossed my mind, that the female polypus stood in some such relation to my host as to warrant her in honoring us with her company. But, instead of doing so, she unceremoniously pushed open a door in the corner, and curtly ejaculated to some unseen occupant, "Get up!" There was a kind of querulous response, and directly a thumping and muttering, as of some person who regarded himself as unreasonably disturbed. Meanwhile we had each finished our first cup of coffee, and were proceeding with a second, when the door in the corner opened, and a black boy, or what an American would be apt to call, a "young darkey," apparently nineteen or twenty years old, shuffled up to the table. He wore only a shirt, unbuttoned at the throat, and cotton pantaloons, scarcely buttoned at all. He nodded to my entertainer with a drawling "Mornin', sir!" and sat down to the third cup of coffee. My host seemed to take no notice of him, and we continued our conversation. Soon after, the sloven youth got up, took his hat, and slowly walked down the path to the river, where I afterward saw him washing his face in the stream.

As I was about leaving, Mr. Bell kindly volunteered his services to me, in any way they might be made available. I thanked him, and suggested that, having no object to accomplish except to "scare up" adventures and seek out novel sights, I should be obliged to him for an introduction to the king, at some future day, after Antonio should have succeeded in rejuvenating my suit of ceremony, now rather rusty from saturation with salt water. He smiled faintly, and said, as for that matter, there need be no delay; and, stepping to the door, shouted to the black youth by the river, and beckoned to him to come up the bank. The youth put on his hat hurriedly, and obeyed. "Perhaps you are not aware *that* is the king?" observed my host, with a contemptuous smile. I made no reply, as the youth was at hand. He took off his hat respectfully, but there was no introduction in the case, beyond the quiet observation, "George, this gentleman has come to see you; sit down!"

I soon saw who was the real "king" in Bluefields. "George," I think, had also a notion of his own on the subject, but was kept in such strict subordination that he never manifested it by words. I found him shy, but not without the elements of an ordinary English education, which he had received in England. He is nothing more or less than a negro, with hardly a perceptible trace of Indian blood, and would pass at the South for "a likely young fellow, worth twelve hundred dollars as a body-servant!"

The second day after my arrival was Sunday, and

in the forenoon, Mr. Bell read the service of the English Church, in the "House of Justice." There were perhaps a dozen persons present, among them the king, who was now dressed plainly and becomingly, and who conducted himself with entire propriety. I could not see that he was treated with any special consideration; while Mr. Bell received marked deference.

It is a curious fact that although the English have had relations, more or less intimate, with this shore, ever since the pirates made it their retreat, during the glorious days of the buccaneers, they have never introduced the Gospel. The religion of the "kingdom" was declared by the late king, in his will, to be "the Established Church of England," but the Established Church has never taken steps to bring the natives within its aristocratic fold. Several dissenting missionaries have made attempts to settle on the coast, but as the British officers and agents never favored them, they have met with no success. Besides, the Sambos are strongly attached to heathenish rites, half African and half Indian, in which what they call "*big drunk*" is not the least remarkable feature. Some years ago a missionary, named Pilley, arrived at Sandy Bay, for the purpose of reclaiming the "lost sheep." A house was found for him, and he commenced preaching, and for a few Sundays enticed some of the leading Sambos to hear him, by giving them each a glass of grog. At length, one Sabbath afternoon, a considerable number of the natives attended to hear the stranger talk, and to receive the usual spiritual consolation. But the demijohn of the worthy minister had been exhausted. He nevertheless sought to compensate for the deficiency by a more vehement display of eloquence, and for a time flattered himself that he was producing a lasting impression. His discourse, however, was suddenly interrupted by one of the chiefs, who rose and indignantly exclaimed, "All preach—no grog—no good!" and with a responsive "No good!" the audience followed him, as he stalked away, leaving the astonished preacher to finish his discourse to two or three Englishmen present.

In Bluefields the natives are kept in more restraint than elsewhere on the coast; but even here it has been found impossible to suppress their traditional practices, especially when connected with their superstitions. My venerable friend Hodgson, after "service," informed me that a funeral was to take place, at a small settlement, a few miles up the river, and volunteered to escort me thither in his pitpan, if Antonio would undertake to do the paddling. The suggestion was very acceptable, and after a very frugal dinner, on roast fish and boiled plantains, we set out. But we were not alone; we found dozens of pitpans starting for the same destination, filled with men and women. It is impossible to imagine a more picturesque spectacle than these light and graceful boats, with occupants dressed in the brightest colors, darting over the placid waters of the river, now gay in the sunlight, and anon sobered in the shadows of the trees which studded the banks. There was a keen strife among the rowers, who, amid shouts and screeches, in which both men and women joined, exerted themselves to the utmost. Even Antonio smiled at the scene, but it was half contemptuously, for he maintained, in respect to these mongrels, the reserve of conscious superiority.

GOING TO THE FUNERAL.

Less than an hour brought us in view of a little collection of huts, grouped on the shore, under the shadow of a cluster of palm-trees, which, from a distance, presented a picture of entrancing beauty. A large group of natives had already collected on the shore, and, as we came near, we heard the monotonous beating of the native drum, or *tum-*

tum, relieved by an occasional low, deep blast on a large hollow pipe, which sounded more like the distant bellowing of an ox than any thing else I ever heard. In the pauses, we distinguished suppressed wails, which continued for a minute perhaps, and were then followed by the monotonous drum and droning pipe. The descriptions of similar scenes in Central Africa, given to us by Clapperton and Mungo Park, recurred to me with wonderful vividness, and left the impression that the ceremonies going on were rather African than American in their origin.

On advancing to the huts, and the centre of the group, I found a small pitpan cut in half, in one part of which, wrapped in cotton cloth, was the dead body of a man of middle age, much emaciated, and horribly disfigured by what is called the *bulpis*, a species of syphilitic leprosy, which is almost universal on the coast, and which, with the aid of rum, has already reduced the population to one half what it was twenty years ago. This disgusting disease is held in such terror by the Indians of the interior, that they have prohibited all sexual relations, between their people and the Sambos of the coast, under the penalty of death.

Around the pitpan were stationed a number of women, with palm branches, to keep off the flies, which swarmed around the already festering corpse. Their frizzled hair started from their heads like the snakes on the brow of the fabled Gorgon, and they swayed their bodies to and fro, keeping a kind of

A MOSQUITO BURIAL.

tread-mill step to the measure of the doleful *tum-tum*. With the exception of the men who beat the drum and blew the pipe, these women appeared to be the only persons at all interested in the proceedings. The rest were standing in groups, or squatted at the roots of the palm-trees. I was beginning to get tired of the performance, when, with a suddenness which startled even the women around the corpse, four men, entirely naked excepting a cloth wrapped round their loins, and daubed over with variously-colored clays, rushed from the interior of one of the huts, and hastily fastening a piece of rope to the half of the pitpan containing the corpse, dashed away towards the woods, dragging it after them, like a sledge. The women with the Gorgon heads, and the men with the drum and trumpet, followed them on the run, each keeping time on his respective instrument. The spectators all hurried after, in a confused mass, while a big negro, catching up the remaining half of the pitpan, placed it on his head, and trotted behind the crowd.

The men bearing the corpse entered the woods, and the mass of the spectators, jostling each other in the narrow path, kept up the same rapid pace. At the distance of perhaps two hundred yards, there was an open place, covered with low, dank, tangled underbush, still wet from the rain of the preceding night, which, although unmarked by any sign, I took to be the burial place. When I came up, the half of the pitpan containing the body had been put in a shallow trench. The other half was then inverted over it. The Gorgon-headed women threw in their palm-branches, and the painted negroes rapidly filled in the earth. While this was going on, some men were collecting sticks and palm-branches, with which a little hut was hastily built over the grave. In this was placed an earthen vessel, filled with water. The turtle-spear of the dead man was stuck deep in the ground at his head, and a fantastic fellow, with an old musket, discharged three or four rounds over the spot.

This done, the entire crowd started back in the same manner it had come. No sooner, however, did the painted men reach the village, than, seizing some heavy *machetes,* they commenced cutting down the palm-trees which stood around the hut that had been occupied by the dead Sambo. It was done silently, in the most hasty manner, and when finished, they ran down to the river, and plunged out of sight in the water—a kind of lustration or purifying rite. They remained in the water a few moments, then hurried back to the hut from which they had issued, and disappeared.

This savage and apparently unmeaning ceremony was explained to me by Hodgson, as follows: Death is supposed by the Sambos to result from the influences of a demon, called *Wulasha,* who, ogre-like, feeds upon the bodies of the dead. To rescue the corpse from this fate, it is necessary to lull the demon to sleep, and then steal away the body and bury it, after which it is safe. To this end they bring in the aid of the drowsy drum and droning pipe, and the women go through a slow and soothing dance. Meanwhile, in the recesses of some hut, where they cannot be seen by *Wulasha*, a certain number of men carefully disguise themselves, so that they may not afterwards be recognized and tormented; and when the demon is supposed to have been lulled to sleep, they seize the moment to bury the body. I could not ascertain any reason for cutting down the palm-trees, except that it had always been practiced by their ancestors. As the palm-tree is of slow growth, it has resulted, from this custom, that they have nearly disappeared from some parts of the coast. I could not learn that it was the habit to plant a cocoa-nut tree upon the birth of a child, as in some parts of Africa, where the tree receives a common name with the infant, and the annual rings on its trunk mark his age.

If the water disappears from the earthen vessel placed on the grave,—which, as the ware is porous, it seldom fails to do in the course of a few days,—it is taken as evidence that it has been consumed by the dead man, and that he has escaped the maw of *Wulasha*. This ascertained, preparations are at once made for what is called a *Seekroe*, or Feast of the Dead—an orgie which I afterwards witnessed higher up the coast, and which will be described in due course.

The negroes brought originally from Jamaica, as also most of their descendants, hold these barbarous practices in contempt, and bury their dead, as they say, "English-gentleman fashion." But while these practices are discountenanced and prohibited in Bluefields proper, they are, nevertheless, universal elsewhere on the Mosquito Shore.

I cannot omit mentioning here, that I paid a visit both to the establishment and the burial-place of the ill-fated Prussian colony. Many of the houses, now rotting down, had been brought out from Europe, and all around them were wheels of carts falling in pieces, harnesses dropping apart, and plows and instruments of cultivation rusting away, or slowly burying themselves in the earth. They told a sad story of ignorance on the part of the projectors of the establishment, and of the disappointments and sufferings of their victims. The folly of attempting to plant an agricultural colony, from the north of Europe, on low, murky, tropical shores, is inconceivable. Again and again the attempt has been made, on this coast, and as often it has terminated in disaster and death. It was tried by the French at Tehuantepec and Cape Gracias; by the English at Vera Paz and Black River; and by the Belgians and Prussians at Santo Tomas and Bluefields. In no instance did these establishments survive a second year, nor in a single instance did a tenth of the poor colonists escape the grave. The Prussians at Bluefields suffered fearfully. At one time, within four months after their arrival, out of more than a hundred, there were not enough retaining their health to bury the dead, much less to attend to the sick. The natives, jealous of the strangers, would neither assist nor come near them, and absolutely refused to sell them the scanty food requisite for their subsistence. This feeling was rather encouraged than otherwise, by the traders on the coast, who desired to retain the monopoly of trade, as they had always done a preponderance of influence among the natives. They procured the revocation of the grant which had been made to the Messrs. Shepherd of San Juan, from whom the Prussians had purchased a doubtful title, and threatened the stricken strangers with forcible expulsion. Death, however, soon relieved them from taking overt measures ; and, at the time of my visit, two or three haggard wretches, whose languid blue eyes and flaxen hair contrasted painfully with the blotched visages of the brutal Sambos, were all that remained of the unfortunate Prussian colony. The burying place was a small opening in the bush, where rank vines sweltered over the sunken graves, a spot reeking with miasmatic damps, from which I retreated with a shudder. I could wish no worse punishment to the originators of that fatal, not to say, criminal enterprise, than that they should stand there, as I stood, that Conscience might hiss in their ears, "Behold thy work !"

Chapter V.

I MADE many inquiries in Bluefields, in order to decide on my future movements, to all of which Mr. Bell gave me most intelligent answers. At first, I proposed to ascend the Bluefields river, which takes its rise in the mountainous district of Segovia in Nicaragua, and which is reported to be navigable, for canoes, to within a short distance of the great lakes of that State, from which it is only separated by a narrow range of mountains. Upon its banks dwell several tribes of pure Indians, the Cookras, now but few in number, and the Ramas, a large and docile tribe. Several of the latter visited Bluefields while I was there, bringing down dories and pitpans rudely blocked out, which are afterwards finished by persons expert in that art. They generally speak Spanish, but I could not learn from them that their country was in any respect remarkable, or that it held out any prospect of compensation for a visit, unless it were an indefinite amount of hunger and hard work. So, although I had purchased a canoe, and made other preparations for ascending the river, I determined to proceed northward along the coast, and, embarking in some turtling vessel from Cape Gracias, proceed to San Juan, and penetrate into the interior by the river of the same name.

This, I ascertained, was all the more easy to accomplish, since the whole Mosquito shore is lined with lagoons, only separated from the sea by narrow strips of land, and so connected with each other as to afford an interior navigation, for canoes, from Bluefields to Gracias. So, procuring the additional services of a young Poyas or Paya Indian, who had been left from a trading schooner, I bade "His Mosquito Majesty" and *his* governor good-by, took an affectionate farewell of old Hodgson, and, with Antonio, sailed away to the northern extremity of the lagoon, having spent exactly a week in Bluefields.

It was a bright morning, and our little sail, filled with the fresh sea-breeze, carried us gayly through the water. Antonio carefully steered the boat, and my Poyer boy sat, like a bronze figure-head, in the bow, while I reclined in the centre, luxuriously smoking a cigar. The white herons flapped lazily around us, and flocks of screaming curlews whirled rapidly over our heads. I could scarcely comprehend the novel reality of my position. The Robinson Crusoe-ish feeling of my youth came back in all of its freshness ; I had my own boat, and for companions a descendant of an aboriginal prince, the possessor of a mysterious talisman, devotedly attached to me, half friend, half protector, and a second strange Indian, from some unknown interior, silent as the unwilling genii whom the powerful spell of Solyman kept in obedience to the weird necromancers of the East. It was a strange position and fellowship for one who, scarcely three months before, had carefully cultivated the friendly interest of Mr. Sly, with sinister designs on the plethoric treasury of the Art Union, in New York !

I gave myself up to the delicious novelty, and that sense of absolute independence which only a complete separation from the moving world can inspire, and passed the entire day in a trance of dreamy delight. I subsequently passed many similar days, but this stands out in the long perspective, as one of unalloyed happiness. "'Twas worth ten years of common life," and neither age nor suffering can efface its bright impress from the crowded tablet of my memory !

It was about four o'clock in the afternoon, when we reached the northern extremity of the lagoon, at a place called the *Haulover*, from the circumstance that, to avoid going outside in the open sea, it is customary for the natives to drag their canoes across the narrow neck of sand which separates Bluefields from the next northern or Pearl Kay Lagoon. Occasionally, after long and heavy winds from the eastward, the waters are forced into the lagoons, so as to overflow the belt of land which divides them, when the navigation is uninterrupted.

In order to be able to renew our voyage early next morning, our few effects and stores were carried across the portage, over which our united strength was sufficient to drag the dory, without difficulty. All this was done with prompt alacrity on the part of Antonio and the Poyer boy, who would not allow me to exert myself in the slightest. The transit was effected in less than an hour, and then we proceeded to make our camp for the night, on the beach. Our little sail, supported over the canoe by poles, answered the purpose of a tent. And as for food, without going fifty yards from our fire, I shot half a dozen curlews, which, when broiled, are certainly a passable bird. Meanwhile, the Poyer boy, carefully wading in the lagoon, with a light spear, had struck several fish, of varieties known as *snook* and *grouper* ; and Antonio had collected a bag full of oysters, of which there appeared to be vast banks, covered only by a foot or two of water. They were not pearl oysters, as might be inferred from the name of the lagoon, but similar to those found on our own shores, except smaller, and growing in clusters of ten or a dozen each. Eaten with that relishing sauce, known among travelers as "hunger sauce," I found them something more than excellent,—they were delicious.

While I opened oysters, by way of helping myself to my princely first course, the Indians busied themselves with the fish and birds. I watched their proceedings with no little interest, and as their mode of baking fish has never been set forth in the cookery books, I give it for the benefit of the gastronomic world in general, which, I take it, is not above learning a good thing, even from a Poyer Indian boy. A hole having been dug in the sand, it was filled with dry branches, which were set on fire. In a few minutes the fire subsided in a bed of glowing coals. The largest of the fish, a *grouper*, weighing perhaps five pounds, had been cleaned and stuffed with pieces of the smaller fish, a few oysters, some sliced plantains, and some slips of the bark of the pimento or pepper-tree. Duly sprinkled with salt, it was carefully wrapped in the broad green leaves of the plantain, and the coals raked open, put in the centre of the glowing embers, with which it was rapidly covered. Half an hour afterward, by which time I began to believe it had been reduced to ashes, the bed was raked open again and the fish taken out. The outer leaves of the wrapper were burned, but the inner folds were entire, and when they were unrolled, like the cerements of a mummy, they revealed the fish, "cooked to a charm," and preserving all the rich juices absorbed in the flesh, which would have been carried off by the heat, in the ordinary modes of cooking. I afterward adopted the same process with nearly every variety of large game, and found it, like patent medicines, of "universal application." Commend me to a young *waree* "done brown" in like manner, as a dish fit for a king. But of that anon.

By and by the night came on, but not as it comes in our northern latitudes. Night, under the tropics, falls like a curtain. The sun goes down with a glow, intense, but brief. There are no soft and lingering twilight adieus, and stars lighting up one by one. They come, a laughing group, trooping over the skies, like bright-eyed children relieved from school. Reflected in the lagoon, they seemed to chase each other in amorous play, printing sparkling kisses on each other's luminous lips. The low shores, lined with the heavy-foliaged mangroves, looked like a frame of massive, antique carving, around the vast mirror of the lagoon, across whose surface streamed a silvery shaft of light from the evening star, palpitating like a young bride, low in the horizon. Then there were whispered "voices of the night," the drowsy winds talking themselves to sleep among the trees, and the little ripples of the lagoon pattering with liquid feet along the sandy shore. The distant monotonous beatings of the sea, and an occasional sullen plunge of some marine animal, which served to open momentarily the eyelids drooping in slumbrous sympathy with the scene—these were the elements which entranced me during the long, delicious hours of my first evening, alone with Nature, on the Mosquito Shore!

My dreams that night so blended themselves with the reality, that I could not now separate them if I would, and to this day I hardly know if I slept at all. So completely did my soul go out, and melt, and harmonize itself with the scene, that I began to comprehend the Oriental doctrine of emanations and absorptions, which teaches that, as the body of man springs from the earth, and after a brief space, mingles again with it; so his soul, part of the Great Spirit of the Universe, flutters away like a dove from its nest, only to return, after a weary flight, to fold its wings and once more melt away in Nature's immortal heart, and uncreated and eternal essence.

Before the dawn of day, the ever-watchful Antonio had prepared the indispensable cup of coffee, which is the tropical specific against the malignant night-damps; and the first rays of the sun shot over the trees only to fall on our sail, bellying with the fresh and invigorating sea-breeze. We laid our course for the mouth of a river called Wawashaan (*hwas* or *wass*, in the dialect of the interior, signifying water), which enters the lagoon, about twenty miles to the northward of the *Haulover*. Here we were told there was a settlement, which I determined to visit. As the day advanced, the breeze subsided, and we made slow progress. So we paddled to the shore of one of the numerous islands in the lagoon, to avoid the hot sun and await the freshening of the breeze in the afternoon. The island on which we landed appeared to be higher than any of the others, and was moreover rendered doubly attractive by a number of tall cocoa-nut palms, that clustered near the beach. We ran our boat ashore in a little cove, where there were traces of fires, and other indications that it was a favorite stopping-place with the natives. A narrow trail led inward to the palm-trees. Leaving the Poyer boy with the canoe, Antonio and myself followed the blind path, and soon came to an open space covered with plantain-trees, now much choked with bushes, but heavily laden with fruit. The palms, too, were clustering with nuts, of which we could not, of course, neglect to take in a supply. Near the trees we found the foundations of a house, after the European plan, and, not far from it, one or two rough grave-stones, on which inscriptions had been rudely traced ; but they were now too much obliterated to be read. I could only make out the figure of a cross on one of them, and the name "San Andres," which is an island off the coast, where it is probable the occupant of this lonely grave was born.

To obtain the cocoa-nuts, which otherwise could only have been got at by cutting down and destroying the trees, Antonio prepared to climb after them. He had brought a kind of sack of coarse netting, which he tied about his neck. He next cut a long section of one of the numerous tough vines which abound in the tropics, with which he commenced braiding a large hoop around one of the trees. After this was done, he slipped it over his head and down to his waist, gave it a few trials of strength, and then began his ascent, literally walking up the tree. It was a curious feat, and worth a description. Leaning back in this hoop, he planted his feet firmly against the trunk, clinging to which, first with one hand, and then with the other, he worked up the hoop, taking a step with every upward movement. Nothing loth to exhibit his skill, in a minute he was sixty feet from the ground, leaning back securely in his hoop, and filling his sack with the nuts. This done, he swung his load over his shoulders, grasped the tree in his arms, let the hoop fall, and slid rapidly to the ground. The whole occupied less time than I have consumed in writing an account of it.

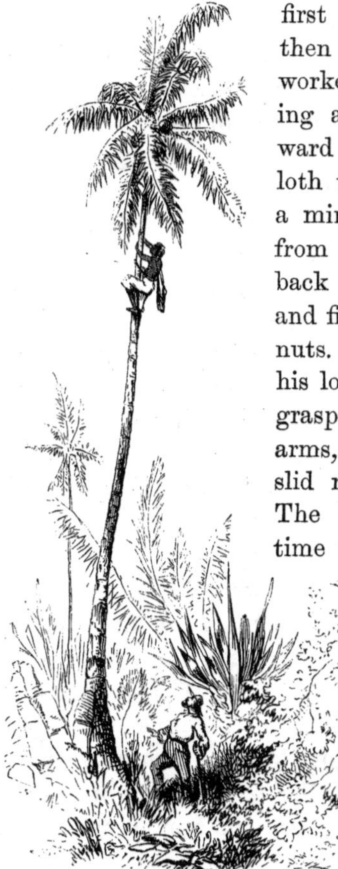

CLIMBING AFTER COCOAS.

Loaded with nuts, plantains, and a species of anona called *soursop,* we returned to the boat, where the water, with which the green cocoa-nuts are filled, tempered with a little Jamaica rum, *para á matar los animalicos,* "to kill the animalculæ," as the Spanish say, made a cooling and refreshing beverage.

In the afternoon we again embarked, and before dark reached the mouth of the Wawashaan, which looked like a narrow arm of the lagoon, but which, we found, when we entered, had considerable current, rendering necessary a brisk use of our paddles.

MANGROVE SWAMP

The banks near the lagoon, were low, and the ground back of them apparently swampy, and densely covered with mangrove trees. This tree is universal on the Mosquito coast, lining the shores of the lagoons and rivers, as high up as the salt water reaches. It is unlike any other tree in the world. Peculiar to lands overflowed by the tides, its trunk starts at a height of from four to eight feet from the ground, supported by a radiating series of smooth, reddish-brown roots, for all the world like the prongs of an inverted candelabrum. These roots interlock with each other in such a manner that it is utterly impossible to penetrate between them, except by laboriously cutting one's way. And even then an active man would hardly be able to advance twenty feet in a day. The trunk is generally tall and straight, the branches numerous, but not long, and the leaves large and thick; on the upper surface of a dark, glistening, unfading green, while below, of the downy, whitish tint of the poplar-leaf. Lining the shore in dense masses, the play of light on the leaves, as they are turned upward by the wind, has the glad, billowy effect of a field of waving grain. The timber of the mangrove is sodden and heavy, and of no great utility; but its bark is astringent, and excellent for tanning. Its manner of propagation is remarkable. The seed consists of a long bean-like stem, about the length and shape of a dipped candle, but thinner. It hangs from the upper limbs in thousands, and, when perfect, drops, point downward, erect in the mud, where it speedily takes root, and shoots up to tangle still more the already tangled mangrove-swamp. Myriads of small oysters, called the mangrove-oysters, cling to the roots, among which active little crabs find shelter from the pursuit of their hereditary enemies, the long-legged and sharp-billed cranes, who have a prodigious hankering after tender and infantile shell-fish.

The Mosquito settlement is some miles up the

river, and we were unable to reach it before dark; so, on arriving at a spot where the ground became higher, and an open space appeared on the bank, we came to a halt for the night. We had this time no fish for supper, but, instead, a couple of *quams*, a species of small turkey, which is not a handsome bird, but, nevertheless, delicate food. Many of these flew down to the shore, as night came on, selecting the tops of the highest, overhanging trees for their roosting-places, and offering fine marks for my faithful double-barreled gun.

The mosquitoes proving rather troublesome at the edge of the water, I abandoned the canoe, and spreading my blanket on the most elevated portion of the bank, near the fire, was soon asleep. Before midnight, however, I was roused by the sensation of innumerable objects, with sharp claws and cold bodies, crawling over me. I leaped up in alarm, and hastily shook off the invaders. I heard a crackling, rustling noise, as of rain on dry leaves, all around me, and by the dim light I saw that the ground was alive with crawling things, moving in an unbroken column toward the river. I felt them in the pockets of my coat, and hanging to my skirts. My nocturnal interview with the turtles at "El Roncador" recurred to me, and Coleridge's ghastly lines—

———"The very sea did rot—
Oh Christ, that this should be!—
And slimy things did crawl with legs
Upon the slimy sea!"

Half fearing that it might be my own disordered fancy, I shouted to Antonio, who, quick as light, was at my side. He stirred up the fire, and laughed outright! We had been invaded by an army of soldier-crabs, moving down from the high back-grounds. Antonio had selected his bed for the night nearest the river, and the fire, dividing the host, had protected him, while it had turned a double column upon me. I could not myself help laughing at the incident, which certainly had the quality of novelty. I watched the moving legion for an hour, but there was no perceptible decrease in the numbers. So I laid down again by the side of Antonio, and slept quietly until morning, when there were no more crabs to be seen, nor a trace of them, except that the ground had been minutely punctured all over, by their sharp, multitudinous claws.

It was rather late when we started up the river. We had not proceeded far before we came to an open space, where there were some rude huts, with canoes drawn up on the bank, in front. A few men, nearly naked, shouted at us as we passed, inquiring, in broken English, what we had to sell, evidently thinking that the white man could have no purpose there unless to trade. We passed other huts at intervals, which, however, had no signs of cultivation around them, except a few palm and plantain-trees, and an occasional small patch of yucas. The mangroves had now disappeared, and the banks began to look inviting, covered, as they were, with large trees, including the *caoba*, or mahogany, and the gigantic ceiba, all loaded down with vines. Thousands of parrots passed over, with their peculiar short, heavy flutter, and loud, querulous note. In the early morning, and toward night, they keep up the most vehement chattering, all talking and none listening, after the manner of a Woman's Rights Convention. There were also gaudy macaws, which floated past like fragments of a rainbow. In common with the parrots, they always go in pairs, and when one is found alone, he is always silent and sad, and acts as if he were a lone widower, and meditated suicide.

On the occasional sandy reaches, we saw groups of the *Roseate Spoonbills*, with their splendid plumage. The whole body is rose-colored; but the wings, toward the shoulders, and the feathers around the base of the neck, are of a bright scarlet, deepening to blood-red. But they form no exception to the law of compensations—in mechanics, called equilibrium, and in mathematics equations, since, while beautiful in plumage, they are sinfully ugly in shape. And I could not help fancying, when I saw them standing silent and melancholy on snags, contemplating themselves in the water, that, as with some other kinds of birds, their brilliant colors gave them no joy, coupled with so serious a drawback in form. I shot several, from which the Poyer boy

"THE SPOONBILL."

selected the most beautiful feathers, which he afterward interwove with others from the macaw, parrot, and egret, in a gorgeous head-dress, as a present to me.

Toward noon we came to a cleared space, much the largest I had seen on the coast ; and, as we approached nearer, I saw a house of European construction, and a large field of sugar-cane. In striking contrast with these evidences of industry and civilization, a Sambo or Mosquito village, made up of squalid huts, half buried in the forest, filled out the foreground. I recognized it as the village of Wasswatla (literally Watertown), the place of our destination. It, nevertheless, looked so uninviting and miserable, that had I not been attracted by the Christian establishment in the distance, I should have returned incontinently to the lagoon.

My unfavorable impressions were heightened on a nearer approach. As we pushed up our canoe to the shore, among a great variety of dories and other boats, the population of the village, including a large number of dogs of low degree, swarmed down to survey us. The juveniles were utterly naked, and most of the adults of both sexes had nothing more than a strip of a species of cloth, made of the inner bark of the *ule* or India-rubber tree (resembling the *tappa* of the Society Islanders), wrapped around their loins. There was scarcely one who was not disfigured by the blotches of the *bulpis*, and the hair of each stood out in frightful frizzles, " like the quills on the fretful porcupine." Most of the men carried a short spear, pointed with a common triangular file, carefully sharpened by rubbing on the stones, which, as I afterward learned, is used for striking turtle.

Forbidding as was the appearance of the assemblage, none of its individuals evinced hostility, and when I jumped ashore, and saluted them with "Good morning," they all responded, "*Mornin', sir!*" brought out with an indescribable African drawl. Two or three of the number volunteered to help Antonio draw up our boat, while I gave various orders, in default of knowing what else to do. Luckily, it occurred to me to produce a document, or pass, with which Mr. Bell had kindly furnished me before leaving Bluefields, and which all seemed to recognize, pointing to it respectfully, and ejaculating, "King paper! King paper!" It was frequently called afterward, "the paper that talks." This precious document, well engrossed on a sheet of fools-cap, with a broad seal at the bottom, ran as follows:—

"**Mosquito Kingdom.**

"GEORGE WILLIAM CLARENCE, by the Grace of God, King of the Mosquito Territory, to our trusty and well-beloved officers and subjects, Greeting! We, by these presents, do give pass and license to Samuel A. Bard Esquire, to go freely through our kingdom, and to dwell therein; and do furthermore exhort and command our well-beloved officers and subjects aforesaid, to give aid and hospitality to the aforesaid Samuel A. Bard Esquire, whom we hold of high esteem and consideration. Given at Blue-fields, this —— day of ——, in this the tenth year of our reign."

(Signed,) "George R."

The ejaculations of "King paper! King paper!" were followed by loud shouts of "Capt'n! Cap-t'n!" while two or three tall fellows ran off in the direction of the huts. I was a little puzzled by the movement, but not long left in doubt as to its object, for, in a few moments, a figure approached, creating hardly less sensation among the people, than he would have done among the "boys" in the Bowery. I at once recognized him as the "Capt'n," whose title had been so vigorously invoked. He was, to start with, far from being a fine-looking darkey; but all natural deficiencies were more than made up by his dress. He had on a most venerable cocked hat, in which was stuck a long, drooping, red plume, that had lost half of its feathers, looking like the plumes of some rake of a rooster, returning, crestfallen and bedraggled, from an unsuccessful attempt on some powerful neighbor's harem. His coat was that of a post-captain in the British navy, and his pantaloons were of blue cloth, with a rusty gold stripe running down each side. They were, furthermore, much too short at both ends, leaving an unseemly projection of ankle, as well as abroad strip

CAPTAIN DRUMMER.

of dark skin between the waistband and the coat. And when I say that the captain wore no shirt, was rather fat, and his pantaloons deficient in buttons wherewith to keep it appropriately closed in front, the active fancy of the reader may be able to complete the picture. He bore, moreover, a huge cavalry sword, which looked all the more formidable from being bent in several places and very rusty. He came forward with deliberation and gravity, and I advanced to meet him, "king paper" in hand.

When I had got near him, he adjusted himself in position, and compressed his lips, with an affectation of severe dignity. Hardly able to restrain laughing outright, I took off my hat, and saluted him with a profound bow, and "Good morning, Captain!" He pulled off his hat in return, and undertook a bow, but the strain was too great on the sole remaining button of his waistband; it gave way, and, to borrow a modest nautical phrase, the nether garment "came down on the run!" The captain, however, no way disconcerted, gathered it up with both hands, and held it in place, while I read the "paper that talked."

The upshot of the ceremony was, that I was welcomed to Wasswatla, and taken to a large vacant hut, which was called the "king's house," and dedicated to the Genius of Hospitality. That is to say, the stranger or trader may take up his abode there, provided he can dislodge the pigs and chickens, who have an obstinate notion of their own on the subject of the proprietorship, and can never be induced to surrender their prescriptive rights. The "king's house" was a simple shed, the ground within trodden into mire by the pigs, and the thatched roof above half blown away by the wind. But, even thus uninviting, it was better than any of the other and drier huts, for the fleas, at least, had been suffocated in the mud. Before night, Antonio had covered the floor, a foot deep, with *cahoon* leaves, and, with the aid of the Poyer boy and one or two natives, seduced thereunto by what they universally call "grog," had restored the roof, and built up a barricade of poles against the pigs. These were not numerous, but hungry and vicious; and, finding the barricade too strong to be rooted down, they tried the dodge of the Jews at Jericho, and of Captain Crockett with the bear, and undertook to squeal it down! They neither ate nor slept, those pigs, I verily believe, during the period of my stay; but kept up an incessant squeal, occasionally relieving their tempers by a spiteful drive at the poles. Between them and pestilent insects of various kinds, my slumbers were none of the sweetest, and I registered a solemn vow that this should be my last trial of Mosquito hospitality.

In the afternoon I had a visit from the captain, who told me that his name was "Lord Nelson Drummer," and that his father had been "Governor" in the section around Pearl-Cay Lagoon. He had laid aside his official suit, and with simple breeches of white cotton cloth, and a straw hat, afforded a favorable contrast to his appearance in the morning. He spoke English—quite as well as the negroes of Jamaica, and generally made himself understood. From him I learned that the house, which I had seen in the clearings, had been built, many years before, by a French Creole from one of the islands of the Antilles, who at one time had there a large plantation of coffee, cotton, and sugar-cane, from the last of which he distilled much rum. Drummer was animated on the subject of the rum, of which there had been, as he said, "much plenty!" But the Frenchmen had died, and although his family kept up the establishment for a little while, they were obliged to abandon it in the end. The negroes who had been brought out, soon caught the infection of the coast, and, slavery having been prohibited (by the British Superintendent at Belize!), became idle, drunken, and worthless. Some of them still lingered around Wasswatla, gathering for sale to the occasional trader, a few pounds of coffee from the trees on the plantation, which, in spite of years of utter neglect, still bore fruit. The abandoned cane-fields furnished a supply of canes, at which all the inhabitants of Wasswatla, old and young, were constantly gnawing. In fact, this appeared to be their principal occupation. I subsequently visited the abandoned estate. It was overgrown with vines and bushes, among which the orange, lime, and coffee-trees struggled for existence. The house was tumbling into ruin, and the boilers in which the sugar had been made, were full of stagnating water. I re-

5

turned to the squalid village, having learned another philosophy in the science of philanthropy; and with a diminishing inclination to tolerate the common cant about "universal brotherhood!"

The soil on the Wawashaan is rich and productive. It seems well adapted to cotton and sugar. The climate is hot and humid, and I saw many of the natives much reduced, and suffering greatly from fevers, which, if not violent, appear, nevertheless, to be persistent, and exceedingly debilitating. The natural products are numerous and valuable. I observed many indian-rubber trees, and, for the first time, the vanilla. It is produced on a vine, which climbs to the tops of the loftiest trees. Its leaves somewhat resemble those of the grape; the flowers are red and yellow, and when they fall off are succeeded by the pods, which grow in clusters, like our ordinary beans. Green at first, they change to yellow, and finally to a dark brown. To be preserved, they are gathered when yellow, and put in heaps, for a few days, to ferment. They are afterward placed in the sun to dry, flattened by the hand, and carefully rubbed with cocoa-nut oil, and then packed in dry plantain-leaves, so as to confine their powerful aromatic odor. The vanilla might be made a considerable article of trade on the coast; but, at present, only a few dozen packages are exported.

Lord Nelson, as I invariably called the captain, domesticated himself with me from the first day, and ate and drank with me—"especially the latter." And I soon found out that there was a direct and intimate relation, between his degree of thirst and his protestations of attachment. He even hinted his intention to get up a *mushla* feast for me, but I would not agree to stay for a sufficient length of time.

Finally, however, a grand fishing expedition to the lagoon was determined on, and I was surprised to see with how much alacrity the proposition was taken up. The day previous to starting was devoted to sharpening spears, cleaning the boats, and making paddles, in all of which operations the women worked indiscriminately with the men. Plantains were gathered, and, as it seemed to me, no end of sugar-canes from the deserted plantation. In the evening, which happened to prove clear, the big drum was got out, fires lighted, and there was a dance, as Lord Nelson said, "Mosquito fashion." My part of the performance consisted in keeping up the spirit of the drummers, by pouring spirits down, which service was responded to by a vehemence of pounding that would have done credit to a militia training. I was surprised to find how much skill the performers had attained; but afterward discovered that the drum is the favorite instrument on the coast, and is called in requisition on all occasions of festivity or ceremony. The dance was uncouth, without the merit of being grotesque; and long before it was finished, the performers, of both sexes, had thrown aside their *tournous*, and abandoned every shadow of decency in their actions.

Lord Nelson began to grow torpid early in the evening, and, before I left the scene, had been carried off dead drunk. Next morning he looked rather downcast, and complained that the rum "*had spoiled his head.*"

It was quite late when our flotilla got under way, with a large dory, carrying the big drum, leading the van. There were some twenty-odd boats, containing nearly the entire population of the village. This number was increased from the huts lower down, the occupants of which hailed us with loud shouts, and hastened after us with their canoes. We went down the river with the current very rapidly, the men paddling in the maddest way, and shouting to each other at the top of their voices. Occasionally the boats got foul, when the rivals used the flat of their paddles over each other's heads without scruple. I was considerably in the rear, and, from the sound of the blows, imagined that every skull had been crushed; but next moment their owners were paddling and shouting as if nothing had happened. From that day, I had a morbid curiosity to get a Mosquito skull!

We all encamped at night, on the sandy beach of a large island, in the centre of the lagoon. The reader may be sure that I made my own camp at a respectable distance from the rest of the party, where I had a quiet supper, patronized, as usual, by Captain Drummer. As soon as it became dark, the preparations for fishing commenced. The women were left on the beach, and three men apportioned to each boat. One was detailed to paddle, another to hold the torch, and the third, and most skillful, acted as striker or spearsman. The torches were made of splinters of the fat yellow pine, which abounds in the interior. The spears, I observed, were of two kinds; one firmly fixed by a shank at the end of a long light pole, called *sinnock*, which is not allowed to escape the hand of the striker. The other, called *waisko-dusa*, is much shorter. The staff is hollow, and the iron spear-head, or harpoon, is fastened to a line which passes through rings by the side of the shaft, and is wound to a piece of light-wood, designed to act as a float. When thrown, the head remains in the fish, while the line unwinds, and the float rises to the surface, to be seized again by the fisherman, who then hauls in his fish at his leisure. When the fish is large and active, the chase after the float becomes animated, and takes the character of what fishermen call "sport."

As I have said, no sooner was it dark than the boats pushed off, in different directions, on the lagoon. My Poyer boy had borrowed a *waisko-dusa*, and with him to strike, and Antonio to paddle, I took a torch, and also glided out on the water. My torch was tied to a pole, which I held over the bow. Antonio paddled slowly, while the Poyer boy, entirely naked (for the strikers often go overboard after their own spears), stood in the bow, with his spear poised in his right hand, eagerly inclining forward, and motionless as a statue. He was perfect in form, and his bronze limbs, just tense enough to display without distorting the muscles, were brought in clear outline against the darkness by the light of the torch—revealing a figure and pose that would shame the highest achievements of the sculptor. It was so admirable that I quite forgot the fisher in the artist, when, rapid as light, the arm of the Poyer boy fell, and the spear entered the water eight or nine feet ahead of the boat. The motion was so sudden, that it nearly startled me overboard. At first, I thought he had missed his mark, but I soon saw the white float, now dipping under the water, now jerked this way, now that, evincing clearly that the spearsman had been true in his aim. A few strokes of Antonio's paddle brought the float within reach of the striker, who began, in sporting phrase, to "land" the fish. It made a desperate struggle, and, for awhile, it was what is called a "tight pull" between the boy and the fish. Nevertheless, he was finally got in, and proved to be what is called a *June*, or *Jew-fish* (*Coracinus*), by the English, and *Palpa* by the natives. In point of delicacy and richness of flavor, this fish is unequaled by any other found in these seas. The one which we obtained weighed not far from eighty pounds. Some of them have been known to weigh two or three hundred pounds. Our prize made a great disturbance in our little canoe, to which Antonio put a stop by disemboweling him on the spot, after which we resumed our sport. We were successful in obtaining a number of rock-fish, and several *sikoko,* or sheep's-heads. Ambitious to try my skill, I took the Poyer boy's place for awhile. I was astonished to find how perfectly clear the water proved to be, under the light of the torch. The bottom, which, in the broad daylight, had been utterly invisible, now revealed all of its mysteries, its shells, and plants, and stones, with wonderful distinctness. I observed also that the fish seemed to be attracted by the light, and, instead of darting away, rose toward the surface and approached the boat. I allowed several opportunities of throwing the spear to slip. Finally, a fine sheep's-head rose just in front of me ; I aimed my spear, and threw it with such an excess of force as literally to drive the dory from beneath my feet, precipitating myself in the water, and knocking down and extinguishing the torch in my ungraceful tumble. The spear was recovered, and I felt rather disappointed to find that it was innocent of a fish. Antonio suggested that he had broken loose, which was kind of him, but it would n't do. As we were without light, and, moreover, had as many fish as we could possibly dispose of, we paddled ashore.

Up to this time, I had been so much absorbed with our own sport, that I had not noticed the other fishers. It was a strange scene. Each torch glowed at the apex of a trembling pyramid of red light, which, as the boats could not be seen, seemed to be inspired with life. Some moved on stately and slow, while others, where the boats were rapidly whirled in pursuit of the stricken fish, seemed to be chasing each other in fiery glee. Every successful throw was hailed with vehement shouts, heightened by loud blows made by striking the flat of the paddle on the surface of the water. All along the shore, the women had lighted fires whereat to dry the fish, which, in this climate, can not be kept long without spoiling. The light from these fires caught on the heavy foliage of the shore, and revealing the groups of half-naked women and children, helped to make up a scene which it is difficult to paint in words, but which can never be forgotten by one who has witnessed it.

It was past midnight before the boats all returned to the shore; and then commenced the drying of the fish. Over all the fires, just out of reach of the flames, were raised frame-works of canes, like grid-irons, on which the fish, thinly sliced lengthwise, and rubbed with salt, were laid. They were repeatedly turned, so that, with the salt, smoke and heat, they were so far cured in the morning, as to require no further attention than a day or two of exposure to the sun. Our Jew-fish was thus prepared, and afterward stood us in good stead, much resembling smoked salmon, but less salt. While Antonio superintended this operation, I cooked the head and shoulders of the big fish in the sand, after the manner I have already described, and achieved a signal success, inasmuch as the dish was well seasoned with "hunger sauce."

OFF the mouth of Pearl-Cay Lagoon are numerous cays, which, in fact, give their name to the lagoon. They are celebrated for the number and variety of turtles found on and around them. I was so much delighted with our torch-light fishing, that I became eager to witness the sport of turtle-hunting, which is regarded by the Mosquitos as their noblest art, and in which they have acquired proverbial expertness. Drummer required only a little persuasion and a taste of rum, to undertake an expedition to the cays. As this involved going out in the open sea, he selected four of the largest pitpans, to each of which he assigned the requisite number of able-bodied and expert men. The women and remaining men were left to continue their fishing in the lagoon. My canoe was much too small to venture off, and accordingly was left in charge of the Poyer boy, who, armed with my double-barreled gun, felt himself a host. With Antonio, I was given a place in the largest pitpan, commanded by Harris, Captain Drummer's "quarter-master," who was much the finest specimen of physical beauty that I had seen among the Sambos.

I was quite concerned on finding how little provisions were taken in the boats, since bad weather often keeps the fishermen out for two or three weeks. But Drummer insisted that we should find plenty to eat, and we embarked. We caught the land-breeze as soon as we got from under the lee of the shore, and drove rapidly on our course. Although the sea was comparatively smooth, yet the boats all carried such an amount of sail as to keep me in a state of constant nervousness. One would scarcely believe that the Mosquito men venture out in their pitpans, in the roughest weather with impunity, riding the waves like sea-gulls. If upset, they right their boats in a moment, and with their broad paddle-blades clear them of water in an incredibly short space of time.

We went, literally, with the wind ; and in four hours after leaving the shore, were among the cays. These are very numerous, surrounded by reefs, through which wind intricate channels, all well known to the fishers. Some of the cays are mere heaps of sand, and half-disintegrated coral-rock, others are larger, and a few have bushes, and an occasional palm-tree upon them, much resembling "El Roncador." It was on one of the latter, where there were the ruins of a rude hut, and a place scooped in the sand, containing brackish water, that we landed, and made our encampment. No sooner was this done than Harris started out with his boat after turtle, leaving the rest to repair the hut, and arrange matters for the night. Of course I accompanied Harris.

The apparatus for striking the turtle is exceedingly simple, corresponding exactly with the *waiskodusa*, which I have described, except that instead of being barbed, the point is an ordinary triangular file, ground exceedingly sharp. This, it has been found, is the only thing which will pierce the thick armor of the turtle; and, moreover, it makes so small a hole, that it seldom kills the green turtle, and very slightly injures the scales of the hawkbill variety, which furnishes the shell of commerce.

Harris stood in the bow of the pitpan, keeping a sharp look out, holding his spear in his right hand, with his left hand behind him, where it answered the purpose of a telegraph to the two men who paddled. They kept their eyes fixed on the signal, and regulated their strokes, and the course and speed of the boat, accordingly. Not a word was said, as it is supposed that the turtle is sharp of hearing. In this manner we paddled among the cays for half an hour, when, on a slight motion of Harris' hand, the men altered their course a little, and worked their paddles so slowly and quietly as scarcely to cause a ripple. I peered ahead, but saw only what I supposed was a rock, projecting above the water. It was, nevertheless, a turtle, floating lazily on the surface, as turtles are wont to do. Notwithstanding the caution of our approach, he either heard us, or caught sight of the boat, and sank while we were yet fifty yards distant. There was a quick motion of Harris' manual telegraph, and the men began to paddle with the utmost rapidity, striking their paddles deep in the water. In an instant the boat had darted over the spot where the turtle had disappeared, and I caught a hurried glimpse of him, making his way with a speed which quite upset my notions of the ability of turtles in that line, predicated upon their unwieldiness on land. He literally seemed to *slide* through the water.

And now commenced a novel and exciting chase. Harris had his eyes on the turtle, and the men theirs on Harris' telegraphic hand. Now we darted this way, then that; slow one moment, rapid the next, and anon stock still. The water was not so deep as to permit our scaly friend to get entirely out of reach of Harris' practiced eye, although to me the bottom appeared to be a hopeless maze. As the turtle must rise to the surface sooner or later to breathe, the object of the pursuer is to keep near enough to transfix him when he appears. Finally, after half an hour of dodging about, the boat was stopped with a jerk, and down darted the spear. As the whole of the shaft did not go under, I saw it had not failed of its object. A moment more, and Harris had hold of the line. After a few struggles and spasmodic attempts to get away, his spirit gave in, and the tired turtle tamely allowed himself to be conducted to the shore. A few sharp strokes disengaged the file, and he was turned over on his back on the sand, the very picture of utter helplessness, to await our return. I have a fancy that the expression of a turtle's head, and half-closed eyes, under such circumstances, is the superlative of saintly resignation; to which a few depreciatory movements of his flippers come in as a sanctimonious accessory, like the upraised palms of a well-fed parson.

STRIKING TURTLE.

This "specimen," as the naturalists would say, proved to be of the smaller, or hawk-bill variety, the flesh of which is inferior to that of the green turtle, although hawk-bills are most valuable on account of their shells. So we paddled off again, keeping close to the cays and reefs, where the water is shallow. It was nearly dark before Harris got a chance at another turtle, which he struck on the bottom, at least eight feet below the surface. This was of the green variety ; he was lifted in the boat, and his head unceremoniously chopped off, lest he should take a spiteful nip at the hams of the paddlers.

We wound our way back to the rendezvous, picking up our hawk-bill, who was that night unmercifully put through the cruel process, which I have already had occasion to describe, for separating the scales from the shell, after which he was permitted to take himself off. I may here mention, that besides the two varieties of turtle which I have named, there is another and larger kind, called the loggerhead turtle (*Testudo Caretta*), which resembles the green turtle, but is distinguished by the superior size of the head, greater breadth of shell, and by its deeper and more variegated colors. It grows to be of great size, sometimes reaching one thousand or twelve hundred pounds ; but its flesh is rank and coarse, and the laminæ of its shell too thin for use. It, nevertheless, supplies a good oil, proper for a variety of purposes.

That evening, we had turtle steaks, and turtle eggs, roasted turtle flippers, and *callipash* and *callipee* (the two latter in the form of soup),—in fact, turtle in every form known to the Mosquito men, who well deserve the name of turtle-men. The turtle conceals its eggs in the sand, but the natives are ready to detect indications of a deposit, which they verify by thrusting in the sand the iron ramrod of a musket, an operation which they call "feeling for eggs."

About midnight, it came on to rain heavily, and continued all the next day, so that nothing could be done. The time was "put in" *talking turtle,* and Harris got so warmed up as to promise to show me what the Mosquito men regard as the *ne plus ultra* of skill in turtle craft, namely, "jumping turtle." He did not explain to me what this meant, but gave me a significant wag of the head, which is a Mosquito synonym for *nous verrons.*

The third day proved propitious, and Harris was successful in obtaining several fine turtles. About noon he laid aside his spear, and took his position, entirely naked, keeping up, nevertheless, his usual look-out. We were not long in getting on the track of a turtle. After a world of maneuvering, apparently with the object of driving him into shallow water, Harris made a sudden dive overboard. The water boiled and bubbled for a few moments, when he reappeared, holding a fine hawk-bill in his outstretched hands. And that feat proved to be what is called "jumping a turtle." It often happens that bungling fishermen get badly bitten in these attempts, which are not without their dangers from the sharp coral rocks and spiny sea-eggs.

During the afternoon of the fourth day, we returned to the lagoon, taking with us eight green turtles, and about ninety pounds of fine shell. We found that most of the party which we had left had gone back to the village, whither Drummer and his "quarter-master" were urgent I should return with them. But Wasswatla had no further attractions for me, and I was firm in my purpose of proceeding straightway up the coast.

With many last turns at the grog, I parted—not without regret—with Drummer and Harris, giving them each a gaudy silk handkerchief, in acknowledgment of two fine turtles which they insisted on my accepting. Harris also gave me his turtle-spear, and was much exalted when I told him that I should have it engraved with his name, and hung up in my *watla* (house) at home.

Pearl-Cay Lagoon is upward of forty miles long, by, perhaps, ten miles wide at its broadest part. There are three or four settlements upon it, the principal of which are called Kirka, and English Bank. I did not visit any of these, but took my course direct for the upper end of the lagoon, where, as the chain of salt lakes is here interrupted for a considerable distance, there is another *haulover* from the lagoon to the sea. I saw several collections of huts on the western shore, and on a small island, where we stopped during the mid-day heats, I gathered a few stalks of the *jiquilite* (*Indigofera disperma*), or indigenous indigo-plant, which may be ranked as one of the prospective sources of wealth on the coast.

We arrived at the *haulover* in the midst of a drenching thunder-storm, which lasted into the night. It was impossible to light a fire, and so we drew up the canoe on the beach, and, piling our traps in the centre, I perched myself on the top, where, with the sail thrown over my head, I enacted the part of a tent-pole for the live-long night! My Indian companions stripped themselves naked, rubbed their bodies with palm oil, and took the pelting with all the nonchalance of ducks. For want of any thing better to do, I ate plantains and dried fish, and, after the rain subsided, watched the brilliant fire-flies, of which hundreds moved about lazily under the lee of the bushes. The atmosphere, after the storm had subsided, was murky and sultry, making respiration difficult, and inducing a sense of extreme lassitude and fatigue. Every thing was damp and sticky, and so saturated with water, that it was impossible for me to lie down. I applied to my Jamaica for comfort, but, in spite of it, relapsed into a fit of *glums*, or "blue-devils." To add to my discomfort, innumerable sand-flies came out, and, soon after, a cloud of mosquitos, while a forest-full of some kind of tree-toad struck up a doleful piping, which proved too much for even my tried equanimity. I got up, and strode back and forth on the narrow sand-beach, in a vehement and intemperate manner, wishing myself in New York, any where, even in Jamaica! The remembrance of my first night on the shores of the lagoon only served to make me feel the more wretched, and I longed to have "some gentleman do me the favor to thread on the tail of me coat!"

Toward daylight, however, my companions had contrived to make up a sickly fire, in the smoke of which I sought refuge from the mosquitoes and sand-flies, and became soothed and sooty at the same time. Day came at last, but the sun was obscured, and things wore but slight improvement on the night. I found that we were on a narrow strip of sand, scarcely two hundred yards wide, covered with scrubby bushes, interspersed with a few twisted trees, looking like weather-beaten skeletons, beyond which was the sea, dark and threatening, under a gray, filmy sky. Antonio predicted a storm, what he called a *temporal*, during which it often rains steadily for a week. Under the circumstances, it became a pregnant question what to do: whether to return down the lagoon to some more eligible spot for an encampment, or to push out boldly on the ocean, and make an effort to gain the mouth of a large river, some miles up the coast, called Rio Grande or Great River.

I resolved upon the latter course, and we dragged the canoe across the *haulover*. Although the surf was not high, we had great difficulty in launching our boat, which was effected by my companions, who, stationed one on each side, seized a favorable moment, as the waves fell, to drag it beyond the line of breakers. While one kept it stationary with his paddle, the other, watching his opportunity, carried off the articles one by one, and finally, stripping myself, I mounted on Antonio's shoulders, and was deposited like a sack in the boat. We paddled out until we got a good offing, then put up our sail, and laid our course north-north-west. The coast was dim and indistinct, but I had great faith in the Poyer boy, whose judgment had thus far never failed. About four o'clock in the afternoon, we came in sight of a knoll or high bank, which, covered with large trees, rises on the north side of the mouth of Great River, constituting an excellent landmark. I was in no wise sorry to find ourselves nearing it rapidly, for the wind began to freshen, and I feared lest it might raise such a surf on the bar of the river as to prevent us from entering. In fact, the waves had begun to break at the shallower places on the bar, while elsewhere the north-east wind drove over the water in heavy swells. The sail was hastily gathered in, and my Indians, seizing their paddles, watched the seventh, or crowning wave, and, by vigorous exertion, cheering each other with shouts, kept the canoe at its crest, and thus we were swept majestically over the bar, into the comparatively quiet water beyond it. Half an hour afterward, the great waves broke on the very spot where we had crossed, in clouds of spray, and with the noise of thunder!

The mouth of Great River is broad, but entirely exposed to the north-east; and, although it is a large stream, the water on its bar is not more than five or six feet deep, shutting out all large vessels, which otherwise might go up a long way into the country. There are several islands near the mouth. On the innermost one, which toward the sea is bluff and high, we made our encampment. It appeared to me as favorable a spot as we could find, whereon to await the *temporal* which Antonio had predicted, and the approach of which became apparent to even the most unpracticed observer. Fortunately, with Harris' turtles, we felt easy on the score of food. So we dragged the canoe high up on the bank, and while I kindled a fire, my companions busied themselves in constructing a shelter over the boat. Stout forked stakes were planted at each end of the canoe, to support a ridge-pole, with other shorter ones supporting the outer poles. To these, canes were lashed transversely, and over all was woven a thatch of *cahoon*, or palmetto-leaves. Outside, and on a line with the eaves, a little trench was dug, to carry off the water, and preserve the interior from being flooded by what might run down the slope of the ground. So rapidly was all this done, that before it was quite dark the hut was so far advanced as to enable us to defy the rain, which soon began to fall in torrents. The strong sea wind drove off the mosquitos to the bush on the main-land, so that I slept comfortably and well, in spite of the thunder of the sea and the roaring of the wind.

For eight days it rained almost uninterruptedly. Sometimes, between nine and eleven o'clock, and for perhaps an hour near sunset, there would be a pause, and a lull in the wind, and a general lighting up of the leaden sky, as if the sun were about to break through. But the clouds would gather again darker than ever, and the rain set in with a steady pouring unknown in northern latitudes. For eight mortal days we had no ray of sun, or moon, or star! Every iron thing became thickly coated with rust; our plantains began to spot, and our dried fish to grow soft and mouldy, requiring to be hung over the small fire which we contrived to keep alive, in one corner of our extemporaneous hut.

TEMPORAL CAMP.

After the third day, the water in the river began to rise, and during the night rose more than eight feet. On the fifth day the current was full of large trees, their leaves still green, which seemed to be bound together with vines. In the afternoon down came the entire thatched roof of a native hut, which lodged against our island, bringing us a most acceptable freight, in the shape of a plump two-months old pig. His fellow-voyager—strange companionship!—was a tame parrot, with clipped wings, who looked melancholy enough when rescued, but who, after getting dry in our hut, and soothing his appetite on my plantains, first became mirthful, then boisterous, and finally mischievous. He was immediately installed as one of the party, and made more noise in the world than all the rest. To me he proved an unfailing source of amusement. He was respectful toward Antonio, but vicious toward the Poyer boy, and never happy except when cautiously stealing to get a bite at his toes. When successful in this he became wild with delight, and as noisy and vehement as a lucky Frenchman. It was one of his prime delights to gnaw off the corks of my bottles; and he was possessed of a most insane desire to get inside of my demijohn, mistaking it, perhaps, for a wicker cage, from which he imagined himself wrongfully excluded. Antonio called him "El Moro," the Moor, for what reason I did not understand, and the name suiting me as well as any other, I baptized him with water, "El Moro," and got an ugly pinch on the wrist for my blasphemy.

Our young porker escaped drowning only to fall into the hands of the Philistines; we had nothing to feed him; he might get away; he was, moreover, invitingly fat; so we incontinently cut his throat, and ate him up!

During our imprisonment, my companions were not idle. Upon the island were many *mohoe*-trees, the bark of which is tough, and of a fine, soft, white fibre. Of this they collected considerable quantities, which the Poyer boy braided into a sort of cap, designed as the foundation of the elegant feather head-dress which he afterward gave me ; while Antonio, more utilitarian, wove a small net, not unlike that which we use to catch crabs. He at once put it into requisition to catch craw-fish, which abounded among the rocks to the seaward of the island. But before entering upon the subject of craw-fish, I may say that the *mohoe* bark, from its fine quality, and the abundance in which it may be procured, might be made exceedingly useful for the manufacture of paper—an article now becoming scarce and dear.

The *cray* or *craw-fish* resemble the lobster, but are smaller in size, and want the two great claws. Their flesh has more flavor than that of either the crab or lobster, and we found them an acceptable addition to our commissariat. There were many wood-pigeons and parrots on the island, but my gun had got in such a state, from the damp, that I did not attempt to use it.

Our protracted stay made a large draft on our yucas and plantains, and it became important to us to look out for fruit and vegetables. The current in the river was too strong, and too much obstructed with floating timber, to permit us to use our boat. The water, even at the broadest part of the stream, had risen upward of fifteen feet, equivalent to a rise of twenty or twenty-five feet in the interior! The banks were overflowed; the low islands outside of us completely submerged and our own space much circumscribed. A few plantain-trees, which we had observed on the first evening, had been broken down or swept away, and we were fain to put ourselves on a short allowance of vegetables. One morning, during a pause in the rain, I ventured out; and, after a little search, found a tree, resembling a pear-tree, and bearing a large quantity of a small fruit, of the size and shape of a crab-apple, and exactly like it in smell. I cried out delightedly to Antonio, holding up a handful of the supposed apples. To my surprise, he shouted, "Throw them down! throw them down!" explaining that they were the fruit of the *mangeneel* or *manzanilla*, and rank poison. He hurried me away from the tree, assuring me that even the dew or rain-drops which fell from its leaves were poisonous, and that its influence, like that of the fabled *upas*, is so powerful as to swell the faces and limbs of those who may be ignorant or indiscreet enough to sleep beneath its shade! I found out subsequently, that it is with the acrid milky juice of this tree that the Indians poison their arrows. I ever afterward gave it a wide berth. In shape and smell is is so much like the crab-apple that I can readily understand how it might prove dangerous to strangers. Under the tropics, it is safe to let wild fruits alone. Antonio, more successful than myself, found a large quantity of *guavas*, which the natives eat with great relish, but which to me have a disagreeable aromatic, or rather, musky taste. So I stuck to plantains, and left my companions and "El Moro" to enjoy a monopoly of *guavas.*

Finally, the windows of heaven were closed, the rain ceased, and the sun came out with a bright, well-washed face. It was none too soon, for every article which I possessed, clothing, books, food, all had begun to spot and mould from the damp. I had myself a sympathetic feeling, and dreamed at night that I was covered with a green mildew; dreams so vivid that I once got up and went out naked in the rain, to wash it off!

After the leaves had ceased to drip, we stretched lines between the trees, and hung out our scanty wardrobe to dry. I rubbed and brushed at my court suit of black, but in vain. What with salt water at "El Roncador," and mould here, it had acquired a permanent rusty and leprous look, which half inclined me to follow the Poyer boy's suggestion, and soak it in palm oil! Few and simple as were our equipments, it took full two days to redeem them from the effects of the damp. My gun more resembled some of those quaint old fire-locks taken from wrecks, and exhibited in museums, than any thing useful to the present generation. In view of all things, I was fain to ejaculate, Heaven save me from another "*temporal*" on the Mosquito Shore!

6

IT was three days after the rain had ceased, before we could embark on the river, and even then its current was angry and turbid, and filled with floating trees. We hugged the banks in our ascent, darting from one side of the stream to the other, to avail ourselves of the *back-sets*, or eddies, sometimes losing, by an unsuccessful attempt, all we had gained by half an hour of hard paddling. The banks were much torn by the water; in some places they had fallen in, carrying many trees into the stream, where they remained anchored to the shore by the numerous tough vines that twined around them. Elsewhere the trees, half undermined, leaned heavily over the current, in which the long vines hung trailing in mournful masses, like the drooping leaves of the funeral willow. The long grass on the low islands had been beaten down, and was covered with a slimy deposit, over which stalked hungry water-birds, the snow-white ibis, and long-shanked crane, in search of worms and insects, and entangled fish.

We were occupied the whole day, in reaching the first settlement on this river—a picturesque collection of low huts, in a forest of palm, papaya, and plantain-trees. Near it were some considerable patches of maize, and long reaches of yucas, squash, and melon-vines. There were, in short, more evidences of industry and thrift than I had yet seen on the entire coast.

As we approached the bank, in front of the huts, I observed that all the inhabitants were pure Indians, whom my Poyer boy hailed in his own tongue. I afterward found out that they were Woolwas, and spoke a dialect of the same language with the Poyers, and Cookras, to the northward. As at Wasswatla, nearly all the inhabitants crowded down to the shore to meet me, affording, with their slight and symmetrical bodies, and long, well-ordered, glossy black hair, a striking contrast to the large-bellied, and spotted mongrels on the Wawashaan. I produced my "King-paper," and advanced toward a couple of elderly men bearing white wooden wands, which I at once conjectured were insignia of authority. But no sooner did they get sight of my "King-paper," than they motioned me back with tokens of displeasure, exclaiming, "*Sax! sax!*" which I had no difficulty in comprehending meant "take it away!"

So I folded it up, put it in my pocket, and extended my hand, which was taken by each, and shaken in the most formal manner. When the men with the wands had finished, all the others came forward, and went through the same ceremony, most of them ejaculating, interrogatively, *Nakisma?* which appears to be an exact equivalent of the English, "How are you?"

This done, the men with the wands beckoned to me to follow them, which I did, to a large hut, neatly wattled at the sides, and closed by a door of canes. One of them pushed this open, and I entered after him, followed only by those who had wands, the rest clustering like bees around the door, or peering through the openings in the wattled walls. There were several rough blocks of wood in the interior, upon which they seated themselves, placing me between them. All this while there was an unbroken silence, and I was quite in a fog as to whether I was held as a guest or as a prisoner. I looked into the faces of my friends in vain; they were as impassible as stones. I, however, felt reassured when I saw Antonio at the door, his face wearing rather a pleased than alarmed expression.

We sat thus a very long time, as it appeared to me, when there was a movement outside, the crowd separated, and a man entered, bearing a large earthen vessel filled with liquid, followed by two girls, with baskets piled with cakes of corn meal, fragments of some kind of broiled meat, and a quantity of a paste of plantains, having the taste of figs, and called *bisbire.* The eldest of the men of wands filled a small calabash with the liquid, touched it to his lips, and passed it to me. I did the same, and handed it to my next neighbor; but he motioned it back, exclaiming, "*Dis! dis!*" drink, drink! I found it to be a species of palm-wine, with which I afterward became better acquainted. It proved pleasant enough to the taste, and I drained the calabash. Another one of the old men then took up some of the roast meat, tore off and ate a little, and handed the rest to me. Not slow in adaptation, I took all hints, and wound up by making a hearty meal. The remnants were then passed out to Antonio, who, however, was permitted to wait on himself.

I made some observations to Antonio in Spanish, which I perceived was understood by the principal dignitary of the wands, who, after some moments, informed me, in good Spanish, that the hut in which we were, was the *cabildo* of the village, and that it was wholly at my service, so long as I chose to stay. He furthermore pointed out to me a rude drum hanging in one corner, made by stretching the raw skin of some animal over a section of a hollow tree, upon which he instructed me to beat in case I wanted any thing. This done, he rose, and, followed by his companions, ceremoniously retired, leaving me in quiet possession of the largest and best hut in the village. I felt myself quite an important personage, and ordered up my hammock, and the various contents of my canoe, with a degree of satisfaction which I had not experienced when waging a war against the pigs, in the "King's house" at Wasswatla.

I subsequently ascertained that all of the ideas of government which the Indians on this river possess, were derived from the Spaniards, either descending to them from former Spanish establishments here, or obtained from contact with the Spaniards far up in the interior. The principal men were called "*alcaldes*," and many Spanish words were in common use. I discovered no trace of negro blood among them, and found that they entertained a feeling of dislike, amounting to hostility, to the Mosquito men. So far as I could ascertain, while they denied the authority of the Mosquito king, they sent down annually a certain quantity of sarsaparilla, maize, and other articles, less as tribute than as the traditionary price of being let alone by the Sambos. In former times, it appeared, the latter lost no opportunity of kidnapping their children and women, and selling them to the Jamaica traders, as slaves. Indeed, they sometimes undertook armed forays in the Indian territory, for the purpose of taking prisoners, to be sold to men who made this traffic a regular business. This practice continued down to the abolition of slavery in Jamaica—a measure of which the Mosquito men greatly complain, notwithstanding that they were not themselves exempt from being occasionally kidnapped.

The difficulty of entering the Rio Grande, and

the absence of any considerable traffic with the natives on its banks, are among the causes which have contributed to keep them free from the degrading influences that prevail on the Mosquito Shore. They rely chiefly upon agriculture for their support, and fish and hunt but little. They have abundance of maize, yucas, cassava, squashes, plantains, papayas, cocoa-nuts, and other fruits and vegetables, including a few limes and oranges, as also pigs and fowls, and higher up the river, in the savannah country, a few horned cattle. I observed, among the domestic fowls, the true Muscovy duck, and the idigenous hen or *chachalaca*.

The people themselves, though not tall, are well-made, and have a remarkably soft and inoffensive expression. The women—and especially the girls—were exceedingly shy, and always left the huts when I entered. The men universally wore the *ule tournou*, or breech-cloth, but the women had in its place a piece of cotton cloth of their own manufacture, striped with blue and yellow, which hung half-way down the thighs, and was supported above the hips by being tucked under in some simple, but, to me, inexplicable manner.* The young girls were full and symmetrical in form, with fine busts, and large, lustrous, black eyes, which, however, always had to me a startled, deer-like expression. I saw

* The blue dye, used in coloring by these Indians, is made from the *jiquilite*, which, as I have said, is indigenous on the coast. The yellow from the *anotta*, called *achiota*, the same used to give the color known as *nankeen*. The tree producing it is abundant throughout all Central America.

no fire-arms among the men, although they seemed to be acquainted with their use. They had, instead, fine bows and arrows, the latter pointed with iron, or a species of tough wood, hardened in the fire. The boys universally had blow-pipes or reeds, with which they were very expert, killing ducks, curlews, and a kind of red partridge, at the distance of thirty and forty yards. The silence with which the light arrow is sped, enables the practiced hunter frequently to kill the greater part of a flock or *covey*, before the rest take the alarm.

My life in the cabildo was unmarked by any adventure worth notice. I received plantains, fowls, whatever I desired, Aladdin-like, by tapping the drum. This was always promptly responded to by a couple of young Indians, who asked no questions, and made no replies, but did precisely what they were bid. Neither they nor the alcaldes would accept any thing in return for what they furnished me, beyond a few red cotton handkerchiefs, and some small triangular files, of which old Hodgson had wisely instructed me to take in a small supply. They all seemed to be unacquainted with the use of money, although not without some notion of the value of gold and silver. I saw several of the women with rude, light *bangles* of gold, which metal, the alcaldes told me, was found in the sands of the river, very far up, among the mountains.

Among the customs of these Indians, there is one of a very curious nature, with which I was made acquainted by accident. Nearly every day I strolled off in the woods, with a vague hope of some time or other encountering a *waree*, or wild hog (of whose presence in the neighborhood, an occasional foray on the maize fields of the Indians bore witness), or perhaps a *peccary*, or some other large animal. As the bush was thick, I seldom got far from the beaten paths of the natives, and had to content myself with now and then shooting a *curassow*, in lieu of higher game. One day, I ventured rather further up the river than usual, and came suddenly upon an isolated hut. Being thirsty, I approached with a view of obtaining some water. I had got within perhaps twenty paces, when two old women dashed out toward me, with vehement cries, motioning me away with the wildest gestures, and catching up handfuls of leaves and throwing them toward me. I thought this rather inhospitable, and at first was disposed not to leave. But, finally, thinking there must be some reason for all this, and seeing that the women appeared rather distressed than angry, I retracted my steps. I afterward found, upon inquiry, that the hut was what is called *tabooed* by the South Sea Islanders, and devoted to the women of the village, during their confinement. As this period approaches, they retire to this secluded place, where they remain in the care of two old women for two moons, passing through lustrations or purifications unknown to the men. While the woman is so confined to the hut, no one is allowed to approach it, and all persons are especially cautious not to pass it to the windward, for it is imagined that by so doing the wind, which supplies the breath of the newly-born child, would be taken away, and it would die. This singular notion, I afterward discovered, is also entertained by the Mosquito people, who no doubt derived it from their Indian progenitors.

The course of life of the Indians appeared to be exceedingly regular and monotonous. Both men and women found abundant occupation during the day; they went to bed early, and rose with the dawn. Although most of them had hammocks, they universally slept on what are called *crickeries,* or platforms of canes, supported on forked posts, and covered with variously-colored mats, woven of the bark of palm branches. I observed no drunkenness among them, and altogether they were quiet, well-ordered, and industrious. In all their relations with me, they were respectful and obliging, but exceedingly reserved. I endeavored to break through their taciturnity, but without success. Hence, after a few days had passed, and the novelty had worn off, I began to weary of inactivity. So I one day proposed to the principal alcalde, that he should undertake a hunt for the *tilbia,* mountain cow, or *tapir,* and the *peccary,* or Mexican hog. He received the proposition deferentially, but suggested that the *manitus,* or sea-cow, was a more wonderful animal than either of those I had named, and that it would not be difficult to find one in the river. I took up the hint eagerly, as I had already caught one or two glimpses of the manitus, which had greatly roused my curiosity. The drum was thereupon beaten, and the alcaldes convened to consult upon the matter. They all came with their wands, and after due deliberation, fixed upon the next night for the expedition. Boats were accordingly got ready, and the hunters sharpened their lances and harpoons. The latter resembled very much the ordinary whaling harpoons, but were smaller in size. The lances were narrow and sharp, and attached to thin staffs, of a very tough and heavy wood. Notwithstanding that Antonio smiled and shook his head, I cleaned my gun elaborately, and loaded it heavily with ball.

Before narrating our adventure in the pursuit of the manitus, it will not be amiss to explain that this animal is probably the most remarkable one found under the tropics, being amphibious, and the apparent connecting link between quadrupeds and fishes. It may perhaps be better compared to the seal, in its general characteristics, than to any other sea-animal. It has the two fore feet, or rather hands, but the hind feet are wanting, or only appear as rudiments beneath the skin. Its head is thick and heavy, and has something the appearance of that of a hornless cow. It has a broad, flat tail, or integument, spreading out horizontally, like a fan. The skin is dark, corrugated, and so thick and hard that a bullet can scarcely penetrate it. A few scattered hairs appear on its body, which has a general resemblance of that of the hippopotamus. There are several varieties of the manitus, but it is an animal which appears to be little known to naturalists. Its habits are very imperfectly understood, and the natives tell many extraordinary stories about it, alleging, among other things, that it can be tamed. It is herbivorous, feeding on the long tender shoots of grass growing on the banks of the rivers, and will rise nearly half of its length out of water to reach its food. It is never found on the land, where it would be utterly helpless, since it can neither walk nor crawl.

It is commonly from ten to fifteen feet long, huge and unwieldy, and weighing from twelve to fifteen hundred pounds. It has breasts placed between its paws, and suckles its young. The male and female are usually found together. It is extremely acute in its sense of hearing, and immerges itself in the water at the slightest noise. Great tact and caution are therefore necessary to kill it, and a manitee hunt puts in requisition all the craft and skill of the Indians.

The favorite hour for feeding, with the manitus, is the early morning, during the dim, gray dawn. In consequence I was called up to join the hunters not long after midnight. Two large pitpans, each holding four or five men, were put in requisition, and we paddled rapidly up the river, for several hours, to the top of a long reach, where there were a number of low islands, covered with grass, and where the banks were skirted by swampy savannahs. Here many bushes were cut, and thrown lightly over the boats, so as to make them resemble floating trees. We waited patiently until the proper hour arrived, when the boats were cast loose from the shore, and we drifted down with the current. One man was placed in the stern with a paddle to steer, another with a harpoon and line

HUNTING THE MANITUS.

crouched in the bow, while the rest, keeping their long keen lances clear of impediments, knelt on the bottom. We glided down in perfect silence, one boat close to each bank. I kept my eyes opened to the widest, and in the dim light got quite excited over a dozen logs or so, which I mistook for manitee. But the hunters made no sign, and we drifted on, until I got impatient, and began to fear that our expedition might prove a failure. But of a sudden, when I least expected it, the man in the bow launched his harpoon. The movement was followed by a heavy plunge, and in an instant the boat swung round, head to the stream. Before

I could fairly comprehend what was going on, the boughs were all thrown overboard, and the men stood with their long lances poised, ready for instant use. We had run out a large part of the slack of the harpoon-line, which seemed to be fast to some immovable object. The bowsman, however, now began to gather it in, dragging up the boat slowly against the current. Suddenly the manitus, for it was one, left his hold on the bottom, and started diagonally across the river, trailing us rapidly after him. This movement gradually brought him near the surface, as we could see by the commotion of the water. Down darted one of the lances, and under again went the manitus, now taking his course with the current, down the stream. The other boat, meantime, had come to our assistance, hovering in front of us, in order to fasten another harpoon the instant the victim should approach near enough to the surface. An opportunity soon offered, and he received the second harpoon and another lance at the same instant. All this time I had both barrels of my gun cocked, feverishly awaiting my chance for a shot. Soon the struggles of the animal became less violent, and he several times came involuntarily to the surface. I watched my chance, when his broad head rose in sight, and discharged both barrels, at a distance of thirty feet, startling the hunters quite as much as they had disconcerted me. It was the Lord's own mercy that some of them did not get shot in the general scramble!

The manitus, after receiving the second harpoon, became nearly helpless, and the Indians, apparently secure of their object, allowed the boats to drift with him quietly down the river. Occasionally he made an ineffectual attempt to dive to the bottom, dashing the water into foam in his efforts, but long before we reached the village he floated at the surface, quite dead. The morning was bright and clear when we paddled ashore, where we found every inhabitant of the place clustering to meet us. When they saw that we had been successful, they set up loud shouts, and clapped their hands with vigor, whence (as this was the only manifestation of excitement which I had seen) I inferred that the capture of a manitus was regarded as something of a feat, even on the Mosquito Shore.

Ropes were speedily attached to the dead animal, at which every body seemed anxious to get a chance to pull, and it was dragged up the bank triumphantly, amid vehement shouts. I had been somewhat piqued at the contempt in which my gun had been held, and had been not a little ambitious of being able to say that I had killed a manitus, and as, after my shot, the animal had almost entirely ceased its struggles, I thought it possible I had given it the final *coup*, and might conscientiously get up a tolerable brag on my adventure, over Mr. Sly's punch, when I returned to New York. It was with some anxiety, therefore, that I investigated its ugly head, only to find that my balls had hardly penetrated the skin, and that the hide of the manitus is proof against any thing in the shape of firearms, except, perhaps, a Minié rifle. And thus I was cheated out of another chance for immortality! Lest, however, my story that the hide of the manitus is an inch thick, and tough as whalebone, should not be credited, I had a strip of it cut off, which, when dried, became like horn, and a terror to dogs, in all my subsequent rambles. I suspect there are some impertinent curs here, in New York, who entertain stinging recollections of that same strip of manitus-hide! Dr. Pounder, my old schoolmaster, I am sure, would sacrifice his eyes, or perhaps, what is of equal consequence, his spectacles, to obtain it!

But while my balls were thus impotent, I found that the lances of the Indians had literally gone through and through the manitus. The harpoons

MANITEE HARPOON AND LANCES.

did not penetrate far, their purpose being simply to fasten the animal. The lances were the fatal instruments, and I afterwards saw a young Indian drive his completely through the trunk of a full-grown palm-tree. This variety of lance is called *silak*, and is greatly prized.

There were great doings in the village over the

manitus. Beneath the skin there was a deep layer of very sweet fat, below which appeared the flesh, closely resembling beef, but coarser, and streaked throughout with layers of fat. This, when broiled before the fire, proved to be tender, well-flavored, and altogether delicious food. The tail is esteemed the most delicate part, and, as observed by Captain Henderson, who had a trial of it on the same shore, "is a dish of which Apicius might have been proud, and which the discriminating palate of Heliogobalus would have thought entitled to the most distinguished reward!" The better and more substantial part of the animal, namely, the flesh, was carefully cut in strips, rubbed with salt, and, hung in the sun to dry, made into what the Spaniards call *tasajo.* The other portions were distributed among the various huts, and the tail was presented to me. When I came to leave, I found that the cured or *tasajoed* flesh had also been preserved for my use. Broiled on the coals, it proved quite equal to any thing I ever tasted, and as sweet as dried venison. And here I may mention that the flesh of the manitus, like that of the turtle, is not only excellent food, but its effects on the system are beneficial, particularly in the cases of persons afflicted with scorbutic or scrofulous complaints. It is said these find speedy relief from its free use, and that, in the course of a few weeks, the disease entirely disappears.

Chapter VII.

AT the end of two weeks, I signified to my friends that I should be compelled, on the following day, to leave them, and pursue my voyage up the coast. I had supposed that there existed an interior connection between Great River and the lagoons which led to Cape Gracias, but found that they commenced with a stream some twenty miles to the northward, called "Snook Creek," and that it would be necessary to trust our little boat again to the sea.

The announcement of my intended departure was received without the slightest manifestion of feeling, but, during the evening, the inhabitants vied with each other in loading the canoe with fruits and provisions. They were, in fact, so lavish of their presents, that I was unable to accept them all, and had to leave more than half of what they brought me. I, nevertheless, made special room for the *tasajoed* manitus, and took all the *bisbire* which was brought. As I have already explained, the *bisbire* is a paste made of ripe plantains, having about the consistency, and very much the taste, of dried figs. It is made into rolls, closely wrapped in the leaves of the tree on which it grows, which preserve it perfectly, and it thus becomes an article of prime value to the voyager.*

I left the village with as much ceremony as I had entered it. The Alcaldes bearing their wands, escorted me down to the water, where I was obliged to shake hands with all the people, each one exclaiming, "*Disabia!*" equivalent to "Good-bye!"

* The plantain and the banana are varieties of the same plant. They not only constitute marked features in the luxuriant foliage of the tropics, but their fruit supplies the place of bread, and forms the principal part of the food of the people. They thrive best in a rich, moist soil, and are generally grown in regular walks, from shoots or bulbs like those of the air-plant, which continually spring up at the roots of the parent stem. They are very rapid in their growth, producing fruit within a twelvemonth. Moreover, not being dependent upon the seasons, a constant supply is kept up during the year; for, while one stem drops beneath its load of ripe fruit, another throws out its long flower-spike, and a third shows the half-formed cluster. The fruit is very nutritive, and is eaten in a great variety of forms—raw, boiled, roasted, and fried—and in nearly every stage of its growth, as well when green as when yellow and mature. Humboldt tells us, that it affords, in a given extent of ground, forty-four times more nutritive matter than the potato, and one hundred and thirty-three times more than wheat. As it requires little if any care in the cultivation, and produces thus perennially and abundantly, it may be called an "institution for the encouragement of laziness." On the banks of all the rivers on the Mosquito Shore, it is found growing wild, from shoots brought down from the plantations of the Indians, and which have taken root where they were lodged by the current.

They stood on the bank until we were entirely out of sight. I left them with admiration for their primitive habits, and genuine though formal hospitality. Although, in their taciturnity, they were not unlike our own Indians, yet, in all other respects, they afforded a very striking contrast to them. The North American savage disdains to work ; his ambition lies in war and the chase ; but the gentler dweller under the tropics is often industrious, and resorts to hunting only as an accessory to agriculture.

The ceremonies of my departure had occupied so much time that, when we reached the mouth of the river, it was too late to venture outside. So we took up our quarters, for the night, in our old encampment, on the island. The moon was out, and the evening was exceedingly beautiful—so beautiful, indeed, that I might have fallen into heroics, had it not been for a most infernal concert kept up by wild animals on the river's banks. I at first supposed that all the ferocious beasts of the forest had congregated, preparatory to a general fight, and comforted myself that we were separated from them by the river. There were unearthly groans, and angry snarls, and shrieks, so like those of human beings in distress as to send a thrill through every nerve. At times the noises seemed blended, and became sullen and distant, and then so sharp and near that I could hardly persuade myself they were not produced on the island itself. I should have passed the night in alarm, had not Antonio been there to explain to me that most, if not all these sounds came from what the Spaniards call the "*mono colorado*," or howling monkey. I afterward saw a specimen—a large, ugly beast, of a dirty, brick-red color, with a long beard, but otherwise like an African baboon. Different from most other monkeys, they remain in nearly the same places, and have favorite trees, in which an entire troop will take up its quarters at night, and open a horrible serenade, that never fails to fill the mind of the inexperienced traveler with the most dismal fancies. Notwithstanding Antonio's explanations, they so disturbed my slumbers that I got up about midnight, and, going down to the edge of the water, fired both barrels of my gun in the direction of the greatest noise. But I advise no one to try a similar experiment. All the water-birds and wild fowl roosting in the trees gave a sudden flutter, and set up responsive croaks and screams, from which the monkeys seemed to derive great encouragement, and redoubled their howling. I was glad when the unwonted commotion ceased, and the denizens of the forest relapsed again into their chronic serenade.

A large proportion of tropical animals are emphatically "children of the night." It is at night that the tiger and maneless Mexican lion leave their lairs, and range the dense forests in pursuit of their prey, rousing the peccary and tapir from their haunts, and sending them to seek refuge in the thickets, where crashing of bushes and splashings in hidden pools testify to the blind fear of the pursued, and the fierce instincts of the pursuers. A sudden plunge of the alligator from the banks, will startle the wild birds on the overhanging trees, and in an instant the forest resounds to the wild cries of the tiger, the plaints of the frightened monkeys, and the shrieks and croaks of the numerous water-fowl; while the wakeful traveler starts up and hastily grasps his faithful gun, surprised to find the wilderness, which was so still and slumberous under the noonday heats, now terrible with savage and warring life.

Toward morning the commotion in the forest subsided, and I was enabled to snatch a few hours of slumber. I awoke to find the sun just streaking the horizon, and the boat all ready for departure. Antonio had cut two trunks of the buoyant *mohoe* tree, which were lashed to the sides of our boat to act as floats, and prevent us from being overturned by any sudden flaw of the wind. We passed the bar without much trouble, and made a good offing, before laying our course for "Snook Creek." The wind was fresh, and the water bright and playful under the blue and cloudless sky. I leaned over the side of our frail boat—scarce a speck in the broad breast of the ocean—and watched the numerous marine animals and *mollusca* that floated past; the *nautilus*, "small commodore," with its tiny sail and rosy prow, the pulsating *rhizostoma*, and the *bernice*, with its silken hair—most fragile forms of life, and yet unharmed dwellers in the mighty sea, which mocks at the strength of iron, and undermines continents in its wrath!

During the afternoon we came close in shore, keeping a sharp look-out for the mouth of "Snook Creek." There are, however, no landmarks on the

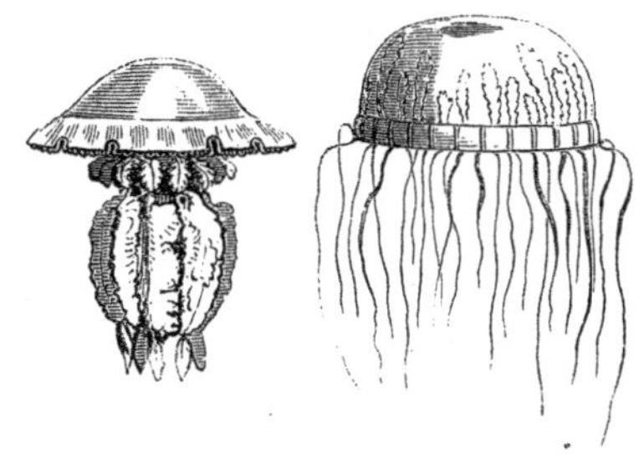

MOLLUSCA OF THE CARIBBEAN SEA.

entire coast; throughout it wore the same flat, monotonous appearance—a narrow strip of sand in front of a low impenetrable forest, in which the fierce north-easters had left no large trees standing. Hence it is almost impossible for voyagers, not intimately acquainted with the shore, to determine their position. My Poyer boy had coasted here but once, and I found, toward evening, that he was of opinion that we had passed the mouth of the creek of which we were in search. So we resolved to stand along the shore for either Walpasixa or Prinza-pulka, where part of the hull of an American ship, wrecked sometime before, still remained as a guide to voyagers.

As the sun went down, the wind fell, and the

moon came up, shedding its light upon the broad, smooth swells of the sea, silver-burnished upon one side, and on the other dark but clear, like the shadows on polished steel. We lowered our useless sail, and my companions took their paddles, keeping time to a kind of chant, led off by Antonio, the Poyer boy joining in the swelling chorus. The melody was very simple, and, like that of all purely Indian chants, sad and plaintive. I have often thought, in listening to them, that they were the wails of a people conscious of their decay, over a continent slipping from their grasp, and a power broken forever!

ON THE MOONLIT SEA!

I lay long, watching the shore as it glided past, and listening to the tinkle of the water under our prow, but finally fell into a deep and dreamless slumber, rocked by the ocean in its gentlest mood. When I awoke we had already passed the Prinzapulka bar, and were fastened to the branches of a large tree, which had become entanged among the mangroves, on the banks of the river. It was with no small degree of satisfaction that I found we had now an uninterrupted river and lagoon navigation to Cape Gracias, and that we should not again be obliged to venture, with our little boat, upon the open sea.

The Prinza-pulka seemed rather an estuary than a river, and was lined with an impenetrable forest of mangroves. These were covered with flocks of the white ibis, and, as we advanced up the stream, we came upon others of a rose color, looking like *bouquets* of flowers among the green leaves of the trees.

At the distance of three miles, the river banks grew higher, although densely covered with wild plants and vines, which seemed to have subdued the forest. The few trees that were left were clustered all over with twining rope-plants, or *lianes*, sometimes hanging down and swinging in mid-air, and again stretched to the ground, like the cordage of a ship, supporting in turn, hundreds of creepers, with leaves of translucent green, and loaded with clusters of bright flowers. An occasional fan-palm thrust itself above the tangled verdure, as if struggling for light and air; while the broad leaves of the wild plantain emerged here and there in groups, and the slender stalks of the bamboo-cane, fringed with delicate leaves like those of the willow, bent gracefully over the water. At the foot of this emerald wall was a strip of slimy earth, and I observed occasional holes, or tunnel-like apertures, through which the alligator trailed his hideous length, or the larger land-animals came down to the water to drink. As we glided by one of these openings, a tapir suddenly projected his head and ugly proboscis, but, startled by our canoe, as suddenly withdrew it, and disappeared in the dark recesses of the impenetrable jungle, in which it is beyond the power of man to penetrate, except he laboriously carves his way, foot by foot, in the matted mass.

About ten o'clock we reached the mouth of a narrow creek, or stream, diverging from the river under a complete canopy of verdure. Up this creek, my Poyer assured me, the Prinza-pulka village was situated. So we paddled in, and, after many windings, finally came where the vegetation was less rank, and the banks were higher and firmer. I began to breathe freer, for the air within these tropical fastnesses seemed to me loaded with miasmatic damps, like the atmosphere of a vault. As we proceeded, the country became more and more open, and the water clearer, revealing a gravelly bottom, until, at last, to my surprise, we came upon broad savannahs, fringed, along the water, by narrow belts of trees. Through these I caught glimpses of gentle swells and undulations of land, upon which, to my further amazement, I saw clumps of pine-trees! I had supposed the pine to be found only in high, temperate latitudes, and could scarcely believe that it grew here, side by side with the palm, almost on a level with the sea, until I was assured by my Poyer that it abounded in all the savannahs, and covered all the *plateaus* and mountains of the interior.

A bend in the creek brought us suddenly in view of a group of canoes, drawn up on the shore, in front of a few scattered huts. One or two women, engaged in some occupation at the edge of the water, fled when they saw us, scrambling up the bank in evident alarm. As we approached nearer, I saw through the bushes a number of men hurrying back and forth, and calling to each other in excited voices. Before we had fairly reached the landing-place, they had collected among the canoes, whence they motioned us back with violent gestures. Some were armed with spears, others had bows and arrows, and two or three carried muskets, which they pointed at us in a very careless and unpleasant manner. I observed that they were Sambos, like those at Wasswatla, equally frizzled about the head, and spotted with the *bulpis*. Whenever we attempted to approach, they shouted "*Bus! bus!*" and raised their weapons. The Poyer boy responded by calling "*Wita*," *i. e.*, chief, or head man. Hereupon one of the number came forward a little, and inquired "*Inglis? Inglis?*" pointing to me. I held up my pass, and, remembering Wasswatla, pointed to it, exclaiming, "King paper! king paper!" This seemed to produce an impression, and we made a movement to land, but up came the guns again, their muzzles looking as large as church doors. Things certainly appeared squally, and I was a little puzzled what to do. Prudence suggested that we should retreat, but then that might be understood as an evidence of fear, which, with savages, as with wild beasts, is a sure way of inviting attack. I preferred, therefore, to await quietly the result of a conference which seemed to be going on, and in which I noticed I was frequently pointed out, with very suggestive gestures. While this was going on, Antonio carefully got out my gun and revolver, handing me the latter in such a manner as not to attract notice. He had evinced a high consideration for it, ever since it had played so large a part in my first interview with the patron at "El Roncador."

After much debate, two of the Sambos, including the head man, pushed off to us in a canoe, under the cover of the weapons of those on shore. They, however, fell back in evident alarm when they caught sight of my revolver. I therefore laid it down, extended both open hands, and hailed them with the Mosquito salutation, which applies equally at all hours of the day and night, "Good morning!" They replied, with the universal drawl, "*Mornin', sir!*" I put my "king paper" forward, very conspicuously, and read it through to them, no doubt to their edification. The head man said, "Good! good!" when I had finished, but nevertheless seemed suspicious of the contents of our boat, inquiring, in a broken way, for "Osnabergs," and "*pauda*," or powder. I explained to them, as well as I could, that we were not traders, which piece of information did not seem to please them. But when they caught sight of my demijohn, they evinced more amiability, which I hastened to heighten by giving them a calabash of the contents.

They afterward signified their willingness to let me go ashore, if I would first give them my gun and revolver, which I sternly and peremptorily refused to do. They finally paddled to the shore, motioning for us to follow. Upon landing, I gave them each a dram, which was swallowed in a breath, with unequivocal signs of relish. The head men,

VILLAGE OF QUAMWATLA.

after another ineffectual attempt to induce me to surrender my revolver, led the way up the bank, Antonio and the Poyer boy remaining with the canoe.

The village was very straggling and squalid, although the position was one of great beauty. It stood on the edge of an extensive savannah, covered thickly with coarse grass, and dotted over with little clusters of bushes, and clumps of dark pines, more resembling a rich park, laid out with consummate skill, than a scene on a wild and unknown shore, under the tropics. As we advanced, I observed that the huts were all comparatively new, and that there were many burnt spots, marked by charred posts and half-burned thatch-poles. Among the rubbish, in one or two places, I noticed fragments of earthenware of European manufacture, and pieces of copper sheathing, evidently from some vessel.

I was conducted to the head man's hut, where room was made for me to sit down on one of the crickeries. Some kind of fermented drink was brought for me, which I had great difficulty in declining. In fact, I did not like the general aspect of things. In the first place, there were no women visible, and then the ugly customers with the guns and spears, when not scrutinizing me or my revolver—which seemed to have a strange fascination in their eyes—were engaged in a very sinister kind of consultation.

The head man seemed particularly anxious to know my destination, and the purposes of my visit. My suspicions had been roused, and I represented myself as a little in advance of a large party from the Cape, bound down the coast, and inquired, in return, what kind of accommodations could be provided for my companions when they arrived. This rather disconcerted him, and I thought the opportunity favorable to fall back to the boat, now fully convinced that some kind of treachery was meditated. A movement was made to intercept me at the door, but the presented muzzle of my revolver opened the way in an instant, and I walked slowly down to the landing, the armed men following, and calling out angrily, "*Mer'ka man! Mer'ka man!*" Antonio stood at the top of the bank, with my gun, his face wearing an anxious expression. He whispered to me hurriedly, in Spanish, that half a dozen armed men had gone down the creek in a boat, and that he had no doubt the intention was to attack us.

In fact the cowardly wretches were now brandishing their weapons, and uttering savage shouts. I at once saw that there was but one avenue of escape open, namely, to take to our boat, and get away as fast as possible. I waited until my companions had taken their places, and then walked down the bank deliberately, and entered the canoe. A few rapid strokes of the paddles carried us well clear of the shore, before the Sambos reached the top of the bank. I brought my gun to bear upon them, determined to fire the instant they should manifest any overt act of hostility. They seemed to comprehend this, and contented themselves with running after us, along the bank, shouting "Mer'ka man!" and pointing their weapons at us, through the openings in the bushes.

We were not long in getting beyond their reach, but they nevertheless kept up loud, taunting shouts, while we were within hearing. I counted this a lucky escape from the village, but was not at my ease about the party which had gone down the creek. I felt sure that they were in ambush in some of the dark recesses of the banks, and that we might be attacked at any moment. Both Antonio and myself, therefore, sat down in the bottom of the canoe, closely watching the shores, while the Poyer boy paddled noiselessly in the stern. It was now near night, and the shadows gathered so darkly over the narrow stream that we could see nothing distinctly. On we went, stealthily and watchfully. We had reached the darkest covert on the creek, a short distance above its junction with the river, when a large canoe shot from the bank across our bows, with the evident purpose of intercepting us. At the same instant a flight of arrows whizzed past us, one or two striking in the canoe, while the others spattered the water close by. I at once commenced firing my revolver, while Antonio, seizing the long manitee-spear, sprang to the bow. At the same instant our canoe struck the opposing boat, as the saying is, "head on," crushing in its rotten sides, and swamping it in a moment. Antonio gave a wild shout of triumph, driving his spear at the struggling wretches, some of whom endeavored to save themselves by climbing into our canoe. I heard the dull *tchug* of the lance as it struck the body of one of the victims, and, with a sickening sensation, cried to the Poyer, who had also seized a lance to join in the slaughter, to resume his paddle. He did so, and in a few seconds we were clear of the

THE FIGHT NEAR QUAMWATLA.

scene of our encounter, and gliding away in the darkness. I caught a glimpse of the struggling figures clinging to their shattered boat, and uttering the wildest cries of alarm and distress. The quick ear of Antonio caught responsive shouts, and it soon became evident that we had been followed by boats from the village.

Convinced that we would be pursued, and that if overtaken we should be borne down by numbers, the question of our safety became one of superior craft, or superior speed. I was disposed to try the latter, but yielded to Antonio, who, watching an opportunity, ran our boat under an overhanging tree, where the tangled bank cast an impenetrable shadow on the water. Here we breathlessly awaited the course of events. It was not long before we heard a slight ripple, and through the uncertain light I saw three canoes dart rapidly and silently past. The pursuers evidently thought we had reached the river, where the mangroves and impenetrable jungles on the banks would effectually prevent concealment or escape. Relieved from the sense of immediate danger, it became a vital question what we should next do to secure our ultimate safety. The moon would soon be up, and our pursuers, not finding us on the river, would at once divine our trick, and, placing us between themselves and the town, render escape impossible. To abandon our boat was to court a miserable death in the woods. Antonio suggested the only feasible alternative. There were but three canoes, and when they reached the river, he shrewdly reasoned, two would follow our most probable track down the stream, while the third would doubtless search for us above. Our policy, then, was to follow in the wake of the latter, until it should be as widely separated from aid as possible, and then, by a sudden *coup-de-main*, either disable or paralyze our opponents, and make the best of our way into the interior, where we could not fail to find creeks, and other places of refuge from pursuit.

My companions stripped themselves, so as not to be encumbered in the water, in case of accident, and I followed their example, retaining only my dark shirt, lest my white body should prove too conspicuous a mark. I carefully loaded my pistols, put a handful of buck-shot in each barrel of my gun, and we started down the creek. A few moments brought us to the river, but we could neither see nor hear the canoes of our enemies. We turned up the stream, paddling rapidly, but silently, and keeping close to the shore. Every few minutes Antonio would stop to listen. Meantime, I hailed with joy some heavy clouds in the East, which promised to prolong the obscurity, by hiding the light of the rising moon.

The excitement of the night of the terrible storm, in which I was wrecked on "El Roncador," was trifling to what I experienced that evening, paddling up the dark and sullen river. I exulted in every boat's length which we gained, as tending to make the inevitable contest more equal, and welcomed every ebon fold of cloud which gathered in the horizon. I felt that a thunder-storm was brooding; and the marshaling of the elements roused still more the savage desperation which gradually absorbed every other feeling and sentiment. At first, every nerve in my system vibrated, and I trembled in every limb; I felt like one in an ague fit; but this soon passed away—every muscle became tense, and I felt the strong pulsations in my temples, as if molten iron was coursing through the veins. I no longer sought to avoid a contest, but longed for the hour to come when I could shed blood. Every moment seemed an age, and I know not how I subdued my impatience.

Meantime the threatened storm gathered, with a rapidity peculiar to the tropics on the eve of a fervid day, and the darkness became so dense that we several times run our boat against the bank, from sheer inability to see. Suddenly the dark vail of heaven was rift, and the lurid lightning fell with a blinding flash, which seemed to sear our eye-balls. An instant after rolled in the deep-voiced thunder, booming awfully among the primeval forests. A few rain-drops followed, which struck with steel-like sharpness on the naked skin, and hot puffs of air came soughing along the river. A moment after the heavens again glowed with the lightnings, glaring on the dark breast of the river, and revealing, but a few yards in advance of us, the hostile canoe, returning from what its occupants no doubt regarded as a hopeless pursuit. Their loud shout of savage defiance and joy was cut short by the heavy roll of the thunder, and, an instant after, the bows of our boats came together. They glanced apart, and I was nearly thrown from my balance into the water, for I had risen, the more surely to pour the contents of my gun into the midst of our assailants. Another shout followed the shock, and I heard the arrows, shot at random in the darkness, hiss past our heads. I reserved my fire until the lightning should fall to guide my aim. I had not long to wait; a third flash revealed the opposing boat; I saw that it was filled with men, and that in their midst stood the treacherous head man of the village. The flash of my gun, and that of the lightning, so far as human senses could discern, were simultaneous; yet instantaneous as the whole transaction must have been, I saw my victim fall, and heard his body plunge in the water, before the report had been caught up by the echo, or drowned by the thunder. I shall never forget the shriek of terror and of rage that rung out from that boat to swell the angry discord of the elements. Even now, it often startles me from my sleep. But then it inspired me with the wildest joy; I shouted back triumphantly, and tossed my arms exultingly in the face of the unblenching darkness. A few more arrows, a couple of musket-shots, fired at random toward us, and the combat was over. We heard wails and groans, but they grew fainter and more distant, showing that our enemies were dropping down the river. Another flash of lightning disclosed them drifting along the bank, and beyond the reach of our weapons.

Our purpose was now accomplished; our foes were behind us, and before us an unknown mesh of lagoons and rivers. We had no alternative but to advance, perhaps upon other and more formidable dangers. However that might be, we did not stop to consider, but all through the stormy night plied our paddles with incessant energy. About midnight we came to a small lagoon, on the banks of which we observed some fires, but the sky was still overcast, and we escaped notice. Toward morning the moon came out, and we directed our boat close in shore, so as to take refuge in some obscure creek during the day. An opening finally presented itself, and we paddled in. As we advanced it became narrow, and was obstructed by drooping branches and fallen trunks. Under some of them we forced our boat with difficulty, and others we cut away with our *machetes*. After infinite trouble and labor we passed the mangrove-swamp, and came to high grounds, on which were many *coyol* palm-trees, and a few dark pines. Here, exhausted with our extraordinary efforts, and no longer sustained by excitement, we made a hasty encampment. To guard against surprise Antonio undertook the first watch, and, wrapping myself in my blanket, I fell into a profound slumber.

And now, to remove any mystery which might attach to the hostile conduct of the Sambos at *Quamwatla* (for that was the name of the inhospitable village), I may explain that, in September, 1849, the bark "Simeon Draper," from New York, bound for Chagres, with passengers for California, was wrecked on the coast, near the mouth of the Prinza-pulka River. The remains of her hull I have alluded to, as now constituting one of the principal landmarks on that monotonous shore. Her passengers all escaped to the land, and succeeded in recovering most of their effects. They were soon discovered by the Sambos of Quamwatla, who, affecting friendship, nevertheless committed extensive depredations on the property of the passengers. Strong representations were made to the head man, but without effect; in fact, it soon became evident that he was the principal instigator of the robberies. The news of the wreck spread along the coast, and a large number of Sambos gathered at the village. As their numbers increased, they grew bold and hostile, until the position of the passengers became one of danger. They finally received intimations that a concerted attack would soon be made upon them, which they anticipated by an assault upon the Sambo village. The inhabitants, taken by surprise, fled after a few discharges of the rifles and revolvers, and the village was set on fire and burned to the ground. The wrecked Americans were not afterward disturbed, and their condition becoming known in San Juan, a vessel was dispatched to their relief, and they were taken off in safety.

It was not until I arrived at Cape Gracias that I

became acquainted with these facts, which accounted for the appearance of things in Quamwatla, and explained the hostility of the natives. Every Englishman on the coast is a trader, and as I disowned that character, and, moreover, carried a revolver, they were not long in making up their minds that I was an American.

Under all the circumstances of the case, our escape was almost miraculous. I subsequently ascertained that three of our assailants had been killed outright in the two encounters, and that the treacherous head man had died of his wounds.

It is with no feeling of exultation that I mention this fact ; for, so long as I live, I shall not cease to lament the necessity, which circumstances imposed upon me, of taking the life of a human being, however debased or criminal. I know of no sacrifice which I would not now make to restore those miserable wretches to their deserted huts, and to the rude affection of which even savages are capable. The events of that terrible night have left a shadow over my heart, which time rather serves to deepen than to efface.

Chapter VIII.

OUR reception at Quamwatla had certainly not been of a kind to inspire us with the most cheerful anticipations. We knew that a vast net-work of lagoons, rivers, and creeks extended to Cape Gracias, but of the character and disposition of the people, scattered along their tangled shores, we were utterly ignorant. Turning back was not to be thought of; and going ahead was a matter which required caution. Should we be so unfortunate as to get involved in another fight, we could hardly expect to get off so easily as we had done in our last encounter.

Under all the circumstances, we concluded that, inasmuch as our place of refuge seemed secure, and withal was not deficient in resources, it would be the wisest plan to remain where we were until the pursuit, which we were sure would be made, should have been abandoned ; or, at least, until the waning of the moon should afford us a dark night, wherein we could pursue our voyage unobserved. With this sage resolution, we set to work to establish a temporary camp.

As I have said, the little creek, which we had followed, led us to the base of a range of low hills, or rather ridges or swells of land, where the ground was not alluvial, but dry and gravelly. These ridges could hardly be called savannahs, although they were covered with a species of coarse grass, relieved, here and there, by clumps of gum-arabic bushes, groups of pine-trees, and an occasional *coyol*, or spiny-palm. Between these comparatively high grounds and the lagoon, intervened a dense, impenetrable mangrove-swamp, pierced by a few choked channels formed by the small streams coming down from the hills.

I selected the shelter of a clump of fragrant pines for our encampment, where the ground was covered with a soft, brown carpet of fallen leaves. A rope stretched between the trees supported our little sail, which was spread out, tent-wise, by poles. Under this my hammock was suspended, affording a retreat, shady and cool by day, and secure from damps and rains at night.

In a little grassy dell, close by, was a clear spring of water. We lit no fires except at night, lest the smoke might betray us ; and only then in places whence the light could not be reflected.

Accustomed as were my companions to wild and savage life, they seemed to enjoy the danger and the seclusion in which we found ourselves. It gave them an opportunity to display their skill and resources, and they really assumed toward me an air of complacent patronage, something like that of a city *habitué* toward his country cousin, when showing to him the marvels of the metropolis.

One of Antonio's earliest exploits, after our resolution to stop had been taken, was to cut down a number of the rough-looking palm-trees. In the trunks of these, near their tops, where the leaves sprang out, he carefully chiseled a hole, cutting completely through the pulp of the tree, to the outer, or woody shell. This hole was again covered with the piece of rind, which had first been removed, as with a lid. I watched the operation curiously, but asked no questions. In the course of the afternoon, however, he took off one of these covers, and disclosed to me the cavity filled with a frothy liquid, of the faintest straw tinge, looking like delicate Sauterne wine. He presented me with a piece of reed, and with a gratified air motioned me to drink. My early experiments with straws, in the cider-barrels of New England, recurred to me at once, and I laughed to think that I had come to repeat them under the tropics. I found the juice sweet, and slightly pungent, but altogether rich, delicious, and invigorating. As may be supposed, I paid frequent visits to Antonio's reservoirs.

This palm bears the name of *coyol* among the

Spaniards, and of *cockatruce* among the Mosquitos. Its juice is called by the former *Vino de Coyol,* and by the Indians generally *Chicha* (*cheechee*)—a name, however, which is applied to a variety of drinks. When the tree is cut down, the end is plastered with mud, to prevent the juice, with which the core is saturated, from exuding. A hole is then cut near the top, as I have described, in which the liquid is gradually distilled, filling the reservoir in the course of ten or twelve hours. This reservoir may be emptied daily, and yet be constantly replenished, it is said, for upward of a month. On the third day, if the tree be exposed to the sun, the juice begins to ferment, and gradually grows stronger, until, at the end of a couple of weeks, it becomes intoxicating—thus affording to the Sambos a ready means of getting up the "big drunk." The Spaniards affirm that the "vino de coyol" is a specific for indigestion and pains in the stomach.

The nuts of this variety of palm grow in large clusters. They are round, containing a very solid kernel, so saturated with oil as to resemble refined wax. It is in all respects superior to the ordinary cocoa-nut oil, and might be obtained in any desirable quantity, if means could be devised for separating the kernel from the shell. This shell is thick, hard, black, capable of receiving the minutest carving, and most brilliant polish, and is often worked into ornaments by the Indians.

In the moist depressions, or valleys, near our encampment, we also found another variety of palm, which often stands the traveler, under the tropics, in good stead, as a substitute for other and better vegetable food. I mean the *Palmetto Royal* or *Mountain Cabbage* (*Areca oleracea*), which has justly been called the "Queen of the Forest." It grows to a great height, frequently no thicker than a man's thigh, yet rising upward of a hundred and fifty feet in the air. No other tree in the world equals it in height or beauty. The trunk swells moderately a short distance above the root, whence it tapers gently to its emerald crown, sustaining throughout the most elegant proportions.

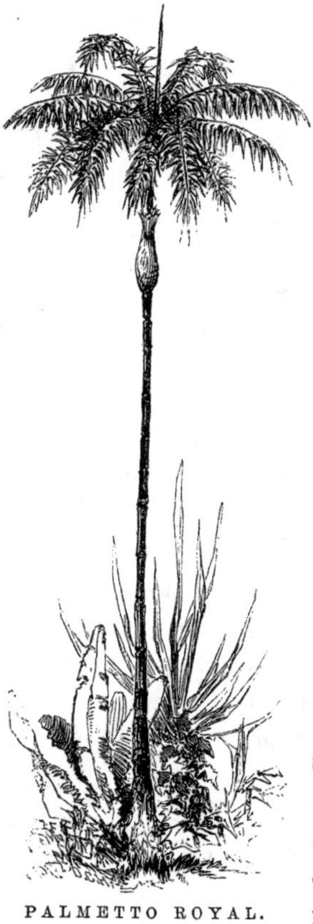

PALMETTO ROYAL.

The edible part, or "cabbage" (as it is called, from some fancied resemblance in taste to that vegetable), constitutes the upper part of the trunk, whence the foliage springs. It resembles a tall Etruscan vase in shape, of the liveliest green color, gently swelling from its pedestal, and diminishing gradually to the top, where it expands in plume-like branches. From the very centre of this natural vase rises a tall, yellowish *spatha*, or sheath, terminating in a sharp point. At the bottom of this, and inclosed in the natural vase which I have described, is found a tender white core, or heart, varying in size with the dimensions of the tree, but usually eight or ten inches in circumference. This may be eaten raw, as a salad, or, if preferred, fried or boiled. In taste it resembles an artichoke, rather than a cabbage.

The Indians climb this palm, and, dexterously inserting their knives, contrive to obtain the edible part without destroying the tree itself. By means of the same contrivance which he made use of in obtaining the cocoa-nuts, on the island in Pearl Cay Lagoon, Antonio kept us supplied with palm cabbages, which were our chief reliance, in the vegetable line. I found that they were most palatable when properly seasoned, and baked in the ground, with some strips of manitee fat, after the manner which I have already described.

The fruits of this tree are small, oblong berries, of a purplish blue, about the size of an olive, inclosing a smooth, brittle nut, which, in turn, covers a cartilaginous kernel.

The pine ridges were not deficient in animal life. A few large cotton-trees grew on the edge of the mangrove-swamp, which were the nightly resort of parrots and paroquets, who came literally in clouds, and then the callings, scoldings, frettings, and screamings that took place would have drowned the confusion of the most vicious rookery extant. In the evening and morning it was really difficult for us to make each other hear, although our camp was distant more than two hundred yards from the roosts. The parrots are often eaten by the natives, in default of other food, but they are tough, hard, dry, and tasteless. Not so, however, with the quails, which were not only numerous, but so tame, or rather so unsuspecting, that we could catch as many as we wanted, in the simplest kind of traps. We adopted this method of procuring such game as the Poyer boy did not kill with his bow, instead of using my gun, the report of which might betray us.

Day by day we extended our excursions farther from the camp, every step revealing to me, at least, something novel and interesting. I think it was the third day after our arrival, when we came upon a patch of low ground, or jungle, densely wooded, and distant perhaps half a mile from our encampment. Attracted by some bright flowers, I penetrated a few yards into the bushes, where, to my surprise, I came upon what appeared to be a well-beaten path, which I followed for some distance, wondering over the various queer tracks which I observed printed, here and there, on the moist ground. While thus engaged, I was startled by the sound of some animal approaching, with a dull and heavy, but rapid tread. Looking up, I saw a lead-colored beast, about the size of a large donkey, its head drooping between its fore-legs, coming toward me at a swinging trot.

Thinking he was charging upon me direct, I leaped into the bushes, with the intention of climbing up a tree. But before I could effect my object, the monster lumbered past, taking not the slightest notice of my presence. I breathed freer, when I saw his broad buttocks and little pig-like tail disappearing down the path, and I made my way out of the jungle, in a manner probably more expeditious than either graceful or valorous. Antonio, who was dodging after a fat currassow, had heard the noise, and was witness of my retreat. He seemed alarmed at first, but only smiled when I explained what I had seen. In fact, he appeared to think it rather a good joke, and hurried off to examine the tracks. He came back in a few minutes, and reported that my monster was *only a dante,* which I took to be some kind of Indian lingo for at least a hippopotamus, or rhinoceros.

"We shall have rare sport," he continued, "in catching this *dante.* It will be equal to hunting the manitus."

I found, upon inquiry, that the *dante* is called, in the Mosquito dialect, *tilba* or *tapia,* which names at once suggested *tapir,* an animal of which I had read, but of which I had very vague notions.

The Poyer boy seemed delighted with the news that there was a *tapir* about, and in less than five minutes after, both he and Antonio were sharpening their spears and lances, with palpable design on my monster's life. They told me that the *tapir* generally keeps quiet during the day, wandering out at night, usually in fixed haunts and by the same paths, to take exercise and obtain his food. I was not a little relieved when they added that he never fights with man or beast, but owes his safety to his speed, thick hide, and ability to take to the water, where he is as much at home as on land, swimming or sinking to the bottom at his pleasure. He is, nevertheless, a headlong beast, and when alarmed or pursued, stops at nothing — vines, bushes, trees, rocks, are all the same to him! He would do well for a crest, with the motto, "*Neck or Nothing!*"

In shape, the *dante* or *tapir* (sometimes called *mountain cow*) is something like a hog, but much larger. He has a similar arched back; his head, however, is thicker, and comes to a sharp ridge at the top. The male has a snout or sort of proboscis hanging over the opening of the mouth, something like the trunk of an elephant, which he uses in like manner. This is wanting in the female. Its ears are rounded, bordered with white, and can be drawn forward at pleasure; its legs are thick and stumpy; its fore-feet or hoofs are divided into three parts or toes, with a sort of false hoof behind; but the hind feet have only three parts or divisions. Its tail is short, and marked by a few stiff hairs; the skin so hard and solid as generally to resist a musket-ball; the hair thin and short, of a dusky brown; and along the top of the neck runs a bristly mane, which extends over the head and down the snout. He has ten cutting-teeth, and an equal number of grinders in each jaw; features which separate him entirely from the ox-kind, and from all other ruminating animals. He lives upon plants and roots, and, as I have said, is perfectly harmless in disposition. The female produces but one young at a birth, of which she is very tender, leading it, at an early age, to the water, and instructing it to swim.

This description finished, the reader is ready to accompany us in our nocturnal expedition against the tapir. Before it became dark, Antonio, accompanied by the boy, went to the thicket which I have described, and felled several stout trees across the path, in such a manner as to form a kind of *cul de sac*. The design of this was to arrest the animal on his return, and enable us to spear him before he could break through or disengage himself. We went to the spot early in the evening, and, as the moon did not rise until late, Antonio caught his hat half-full of fire-flies, which served to guide us in the bush. He then pulled off their wings and scattered them among the fallen trees, where they gave light enough to enable us to distinguish objects with considerable clearness. Notwithstanding Antonio's assurances that the *tapir* was a member of the Peace Society, I could not divest myself of the alarm which he had given me in the morning, and I was not at all sorry to find that my companions had selected a spot for their abattis, where an overhanging tree enabled me to keep out of harm's way, yet near enough to take a sly drive with my lance at the tapir, if he should happen to come that way.

Antonio and the Poyer boy took their stations among the fallen trees; I took mine, and we awaited the *dante's* pleasure. I strained my eyes in vain endeavors to penetrate the gloom, and held my breath full half the time to hear the expected tread. But we peered, and listened, and waited in vain; the fire-flies crawled away in every direction, and yet the *tapir* obstinately kept away. Finally, the moon came up; and by-and-by it rose above the trees—and still no tapir!

My seat on the tree became uncomfortable, and I instituted a comparison between tapir and manitus-hunting, largely to the advantage of the latter; and, finally, when Antonio whispered "He is coming!" I felt a willful disposition to contradict him. But my ear, meanwhile, caught the same dull sound which had arrested my attention in the morning; and, a few moments afterward, I could make out the beast, in the dim light, driving on at the same swinging trot. Right on he came, heedless and headlong. Crash! crash! There was a plunge and struggle, and a crushing and trampling of branches, then a dull sound of the heavy beast striking against the unyielding trunks of the fallen trees. He was now fairly stopped, and with a shout my companions drove down upon him with their lances, which rung out a sharp metallic sound when they struck his thick, hard hide. It was an exciting moment, and my eagerness overcoming my prudence, I slipped down the tree, and joined in the attack. Blow upon blow of the lances, and I could feel that mine struck deeply into the flesh, it seemed to me into the very vitals of the animal. But the strokes only appeared to give him new strength, and gathering back, he drove again full upon the opposing tree, bearing it down before him. I had just leaped upon the trunk, the better to aim my lance, and went down with it headlong, almost under the feet of the struggling animal, one tramp

THE DEATH OF THE TAPIR.

of whose feet would have crushed me like a worm. I could have touched him with my arm, he was so near! I heard the alarmed shriek of Antonio, when he saw me fall; but, in an instant, he leaped to my side, and, shortening his lance, drove it, with desperate force, clean through the animal, bringing him to his knees. This done, he grappled me as he might an infant, and before I was aware of it, had dragged me clear of the fallen timber. The blow of Antonio proved fatal; the tapir fell over on his side, and in a few moments was quite dead.

The Poyer boy was dispatched to the camp for fire and pine splints, which, stuck in the ground around the tapir, answered for torches. By their light my companions proceeded to cut up the spoil, a tedious operation, which occupied them until daylight. I did not wait, but went back to my hammock, leaving them to finish their work, undisturbed by my questions.

When I awoke in the morning, I found Antonio had the tapir's head baking in the ground, from whence rose a hot but fragrant steam. It proved to be very good eating, as did also the feet and the neck, but the flesh of the animal in general was abominably coarse and insipid, although my companions seemed to relish it greatly. I found it, like that of the manitus, exceedingly laxative.

Some idea may be formed of the tapir's tenacity of life, when I say that I counted upward of thirty lance-thrusts in the body of the one we killed, none of which were less than six inches deep, and nearly all penetrating into the cavity of the body! It rarely happens, therefore, that the animal is killed by the individual hunter. The hide is quite as thick, and I think harder than that of the manitus, which, when dried, it closely resembles.

I should weary the reader were I to enter into all the details of our life at the "Tapir Camp," as I called it, in honor of the exploit I have just recounted. During the eight days which we spent there, I learned more of nature and her works than I had known before. I spent hours in watching the paths of the black ants, tracing them to their nests in the trees, which were dark masses, as large as a barrel, made up of fragments of leaves cemented together. From these paths, which were from four to six inches wide, all grass, leaves, sticks, and other obstructions, had been removed, and along them poured an unbroken column of ants, thousands on thousands, those bound from the nest hurrying down one side of the path, and those bound in, each carrying aloft a piece of green leaf, perhaps half an inch square—a mimic army with banners—hurrying up the other. I amused myself, sometimes, by putting obstructions across the path, and watching the surging up of the interrupted columns. Then could be seen fleet couriers hurrying off to the nest, and directly the path would be crowded with a heavy reënforcement, invariably headed by eight or ten ants of larger size, who appeared to be the engineers of the establishment. These would climb over and all around the obstruction, apparently calculating the chances of effecting its removal. If not too heavy, they disposed their regiments, and dragged it away by a grand simultaneous effort.

But if, on examination, they thought its removal impossible, they hurried to lay out a road around it, clearing away the grass, leaves, twigs, and pebbles with consummate skill, each column working toward the other. The best drilled troops could not go more systematically and intelligently to work, nor have executed their task with greater alacrity and energy. No sooner was it done, than, putting themselves at the head of their workies, the engineers hastened back as they came, ready to obey the next requisition upon their strength and skill.

Here I may mention that there is no end of ants under the tropics. They swarm every where, of unnumbered varieties—from little creatures, of microscopic proportions, to those of the size of our wasp. It is always necessary, when on land, to hang one's provisions by cords from the branches of trees, or they would literally be eaten up in a single night. There is one variety, called the *hormegas*, by the Spaniards, which has an insatiate appetite for leather, especially boots, and will eat them full of holes in a few hours. All the varieties of *acacias* teem with a small red, or "fire ant," whose bite is like the prick of a red-hot needle. The unfortunate traveler who gets them in any considerable numbers on his person, is driven to distraction for the time being. It is difficult to imagine keener torment.

Thousands of small, light-colored bees gathered round the fallen trunks of the coyol-palms, to collect the honey-like liquid that exuded here and there, as the juice began to ferment. I soon ascertained that they were stingless, and amused myself in watching their industrious zeal. I gradually came to observe that when each had gathered his supply, he rose, by a succession of circuits, high in the air, and then darted off in a certain direction. Carefully watching their course, I finally traced them to a low, twisted tree, on the edge of the swamp, in the hollow of which they had their depository. Of course, I regarded this as a fortunate discovery, and we were not slow to turn it to our advantage. I had less scruples in cutting down the tree, and turning the busy little dwellers out on the world, since they had no winter to provide for, and could easily take care of themselves. The supply of honey proved to be very small, and seemed to have been collected chiefly for the support of the young bees. We obtained only four bottles full from the tree. In taste it proved to be very unlike our northern honey, having a sharp, pungent, half-fermented flavor, causing, when eaten pure, a choking contraction of the muscles of the throat. Antonio mixed some of it with the "vino de coyol," which, after fermentation, produced a very delicious, but strong, and most intoxicating kind of *liqueur.*

On the afternoon of the eighth day, the moon having reached her last quarter, we packed our little boat, and just as the night fell, worked our way slowly through the little, obstructed canal to the lagoon, which now expanded to the north. We paddled boldly through the middle, the better to avoid observation from the shore. The night was dark, but wonderfully still, and I could hear distinctly the sound of drums and revelry from the villages on the eastern shore, although they must have been fully three miles distant.

I left "Tapir Camp" with real regret. The days had glided by tranquilly, and I had enjoyed a calm content, to which I had before been a stranger. For the first time, I was able to comprehend the feeling, gathering strength with every day, which induces men, sometimes the most brilliant and prosperous, to banish themselves from the world, and seek, in utter retirement, the peace which only flows from a direct converse with nature, and an earnest self-communion.

LONG the coast, from the Prinzapulka river northward, as I have said, stretches a net-work of rivers and lagoons, for a distance of at least one hundred and fifty miles, terminating near Cape Gracias. These lagoons are broad and shallow, and bordered by extensive marshes. Wherever the dry ground does appear, strange to say, it is generally as a sandy savannah, undulating, and supporting few trees except the red, or long-leaved pine. These savannahs are only adapted for grazing, since the soil is too light and poor for cultivation, and fails to support any of the staple products, or any of the many esculent vegetables of the tropics, except the cassava. And although the few scattered inhabitants of the Mosquito Shore, above the Prinzapulka, live upon the borders of the lagoons, selecting generally the savannahs for their villages, it is because they are essentially fishers, and derive their principal support from the sea. The islands of the coast abound with turtle, and the rivers, creeks, and lagoons teem with fish of nearly every variety known under the tropics. The few vegetables which they require are obtained from the banks of the rivers in the back country, where the streams flow through their proper valleys, and before they are lost in the low grounds of the coast. The plantations on these rivers belong to the Indians proper, whose numbers increase toward the interior, and who supply the Sambos, or coast-men, not only with vegetables, but also with the various kinds of boats which are used by them, receiving in exchange a few cottons, axes, trinkets, and other articles which are brought by the foreign traders. The character and habits of these Indians are widely different from those of the coast-men. The latter are drunken, idle, and vicious, while the former are mild, industrious, and temperate. The differences which I have indicated between the Indian settlement on the Rio Grande and the Sambo village of Wasswatla, hold equally true throughout, except that the farther the traveler proceeds northward from Bluefields, the more debased and brutal the Sambos become.

In attempting to thread my way through the maze of waters before us, I kept the facts which I

LIFE AMONG THE LAGOONS.

have recounted constantly in view, and sought rather to penetrate inland, than diverge toward the coast. So, whenever two or more channels presented themselves, I universally took the inside one. This frequently led us into the rivers flowing from the interior, but their current speedily enabled us to correct these mistakes.

No incident relieved the monotony of our first night, after leaving "Tapir Camp." Toward morning we paddled into the first opening in the mangroves that held out promise of concealment. We had the usual difficulties to encounter—fallen trees, and overhanging limbs; but when the morning broke we had worked our way to a spot where the creek expanded into a kind of subordinate lagoon, very shallow, and full of sandy islets, partly covered with grass and water-plants. At one spot on the shore the ground was elevated a few feet, supporting a number of large and ancient trees, heavily draped with vines, under which we encamped.

After a very frugal meal, my hammock was suspended between the trees, and I went to sleep. About noon I awoke, and spent the rest of the day in watching the various forms of animal life which found support in these secluded wilds. It seemed to me as if all the aquatic birds of the world were congregated there, in harmonious conclave. Long-shanked herons, with their necks drawn in, and their yellow bills resting on their breasts, stood meditatively on a single leg; troops of the white and scarlet ibis trotted actively along the open sands;

and round-tailed darters, with their snaky necks and quick eyes, alighted in the trees around us—the only birds of all that assemblage which seemed to notice our intrusion! Then there were cranes, and gaudy, awkward spoon-bills (clownish millionaires!) and occasionally a little squadron of blue-winged teal paddled gracefully by.

Overhead, a few noisy macaws sheltered themselves from the noon-day heats. Among these, I saw, for the first time, the green variety, a more modest, and, to my taste, a far more beautiful bird, than his gaudier cousin. The large trees to which I have alluded, were of the variety known as the *ceiba*, or silk-cotton tree. They were now in their bloom, and crowned with a profusion of flowers of rich and variegated colors, but chiefly a bright carnation. It was a novel spectacle to see a gigantic tree, five or six feet in diameter, and eighty or ninety feet high, sending out long and massive limbs, yet bearing flowers like a rose-bush—a sort of man-milliner! Viewed from beneath, the flowers were scarcely visible, but their fragrance was overpowering, and the ground was carpeted with their gay leaves and delicate petals. But seen from a little distance, the ceiba-tree in bloom is one of the most splendid productions of Nature—a gigantic bouquet, which requires a whole forest to supply the contrasting green! The flowers are rapidly succeeded by a multitude of pods, which grow to the size and shape of a goose-egg. When ripe, they burst open, revealing the interior filled with a very soft, light cotton or silky fibre, attached as floats to diminutive seeds, which are thus wafted far and wide by the winds. This process is repeated three times a year. I am not aware that the cotton has ever been manufactured, or applied to any more useful purpose than that of stuffing pillows and mattresses.

The trunk of the ceiba, however, is invaluable to the natives. The wood is easily worked, and is, moreover, light and buoyant, and not liable to split by exposure to the sun. For these reasons, it is principally used for *dories*, *pitpans*, and the different varieties of boats required on the coast, although, for the smaller canoes, the cedar and mahogany are sometimes substituted. The mahogany boats, however, are rather heavy, while the cedar is liable to split in what is called "beaching." I have seen *dories* hollowed from a single trunk of the cebia, in which a tall man might comfortably lie at length across the bottom, and which were capable of carrying fifty persons.

But the *ceibas* of our encampment supported, besides their own verdure, a mass of *lianes* or climbers, of many varieties, as also, numerous parasitic plants, and among them the wild-pine or rain-plant, which served us a most useful purpose. Several of these grew in the principal forks of the trees, to the height of from four to six feet. Their leaves are broad, and wrap round on themselves, like a roll, forming reservoirs, in which the rain and dew is collected and retained, safe from sun and wind.

Each leaf will hold about a quart of water, which looks clear and tempting in its green, translucent goblet. Had it not been for the rain-plant, we would have suffered very often from thirst, among those brackish lagoons, where fresh water is obtained with difficulty.

With the night, we resumed our stealthy course to the northward, guided by the familiar north star, which here, however, circles so low in the horizon, as hardly to be visible above the trees. The long and narrow lagoon contracted more and more, until it presented a single channel, perhaps a hundred yards wide, closely lined with mangroves, which, rising like a wall on both sides, prevented us from making out the character of the back country. In passing through some of the numerous bends, I nevertheless caught star-light glimpses of distant hills, and high grounds in the direction of the interior. The channel soon began to trend to the north-east, and there was a considerable current in that direction. I was concerned lest, notwithstanding all my caution, I had lost the clew to the lagoons, and taken some one of the outlets into the sea. We nevertheless kept on, steadily and rapidly, discovering no signs of habitations on the banks, until near morning, when my suspicions were confirmed by a monotonous sound, which I had no difficulty in recognizing as the beating of the sea. I was therefore greatly relieved when the narrow channel, which we were traversing, expanded suddenly into a beautiful lagoon, which I subsequently ascertained was called "Tongla Lagoon." It is triangular in shape, extending off to the north-west.

I was weary of dodging the Sambos, and determined, as the wind was blowing fresh, to put up our sail, and standing boldly through the lagoon, take the risk of recognition and pursuit. There never was a brighter day on earth, and our little boat seemed emulous to outstrip the wind. Gathering confidence from our speed, I got out my fishing line, and, attaching a bit of cotton cloth to the hook, trailed it after the boat. It had hardly touched the water before it was caught by a kind of rock-fish, called *snapper* by the English residents, and *cowatucker* by the Mosquitos. It is only from ten to twelve inches in length, but broad and heavy. Antonio recognized it as one of the best of the small fishes, and I continued the sport of catching them, until it would have been wanton waste to have taken more. I found them to be of two varieties, the red and black, of which the latter proved to be the most delicate. I also caught two fish of a larger kind, called *baracouta,* each about twenty inches in length, resembling our blue-fish. It is equally ravenous, and has a like firm and palatable flesh. I am not sure that it is not the true blue-fish, although I afterward caught some in the Bay of Honduras which were between three and four feet in length.

In order to get the full benefit of the land-breeze, we kept well over to the seaward or eastern side of the lagoon. As the lagoon narrowed, our course gradually brought us close in shore. I had observed some palm-trees on the same side of the lagoon, but the ground seemed so low, and tangled with verdure, that I doubted if the trees indicated, as they usually do, a village at their feet. I nevertheless maintained a sharp look-out, and kept the boat as near to the wind as possible, so as to slip by without observation. It was not until we were abreast of the palms, that I saw signs of human habitations. But then I made out a large number of canoes drawn up in a little bay, and, through a narrow vista in the trees, saw distinctly a considerable collection of huts. There were also several of the inhabitants moving about among the canoes.

I observed also that our boat had attracted attention, and that a number of men were hurrying down to the shore. I was in hopes that they would be content with regarding us from a distance, and was not a little annoyed when I saw two large boats push from the landing. We did not stop to speculate upon their purposes, but shook out every thread of our little sail, and each taking a paddle, we fell to work with a determination of giving our pursuers as pretty a chase as ever came off on the Mosquito Shore. It was now three o'clock in the afternoon, and I felt confident that we could not be overtaken, if at all, before night, and then it would be comparatively easy to elude them.

Our pursuers had no sails, but their boats were larger, and numerously manned by men more used to the paddle than either Antonio or myself. While the wind lasted, we rather increased our distance, but as the sun went down the breeze declined, and our sail became useless. So we were obliged to

THE CHASE ON TONGLA LAGOON.

take it in, and trust to our paddles, alone. This gave our pursuers new courage, and I could hear their shouts echoed back from the shores. When night fell they had shortened their distance to less than half what it had been at the outset, and were so near that we could almost make out their words; for, during quiet nights, on these lagoons, voices can be distinguished at the distance of a mile. The lagoon narrowed more and more, and was evidently getting to be as contracted as the channel by which we had entered. This was against us; for, although we had almost lost sight of our pursuers in the gathering darkness, our safety depended entirely upon our slipping, unobserved, into some narrow creek. But we strained our eyes in vain, to discover such a retreat. The mangroves presented one dark, unbroken front.

The conviction was now forced upon me that, in spite of all our efforts to avoid it, we were to be involved in a second fight. I laid aside my paddle, and got out my gun. And now I experienced again the same ague-like sensations which I have described as preceding our struggle on the Prinzapulka. It required the utmost effort to keep my teeth from chattering audibly. I had a singular and painful sensation of fullness about the heart. So decided were all these phenomena, that, notwithstanding our danger, I felt glad it was so dark that my companions could not see my weakness. But soon the veins in my temples began to swell with blood, pulsating with tense sharpness, like the vibration of a bow-string; and then the muscles became rigid, and firm as iron. I was ready for blood! Twice only have I experienced these terrible sensations, and God grant that they may never agonize my nerves again!

Our enemies were now so near that I was on the point of venturing a random long shot at them, when, with a suppressed exclamation of joy, Antonio suddenly turned our canoe into a narrow creek, where the mangroves separated, like walls, on either side. Where we entered, it was scarcely twenty feet wide, and soon contracted to ten or twelve. We glided in rapidly for perhaps two hundred yards, when Antonio stopped to listen. I heard nothing, and gave the word to proceed. But the crafty Indian said "No ;" and, carefully leaning over the edge of the boat, plunged his head in the water. He held it there a few seconds, then started up, exclaiming, "They are coming !" Again we bent to the paddles, and drove the boat up the narrow creek with incredible velocity.

I was so eager to get a shot at our pursuers that I scarcely comprehended what he meant, when, stopping suddenly, Antonio pressed his paddle in my hands, and, exchanging a few hurried words with the Poyer boy, each took a machete in his mouth, and leaped overboard. I felt a sudden suspicion that they had deserted me, and remained for the time motionless. A moment after, they called to me from the shore, "Paddle ! paddle !" and, at the same instant, I heard the blows of their machetes ringing on the trunks of the mangroves. I at once comprehended that they were felling trees across the narrow creek, to obstruct the pursuit ; and I threw aside the paddle, and took my gun again, determined to protect my devoted friends, at any hazard. I never forgave myself for my momentary but ungenerous distrust !

Our pursuers heard the sound of the blows, and, no doubt comprehending what was going on, raised loud shouts, and redoubled their speed. *Kling ! kling !* rang the machetes on the hard wood ! Oh, how I longed to hear the crash of the falling trees ! Soon one of them began to crackle—another blow, and down it fell, the trunk splashing gloriously in the water ! Another crackle, a rapid rustling of branches, and another splash in the water ! It was our turn to shout now !

I gave Antonio and the Poyer boy each a hearty embrace, as, dripping with water, they clambered back into our little boat. We now pushed a few yards up the stream, stopped close to the slimy bank, and awaited our pursuers. "Come on, now," I shouted, "and not one of you shall pass that rude barrier alive !"

The first boat ran boldly up to the fallen trees, but the discharge of a single barrel of my gun sent it back, precipitately, out of reach. We could distinguish a hurried conversation between the occupants of the first boat and of the second, when the latter came up. It did not last long, and when it stopped, Antonio, in a manner evincing more alarm than he had ever before exhibited, caught me by the arm, and explained hurriedly that the second boat was going back, and that the narrow creek, in which we were, no doubt communicated with the principal channel by a second mouth. While one boat was thus blockading us in front, the second was hastening to assail us in the rear ! I comprehended the movement at once. Our deliberation was short, for our lives might depend upon an improvement of the minutes. Stealthily, scarce daring to breathe, yet with the utmost rapidity possible, we pushed up the creek. As Antonio had conjectured, it soon began to curve back toward the estuary. We had pursued our course perhaps ten or fifteen minutes—they seemed hours !—when we overheard the approach of the second boat.

We at once drew ours close to the bank, in the gloomiest covert we could find. On came the boat, the paddlers, secure of the success of their device, straining themselves to the utmost. There was a moment of keen suspense, and, to our inexpressible relief, the boat passed by us. We now resumed our paddles, and hastened on our course. But before we entered the principal channel, my companions clambered into the overhanging mangroves, and in an incredibly short space of time had fallen other trees across the creek, so as completely to shut in the boat which had attempted to surprise us.

The device was successful; we soon emerged from the creek, and the sea-breeze having now set in, favorably to our course, we were able to put up our sail, and defy pursuit. We saw nothing afterward of our eager friends of Tongla Lagoon!

Some time past midnight we came to another and larger lagoon, called "Wava Lagoon," and, weary and exhausted from nearly two days of wakefulness, hard labor, and excitement, we ran our boat ashore on a little island, which presented itself, and dragged it up into the bushes. We kindled a fire, cooked our fish, and then I lay down in the canoe, and went to sleep. I had entire confidence that we would not be pursued further, as we were now a long way from the coast, and in the country of the unmixed Indians, who, so far from recognizing the assumptions of the Sambos, hold an attitude so decidedly hostile toward them that the latter seldom venture into their territory.

9

I awoke near noon, but unrefreshed, with a dull pain in my head, a sensation of chilliness, great lassitude, and an entire absence of appetite. Had our encampment been more favorable, I should not have attempted to move ; but the island was small, without water, and, moreover, too near the channel leading to Tongla Lagoon to be a desirable resting-place. So we embarked about midday, and stood across the lagoon for its western shore, where the ground appeared to rise rapidly, and high blue mountains appeared in the distance. The sun shone out clearly, and the day was sultry, but my chilliness increased momentarily, and, in less than an hour after leaving the island, I found myself lying in the bottom of the canoe, wrapped in my blanket, and for the first time in my life, suffering from the ague. The attack lasted for full two hours, and was followed by a bursting pain in my head, and a high fever. I had also dull pains in my back and limbs, which were more difficult to be borne than others more acute.

At four o'clock in the afternoon, Antonio put the boat in shore—for I was too ill to give directions—where a bluff point ran out into the lagoon, forming a small bay, with a smooth, sandy beach. A little savannah, similar to that which I have described at Tapir Camp, extended back from the bluff, near the centre of which, at its highest point, which commanded a beautiful view of the lagoon, rose a single clump of pines. Here my companions carried me in my hammock, and here they hastily arranged our camp.

When the sun went down, my fever subsided, but was followed by a profuse and most debilitating sweat. Meantime Antonio had collected a few nuts of a kind which, I afterward ascertained, is called by the English of the West Indies *physic-nut* (*jatropha*), which grows on a low bush, on all parts of the coast. These he rapidly prepared, and administered them to me. They operated powerfully, both as an emetic and cathartic. When their effects had ceased, I fell asleep, and slept until morning, when I awoke weak, but free from pain, or any other symptom of illness. I congratulated myself and Antonio, but he dampened my spirits sensibly by explaining that, however well I might feel for that day, I would be pretty sure to have a recurrence of fever on the next. And to mitigate the severity of this, if not entirely to prevent it, he presented to me a calabash of reddish-looking liquid, which he called *cinchona*, and told me to drink deeply. Heavens! I shall never forget the bitter draught, which he commended to my unwilling lips every two hours during that black day in my calendar! I know what it is now, for my Mosquito experiences have entailed upon me a sneaking fever and ague, which avails itself of every pretext to remind me that we are inseparable. Looking to my extensive consumption of quinine, I have marveled, since my return, that the price of the drug has not been doubled! Others may look at the stock quotations, but my principal interest in the commercial department of the morning paper, is the "ruling rate" of *quinine!* Not having, as yet, discovered any considerable advance, I begin to doubt the dogma of the economists, that "the price is regulated by the demand."

Antonio was right. The next day came, and at precisely twelve o'clock came also the chill, the fever, the dull pains, and the perspiration, but all in a more subdued form. I escaped the physic-nuts, but the third day brought a new supply of the bitter liquid, which Antonio told me was decocted from bark taken from the roots of a species of mangrove-tree. I have never seen it mentioned that the cinchona is found in Central America, but, nevertheless, it *is* there, or something so nearly like it, in taste and effects, as to be undistinguishable. Thin slips of the bark, put into a bottle of rum, made a sort of cordial or bitters, of which I took about a wine-glassful every morning and evening, during the remainder of my stay on the coast, with beneficial results.

I had three recurrences of the fever, but the sun passed the meridian on the sixth day without bringing with it an attack—thanks to the rude but effective "healing art" of my Indian companions. Experience had taught them about all, I think, that has ever been learned in the way of treatment of indigenous complaints. It is only exotic diseases, or sweeping epidemics, that carry death and desolation among the aborigines, whose ignorance of their nature and remedies invests them with a terror which enhances the mortality. Not only was the treatment to which I was subjected thoroughly correct, but the dieting was perfect. The only food that was given to me consisted of the seeds of the okra (which is indigenous on the coast), flavored by being boiled with the legs and wings of quails, and small bits of dried manitee flesh. I only outraged the notions of my rude physicians in one respect, *viz.*, in insisting on being allowed to wash myself. The Indians seem to think that the effect of water on the body, or any part of it, during the period of a fever, is little less than mortal—a singular notion, which may have some foundation in experience, if not in reason. The Spaniards, wisely or foolishly, entertain the same prejudice; and, furthermore, shut themselves up closely in dark rooms, when attacked by fever. At such times they scarcely commend themselves pleasantly to any of the senses.

From the open, airy elevation where our camp was established, as I have already said, we had an extensive and beautiful view of the lagoon. We saw canoes, at various times, skirting the western shore, and, from the smoke which rose at intervals, we were satisfied that there were there several Indian villages. As soon, therefore, as I thought myself recovered from my fever, which was precisely at one o'clock past meridian, on the sixth day (the fever due at noon not having "come to time"), I was ready to proceed to the Indian towns. But our departure was delayed for two days more by an unfortunate occurrence, which came near depriving the Poyer boy of his life, and me of a valuable assistant; for, while Antonio was supreme on land, the Poyer boy was the leader on the water. I always called him—Mosquito fashion—"admiral."

It seems that, while engaged in gathering dry wood, he took hold of a fallen branch, under which was coiled a venomous snake, known as the *tamagasa* (called by the English *tommy-goff*, and the Mosquitos *piuta-sura*, or the poison snake). He had scarcely put down his hand when it struck him in the arm. He killed it, grasped it by the tail, and hurried to our camp. I was much alarmed, for his agitation was extreme, and his face and whole body of an ashy color. Antonio was not at hand, and I was at an utter loss what to do, beyond tying a ligature tightly around the arm. The Poyer, however, retained his presence of mind, and, unrolling a mysterious little bundle, which contained his scanty wardrobe, took out a nut of about the size and much the appearance of a horse-chestnut, which he hastily crushed, and, mixing it with water, drank it down. By this time Antonio had returned, and, learning the state of the case, seized his machete, and hastened away to the low grounds on the edge of the savannah, whence he came back, in the course of half an hour, with a quantity of some kind of root, of which I have forgotten the Indian name. It had a strong smell of musk, impossible to distinguish from that of the genuine civet. This he crushed, and formed into a kind of poultice, bound it on the wounded arm, and gave the boy to drink a strong infusion of the same. This done, he led him down to the beach, dug a hole in the moist sand, in which he buried his arm to the shoulder, pressing the sand closely around it. I thought this an emphatic kind of treatment, which might be good for Indians, but which would be pretty sure to kill white men. The boy remained with his arm buried during the entire night, but, next morning, barring being a little pale and weak from the effects of these powerful remedies, he was as well as ever, and resumed his usual occupations. A light blue scratch alone indicated the place where he had been bitten.

The *tamagasa* (a specimen of which I subsequently obtained, and which now occupies a distinguished place among the reptiles in the Philadelphia Academy), is about two feet long. It is of the thickness of a man's thumb, with a large, flat head, and a lump in the neck something like that of the cobra, and is marked with alternate black and dusky white rings. It is reputed one of the most venomous serpents under the tropics, ranking next to the beautiful, but deadly *corral.*

Chapter X

FROM our misfortunes, I named our encampment, on Wava Lagoon, "Fever Camp," although so far from contracting the fever there, I am sure it was its open and elevated position which contributed to my recovery. The fever was rather due to over-exertion, and exposure at night; for the night-damps, on all low coasts under the tropics, are unquestionably deadly, and the traveler cannot be too careful in avoiding them. Early in the afternoon of the day of our departure from "Fever Camp," we entered a large stream, flowing into the lagoon from the north-west, upon the banks of which, judging from the direction of the smoke we had seen, the Indian villages were situated. We were not mistaken. Before night we came to a village larger than that on the Rio Grande, but in other respects much the same, except that it stood upon the edge of an extensive savannah, instead of on the skirt of an impenetrable forest. Around it were extensive plantations of cassava, and other fruits and vegetables, growing in the greatest luxuriance, and indicating that the soil of the inland savannahs does not share the aridity of those nearer the coast. This was further evinced by the scarcity of pines, which were only to be seen on the ridges or gentle elevations with which the surface of the savannah was diversified.

Our appearance here created the same excitement which it had occasioned at the other places we had visited, and our reception was much the same with that which we had experienced on the Rio Grande. Instead, however, of being met by men with wands, we were welcomed by five old men, one of whom vacated his own hut for our accommodation. None here could speak either English or Spanish intelligibly, but the affinity between their language and that of my Poyer enabled him to make known our wants, and obtain all useful information. We were treated hospitably, but with the utmost reserve, and during my whole stay, but a single incident relieved the monotony of the village. This was a marriage—and a very ceremonious affair it was.

These Indians, I should explain, are called Towkas, or Toacas, and have, I presume, all the general characteristics and habits of the Cookras and Woolwas. These do, in fact, constitute a single family, although displaying dialectical differences in their language.

TOWKAS INDIANS.

Among all these Indians, polygamy is an exception, while among the Sambos it is the rule. The instances are few in which a man has more than one wife, and in these cases the eldest is not only the head of the family, but exercises a strict supervision over the others. The betrothals are made at a very early age, by the parents, and the affianced children are marked in a corresponding manner, so that one acquainted with the practice can always point out the various mates. These marks consist of little bands of colored cotton, worn either on the arm, above the elbow, or on the leg, below the knee, which are varied in color and number, so that no two combinations in the village shall be the same. The combinations are made by the old men, who take care that there shall be no confusion. The bands are replaced from time to time, as they become worn and faded. Both boys and girls also wear a necklace of variously-colored shells or beads, to which one is added yearly. When the necklace of the boy counts ten beads or shells, he is called *muhasal*, a word signifying three things, *viz.*, ten, all the fingers, and *half-a-man*. When they number twenty, he is called *'all*, a word which also signifies three things, *viz.*, twenty, both fingers and toes, and *a man*. And he is then effectively regarded as a man. Should his affianced, by that time, have reached the age of fifteen, the marriage ceremony takes place without delay.

As I have said, a sleek young Towka was called upon to add the final bead to his string, and take upon himself the obligations of manhood, during my stay at the village. The event had been anticipated by the preparation of a canoe full of palm-wine, mixed with crushed plantains, and a little honey, which had been fermenting, to the utter disgust of my nostrils, from the date of my arrival. The day was observed as a general holiday. Early in the morning all the men of the village assembled, and with their knives carefully removed every blade of grass which had grown up inside of a circle, perhaps a hundred feet in diameter, situated in the very centre of the village, and indicated by a succession of stones sunk in the ground. The earth was then trampled smooth and hard, after which they proceeded to erect a little hut in the very centre of the circular area, above a large flat stone which was permanently planted there. This hut was made conical, and perfectly close, except an opening at the top, and another at one side, toward the east, which was temporarily closed with a mat, woven of palm-bark. I looked in without hinderance, and saw, piled up on the stone, a quantity of the dry twigs of the copal-tree, covered with the gum of the same. The canoe full of liquor was dragged up to the edge of the circle, and literally covered with small white calabashes, of the size of an ordinary coffee-cup.

At noon, precisely, all the people of the village hurried, without order, to the hut of the bridegroom's father. I joined in the crowd. We found the "happy swain" arrayed in his best, sitting demurely upon a bundle of articles, closely wrapped in a mat. The old men, to whom I have referred, formed in a line in front of him, and the eldest made him a short address. When he had finished, the next followed, until each had had his say. The youth then got up quietly, shouldered his bundle, and, preceded by the old men, and followed by his father, marched off to the hut of the prospective bride. He put down his load before the closed door, and seated himself upon it in silence. The father then rapped at the door, which was partly opened by an old woman, who asked him what he wanted, to which he made some reply which did not appear to be satisfactory, when the door was shut in his face, and he took his seat beside his son. One of the old men then rapped, with precisely the same result, then the next, and so on. But the old women were obdurate. The bridegroom's father tried it again, but the she-dragons would not open the door. The old men then seemed to hold a council, at the end of which a couple of drums (made, as I have already explained, by stretching a raw skin over a section of a hollow tree), and some rude flutes were sent for. The latter were made of pieces of bamboo, and were shaped somewhat like flageolets, each having a mouth-piece, and four stops. The sound was dull and monotonous, although not wholly unmusical.

Certain musicians now appeared, and at once commenced playing on these instruments, breaking out, at long intervals, in a kind of supplicatory chant. After an hour or more of this soothing and rather sleepy kind of music, the inexorable door opened a little, and one of the female inmates glanced out with much affected timidity. Hereupon the musicians redoubled their efforts, and the bridegroom hastened to unroll his bundle. It contained a variety of articles supposed to be acceptable to the parents of the girl. There was, among other things, a *machete*, no inconsiderable present, when it is understood that the cost of one is generally a large *dory*, which it requires months of toil to fashion from the rough trunk of the gigantic ceiba. A string of gay glass beads was also produced from the bundle. All these articles were handed in to the women one by one, by the father of the groom. With every present the door opened wider and wider, until the mat was presented, when it was turned back to its utmost, revealing the bride arrayed in her "prettiest," seated on a crickery, at the remotest corner of the hut. The dragons affected to be absorbed in examining the presents, when the bridegroom, watching his opportunity, dashed into the hut, to the apparent utter horror and dismay of the women ; and, grasping the girl by the waist, shouldered her like a sack, and started off at a trot for the mystic circle, in the centre of the village. The women pursued, as if to overtake him and rescue the girl, uttering cries for help, while all the crowd huddled after. But the youth was too fast for them ; he reached the ring, and lifting the vail of the hut, disappeared within it. The women could not pass the circle, and all stopped short at its edge, and set up a chorus of despairing shrieks, while the men all gathered within the charmed ring, where they squatted themselves, row on row, facing outward. The old men alone remained standing, and a bit of lighted pine having meanwhile been brought, one of them approached the hut, lifted the mat, and, handing in the fire, made a brief speech to the inmates. A few seconds after an aromatic smoke curled up from the opening in the top of the little hut, from which I infer that the copal had been set on fire. What else happened, I am sure I do not know !

When they saw the smoke, the old women grew silent and expectant ; but, by-and-by, when it subsided, they became suddenly gay, and "went in strong" for the festivities, which, up to this time, I must confess, I had thought rather slow. But here I may explain, that although the bridegroom has no choice in the selection of his wife, yet if he have reason for doing so, he may, while the copal is burning, take her in his arms, and cast her outside of the circle, in the open day, before the entire people, and thus rid himself of her forever. But in this case, the matter is carefully investigated by the old men, and woe betide the wretch who, by this public act, has impeached a girl wrongfully! Woe equally betide the girl who is proved to have been "put away" for good reasons. If, however, the copal burns out quietly, the groom is supposed to be satisfied, and the marriage is complete.

The copal, in this instance, burned out in the most satisfactory manner, and then the drums and flutes struck up a most energetic air, the music of which consisted of about eight notes, repeated with different degrees of rapidity, by way of giving variety to the melody. The men all kept their places, while I was installed in a seat of honor beside the old men. The women, who, as I have said, could not come within the circle, now commenced filling the calabashes from the canoe, and passing them to the squatting men, commencing with the ancients and the "distinguished guests"—for Antonio and my Poyer were included in our party. There was nothing said, but the women displayed the greatest activity in filling the emptied calabashes. I soon discovered that every body was deliberately and in cold blood getting up of what Captain Drummer called the "big drunk!" That was part of the performance of the day, and the Indians went at it in the most orderly and expeditious manner. They wasted no time in coyish preliminaries—a practice which might be followed in more civilized countries, to the great economy, not only of time, but of the vinous. It was not from the love of the drink that the Towkas imbibed, I can well believe, for their *chicha* was bad to look at, and worse to taste.

With the fourth round of the calabashes, an occasional shout betrayed the effects of the *chicha* upon some of the weaker heads. These shouts became more and more frequent, and were sometimes uttered with a savage emphasis, which was rather startling. The musicians, too, became more energetic, and as the sun declined, the excitement rose, until, unable to keep quiet any longer, all hands got up, and joined in a slow, swinging step around the circle, beating with their knuckles on the empty calabashes, and joining at intervals in a kind of refrain, at the end of which every man struck the bottom of his calabash against that of his neighbor. Then, as they came round by the canoe, each one dipped his calabash full of the contents. The liquid thus taken up was drunk at a single draught, and then the dance went on, growing more rapid with every dip of the calabash. It got to the stage of a trot, and then a fast pace, and finally into something little short of a gallop, but still in perfect time. The rattling of the calabashes had now grown so rapid, as almost to be continuous, and the motion so involved and quick, that, as I watched it, I felt that kind of giddiness which one often experiences in watching the gliding of a swift current of water. This movement could not be kept up long, even with the aid of *chicha*, and whenever a dancer became exhausted, he would wheel out of line, and throw himself flat on his face on the ground. Finally, every one gave in, except two young follows, who seemed determined to do, in their way, what other fast young men, in other countries, sometimes undertake to accomplish, viz.: drink each other down, or "under the table." They danced and drunk, and were applauded by the women, but were so closely matched that it was impossible to tell which had the best chance of keeping it up longest. In fact, each seemed to despair of the other, and, as if by a common impulse, both threw aside their calabashes, and resolved the contest from a trial of endurance into one of strength, leaping at each other's throats, and fastening their teeth like tigers in each other's flesh.

There was instantly a great uproar, and those of the men who had the ability to stand, clustered around the combatants in a confused mass, shouting at the stretch of their lungs, and evidently, as I thought, regarding it as a "free fight." But there was little damage done, for the old men, though emphatically "tight," had discretion enough to send the women for thongs, with which the pugnacious youths were incontinently bound hand and foot, and dragged close to the hut in the centre, and there left to cool themselves off as they were best able, no one taking the slightest notice of them. "Verily," I ejaculated to myself, "wisdom knoweth no country."

The dance which I have described was resumed from time to time, until it became quite dark, when the women brought a large number of pine splinters, of which the men each took one. These were lighted, and then the dancers paced up to the little hut, and each tore off one of the branches of which it was

THE END OF IT!

built, finally disclosing the newly-married couple sitting demurely side by side. As soon as the hut was demolished, the groom quietly took his bride on his back—literally "shouldering the responsibility!"—and marched off to the hut which had previously been built for his accommodation, escorted by the procession of men with torches. This was the final ceremony of the night, although some of the more dissipated youths returned to the canoe, and kept up a drumming, and piping, and dancing, until morning. Next day every body brought presents of some kind to the newly-married pair, so as to give them a fair start in the world, and enable them to commence life on equal terms with the best in the village.

It would be difficult to find on earth any thing more beautiful than the savannah which spread out, almost as far as the eye could reach, behind the Towkas village. Along the river's bank rose a tangled wall of verdure ; giant ceibas, feathery palms, and the snake-like trunks of the *mata-palo*, all bound together, and draped over with cable-like *lianes*, (the tie-tie of the English,) and the tenacious tendrils of myriads of creeping and flowering plants. Unlike the wearying, monotonous prairies of the West, the savannah was relieved by clumps of acacias—among them the delicate-leaved gum-arabic—palmettos, and dark groups of pines, arranged with such harmonious disorder, and admirable picturesque effect, that I could scarcely believe the hand of art had not lent its aid to heighten the efforts of nature in her happiest mood.

Finding retreats in the dense coverts of the jungles on the river's bank, or among the clustering groups of bushes and trees, the antelope and deer, the Indian rabbit and *gibeonite*, wandered securely over the savannah, nipping the young grass, or chasing each other in mimic alarm. Here, too, might be observed the crested curassow, with his stately step, the plumptitudinous qualm, and the crazy chachalca, (*coquericot*,) besides innumerable quails—all fitting food for omnivorous man, but so seldom disturbed as not to recognize him as their most dangerous enemy. Then night and morning the air was filled with deafening parrots, noisy macaws, and quick-darting, chattering paroquets.

I rose early every day, and with my gun in my hand, strayed far over the savannah, inhaling the freshness of the morning air, and shooting such game as looked fat, tender, and otherwise acceptable to my now fastidious appetite. The curassow, (called *cossu* by the Mosquitos,) is one of the finest birds in the world. It is about the size of the turkey, but has stronger and longer legs. The plumage is dark brown or black, ash-colored about the neck, and of a reddish brown on the breast. On its head it has a crest of white feathers tipped with black, which it raises and depresses at pleasure. The flesh is whiter than that of a turkey, but rather dry, requiring a different mode of cooking than is practiced in the woods, to bring out its qualities in perfection. It is easily tamed, as are also the *qualm* and *chachalaca*. The latter, when old, is tough, but when young, its flesh cannot be surpassed for delicacy and flavor.

The animal called the Indian rabbit is very numerous, and is a variety of what, in South America, is called the *agouti.* It is about the size of a rabbit : body plump ; snout long, and rather sharp ; nose divided at the tip, and upper jaw longer than the lower ; hind legs longer than the anterior ones, and furnished with but three toes ; tail short, and scarcely visible, while its body is covered with a hard, shining, reddish-brown hair, freckled with dark spots. It lives upon vegetables, holds its food in eating, like a squirrel, and has a vicious propensity for biting and gnawing whatever it comes near. For this reason it is a nuisance in the neighborhood of plantations, and, as it multiplies rapidly, it is about the only animal which is hunted systematically by the Indians. Its flesh is only passable.

The *gibeonite* (*cavia-paca*), sometimes called *pig-rabbit,* closely resembles the guinea-pig, but is something larger. The head is round ; the muzzle short and black ; the upper jaw longer than the lower ; the lip divided, like that of a hare ; the nostrils large, and the whiskers long ; eyes brown, large, and prominent ; ears short and naked ; neck thick ; body very plump, larger behind than before, and covered with coarse, short hair, of a dusky brown color, deepest on the back ; the throat, breast, inside of the limbs, and belly dingy white ; and on each side of the body are five rows of dark spots, placed close to each other. The legs are short, the feet have five toes, with strong nails, and the tail is a simple conic projection. Its flesh is peculiarly juicy and rich, and, baked in the ground, the animal makes a dish for an epicure. I believe I did not let a day pass without having a baked *gibeonite.*

Among the Indians of the village, the eggs and flesh of the river turtle were favorite articles of food; and in constantly using them, I thought they evinced a proper appreciation of what is good. There are two varieties of these turtles, one called *bocatoro* (Mosquito *chouswat*), and the other *hecatee.* The latter is seldom more than eighteen inches long, but its shell is very deep. We cooked them by simply separating the lower shell, taking out the entrails, and stuffing the cavity with cassava, pieces of plantain, manitee fat, and various condiments, then wrapping it in plantain leaves, as I have described, and turning it back down, baking it in the ground. It always required a good bed of coals to cook it properly, but when rightly done, the result was a meal preëminently savory and palatable. The Indian boys brought, literally, bushels of the eggs of these turtles from the bars and sand-spits of the river and lagoon. These are very delicate when entirely fresh.

Chapter XI.

WE were not many days in exhausting the resources of the Towkas village, in the way of adventures; and, one sunny afternoon, packed our little boat, and, bidding our entertainers good-by, paddled down the river, on our voyage to Sandy Bay—next to Bluefields, the principal Sambo establishment on the coast. Our course lay, a second time, through Wava Lagoon, which connects, by a narrow and intricate channel or creek, with a larger lagoon to the northward, called Duckwarra. The night was quiet and beautiful—the crescent moon filling the air with a subdued and dreamy light, soothing and slumbrous, and so blending the real with the ideal that I sometimes imagine it might all have been a dream! My companions, if they did not share the influences of the night, at least respected my silence, and we glided on and on, without a sound save the steady dip of the paddles, and the gentle ripple of the water, which closed in mimic whirlpools on our track.

When morning broke, we had already entered Duckwarra Lagoon, the largest we had encountered since leaving Pearl-Cay. It had the same appearance with all the others, and, having nothing to detain us, we steered directly across, only stopping near noon on one of the numerous islets, to cook our breakfast, and escape the midday heats. This islet was, perhaps, two hundred yards across, and elevated in the centre some fifteen or twenty feet above the water. Near the apex were growing a number of ancient palms, and, strolling up to them, I found at their roots a small elevation, or tumulus, perhaps fifteen feet in diameter at the base, and five or six feet high. Its regularity arrested my attention, and led me to believe that it was artificial. I called to Antonio, who at once pronounced it a burying-place of the "Antiguos." I proposed opening it, but my companions seemed loth to disturb the resting-place of the dead. However, finding that I had commenced the work without them, they joined me, and with our machetes and paddles, we rapidly removed the earth. Near the original surface of the ground, we came to some bones, but they were so much decayed that they crumbled beneath the fingers. Uncovering them further, we found at the head of the skeleton a rude vase, which was got out without much damage. Carefully removing the earth from the interior

I found that it contained a number of chalcedonic pebbles, pierced as if for beads, a couple of arrow-heads of similar material, and a small ornament of thin, plate gold, rudely representing a human figure, as shown in the accompanying engraving, which is of the size of the original. At the feet of the skeleton we also discovered another small vase of coarse pottery, which, however, contained no relics. Antonio seemed much interested in the little golden image, but finally, after minute examination, returned it to me, saying, that although his own people in Yucatan often buried beneath tumuli, and had golden idols which they placed with the dead, yet, in workmanship, they were unlike the one we had discovered.

"Ah!" he continued, his eyes lighting with unusual fire, "you should see the works of our ancestors! They were gods, those ancient, holy men! Their temples were built for them by *Kabul*, the Lord of the Powerful Hand, who set the seal of his bloody palm upon them all! You shall go with me to the sacred lake of the Itzaes, where our people are gathered to receive the directions of the Lord of Teaching, whose name is *Votan Balam*, who led our fathers thither, and who has promised to rescue them from their afflictions!"

He stopped suddenly, as if alarmed at what he had said, kissed his talisman, and relapsed again into the quiet, mild-eyed Indian boy, submissively awaiting my orders.

We left Duckworra Lagoon by a creek connecting it with Sandy Bay Lagoon, and on the second afternoon from Wava River, arrived at the Sambo settlement, which is on its southern shore, about eight miles from the sea. It stands upon the edge of a savannah, that rises to the southward and eastward, forming, toward the sea, a series of bluffs, the principal of which is called Bragman's Bluff, and is the most considerable land-mark on the coast.

The town has something the appearance of Bluefields, and contains perhaps five hundred inhabitants, who affect "English fashion" in dress and modes of living. That is to say, many of them wear English hats, even when destitute of every other article of clothing, except the *tournou*, or breech-cloth. These hats are of styles running back for thirty years, and, moreover, crushed into a variety of shapes which are infinitely ludicrous, especially when the wearers affect gravity or dignity. A naked man cannot make himself absolutely ridiculous, for nature never exposes her creations to humiliation; but the attempts at art, in making up the man on the Mosquito Shore, I must confess, were melancholy failures.

Before we got to the village, the beating of drums, and the occasional firing off of muskets, announced that some kind of a feast or celebration was going on. As we approached nearer I saw the English flag displayed upon a tall bamboo, planted in the centre of a group of huts. I saw also a couple of boats, of European construction, drawn up on the beach, from which I inferred that there must be a trading vessel on the coast, and that I was just in time to witness one of the orgies which always follow upon such an event. I had had some misgivings as to the probable reception we should meet, in case the news of our affair with the Quamwatlas had reached here, and felt not a little reassured when I saw indications of the presence of foreigners.

The people were all so absorbed with their festivities that our approach was not noticed; but when we got close to the shore, I fired off both barrels of my gun by way of salute. An instant after, a number of men came out from among the huts, and hurried down to the beach. Meantime I had got out my "King-paper," and leaped ashore.

The crowd that huddled around me would have put Falstaff's tatterdemalion army to shame. The most conspicuous character among them wore a red check shirt, none of the cleanest, and a threadbare undress coat of a British general, but had neither shoes nor breeches. Nor was he equally favored with Captain Drummer in respect of a hat. Instead of a venerable chapeau, like that worn by the captain with so much dignity, he had an ancient bell-crowned "tile," which had once been white, but was now of equivocal color, and which, apparently from having been repeatedly used as a seat, was crushed up bellows' fashion, and cocked forward in a most absurd manner.

The wearer of this imposing garb had already

reached the stage of "big drunk," and his English, none of the best at any time, was now of a very uncertain character. He staggered up, as if to embrace me, slapping his breast with one hand, and druling out "I General Slam—General Peter Slam!" I avoided the intended honor by stepping on one side, the consequence of which was, that if the General had not been caught by Antonio, he certainly would have plunged into the lagoon.

I made a marked display of my "King-paper," and commenced to read it to the General, but he motioned me to put it up, saying, "All good! very great good! I Peter Slam, General!" Meantime the spectators were reinforced from the village, and drums were sent for. They were of English make, and of the biggest. General Slam then insisted on escorting me up from the beach, "English gentleman fashion!" and taking my arm in his unsteady grasp, he headed the procession, with a desperate attempt at steadiness, but nevertheless swaying from side to side, after the immemorial practice of drunken men.

The General was clearly the magnate of Sandy Bay, (called by the Sambos *Sanaby*,) and when we reached the centre of the village, where the feast was going on, we were saluted by a "hurrah!" given "English fashion." Here I noticed a big canoe full of *mishla*, around which the drinking and dancing was uninterrupted. General Slam took me at once to his own house or hut, where the traders in whose honor the feast was got up, were quar-

GENERAL PETER SLAM.

tered. I found there the captain and clerk, and two of the crew of the "London Belle," a trading vessel which had recently arrived at Cape Gracias, from Jamaica. There was also an Englishman, named H——, who lived at the Cape, and who seemed to hold here a corresponding position with Mr. Bell in Bluefields. They were all reclining on crickeries, or in hammocks, and appeared to be on terms of easy familiarity with a number of very sleek young girls, in whose laps they were resting their heads, and whose principal occupation, in the intervals of not over delicate dalliance, was that of passing round glasses of a kind of punch, compounded of Jamaica rum, the juice of the sugar-cane, and a variety of crushed fruits.

The whole party was what is technically called "half-seas-over," and welcomed me with that large liberality which is inseparable from that condition. The general was slapped on the back, and told to "bring in more girls, you bloody rascal, no skulking now!" Whereupon his hat was facetiously crushed down over his eyes by each one of his guests in succession, and he was kicked out of the door by the English captain, a rough brute of a man, who only meant to be playful.

I had barely time to observe that General Slam's house was not entirely without evidences of civilization. Upon one side was a folding table, and ship's sideboard, or locker, both probably from some wreck. In the latter were a quantity of tumblers, decanters, plates, and other articles of Christian use ; and on the walls hung a few rude lithographs, gaudily colored. Among them—strange juxtaposition !—was a picture of Washington.

My survey was interrupted by a great tumult near the hut, and a moment after, half a dozen Sambos, reeking with their filthy *mishla*, staggered in at the door, dragging after them a full-blooded Indian, quite naked, and his body bleeding in several places, from blows and scratches received at the hands of his savage assailants. The Sambos pushed him toward the English captain, ejaculating, "Him ! him !" while the Indian himself stood in perfect silence, his thin lips compressed, and his eyes fixed on the captain. The conduct of the latter was in keeping with that of the drunken wretches who had dragged the Indian to the hut, and who, vociferating some unintelligible jargon, were brandishing their clubs over his head, and occasionally hitting viciously with them at his feet.

"That 's the bloody villain, is it !" said the captain, leaping from his crickery, and striking the Indian a terrible blow in the face, which felled him to the ground. "I 'll learn him proper respect for the King !" This act was followed by stamping his foot heavily on the fallen and apparently insensible Indian.

The entire proceeding was to me inexplicable ; but this last brutality roused my indignation. I grasped the captain by the collar of his coat, and hurled him across the hut. "Do you pretend to be an Englishman," I said, "and yet set such an example to these savages? What has this Indian done?" "I'll let you know what he has done," he shrieked, rather than spoke, in a wild paroxysm of rage; and, grasping a knife from the table, he drove at me, with all his force. Maddened and drunk as he was, I had only to step aside to avoid the blow. Missing his mark, he stumbled over the fallen Indian, and fell upon the knife, which pierced through and through his left arm, just below the shoulder. Quick as lightning the Indian leaped forward, tore the knife from the wound, and in another instant would have driven it to the captain's heart, had I not arrested his arm. He glanced up in my face, dropped the knife, and folding his arms, stood erect and silent.

The captain's companions, with the exception of Mr. H., were much inclined to be belligerent, but the revolver in my belt inspired them with a wholesome discretion.

Meantime, the captain's wound had been bound up, and the Indian had withdrawn. The Sambos had retreated the instant I had interposed against the violence of the trader.

The occasion of this brutal assault was simply this. The Sambos, living on the coast, effectually cut off the Indians from the sea, and, availing themselves of their position, and the advantage of firearms, make exactions of various kinds from them. Thus, if the Indians go off to the cays for turtles, they require from them a certain proportion of the shells, which is called the "king's portion." But as the Jamaica traders always keep the king and chiefs in debt to them, the shells thus collected go directly into their hands. In fact, it is only through the means which they afford, and often by their direct interference, that the nominal authority of the so-called king is kept up. It was alleged that the Indian whom the captain had abused, and who was a very expert fisherman, had not made a fair return; and his want of "proper respect for the king," it turned out, consisted in not having a sufficient quantity of shells to satisfy the cupidity of the trader!

After this occurrence at General Slam's house, I did not find it agreeable to stay there longer, and, accordingly, strolled off in the village. The festival had now become uproarious. Around the *mishla* canoe was a motley assemblage of men, women, and children; some with red caps and frocks, others strutting about with half a shirt, and others entirely naked. A number of men with pipes and drums kept up an incessant noise, while others, with muskets, which they filled with powder almost to the muzzle, fired occasional volleys, when all joined in a general *hurrah*, "English fashion."

At a little distance was built up a rude fence of palm-branches and pine-boughs, behind which there was a crowd of men laughing and shouting in a most convulsive manner. I walked forward, and saw that only males were admitted behind the screen of boughs. Here, in the midst of a large circle of spectators, were two men, dressed in an extraordinary manner, and performing the most absurd antics. Around their necks each had a sort of wooden collar, whence depended a fringe of palm-leaves, hanging nearly to their feet. Their head-dresses terminated in a tall, thin strip of wood, painted in imitation of the beak of a saw-fish, while their faces were daubed with various colors, so as completely to change the expression of the features. In each hand they had a gourd containing pebbles, with which they marked time in their dances. These were entirely peculiar, and certainly very comical. First they approached each other, and bent down their tall head-pieces with the utmost gravity, by way of salute ; then sidled off like crabs, singing a couplet which had both rhythm and rhyme, but, so far as I could discover, no sense. As interpreted to me, afterward, by Mr. H——, it ran thus :—

"Shovel-nosed shark,
 Grandmother, grandmother!
Shovel-nosed shark,
 Grandmother!"

When the performers got tired, their places were taken by others, who exhausted their ingenuity in devising grotesque and ludicrous variations.

When evening came, fires of pine wood were lighted in all directions, and the drinking and dancing went on, growing noisier and more outrageous as the night advanced. Many got dead drunk, and were carried off by the women. Others quarreled, but the women, with wise foresight, had carried off and hidden all their weapons, and thus obliged them to settle their disputes with their fists, "English fashion." To me, these boxing bouts were exceedingly amusing. Instead of parrying each others' strokes, they literally exchanged them. First one would deliver his blow, and then stand still and take that of his opponent, blow for blow, until both became satisfied. Then they would take a drink of *mishla* together, "English fashion," and become friends again.

During the whole of the evening I found myself closely watched by a hideous old woman, who moved around among the revelers like a ghoul. Everybody made way for her when she approached, and none ventured to speak with her. There was something almost fascinating in her repulsiveness. Her hair was long and matted, and her shriveled skin appeared to adhere like that of a mummy to her bones; for she was emaciated to the last degree. The nails of her

SUKIA OF SANDY BAY.

fingers were long and black, and caused her hands to look like the claws of some unclean bird. Her eyes were bloodshot, but bright and intense, and were constantly fixed upon me, like those of some wild beast on its prey. Wherever I moved she followed, even behind the screen concealing the masked dancers, where no other woman was admitted.

I lingered among the revelers until their antics ceased to be amusing, and became simply brutal. Both sexes finally gave themselves up to the grossest and most shameless debauchery, such as I have never heard ascribed to the most bestial of savages.

Disgusted and sickened, I turned away, and went down to the shore, preferring, after what had occurred at Slam's house, to sleep in my boat, to trusting myself in the power of the wounded trader. So we pushed off a few hundred feet from the shore, and anchored for the night. I wrapped myself in my blanket, and, notwithstanding the noisy revels in the village, savage laughter and angry shouts, the beating of drums and firing of guns, I was soon asleep.

It was past midnight; the moon had gone down, the fires of the village were burning low, and the dancers, stupified and exhausted, only broke out in occasional spasmodic shrieks, when I was awakened by Antonio, who placed his finger on my lips in token of silence. I nevertheless started up in something of alarm, for the image of the skinny old hag, who had tracked me with her snaky eyes all the evening, had disturbed my dreams. To my surprise I found the Indian, whom I had rescued from the drunken violence of the trader, crouching in the bottom of the boat. He had already explained to Antonio, through the Poyer, that we were in great danger; that the old woman who had haunted me was a powerful *Sukia,* whose commands were always implicitly obeyed by the superstitious Sambos. Instigated by the discomfited trader, she had demanded our death, and even now her followers were planning the means to accomplish it. Our safety, he urged, depended upon our immediate departure, and then, as if relieved of a burden, he slipped quietly overboard, and swam toward the shore.

I was nothing loth to leave Sandy Bay, and we lost no time in getting up the large stone which served us for an anchor, and taking our departure. By morning we were clear of the lagoon, and in the channel leading from it to Wano Sound, lying about fifteen miles to the nortward of Sandy Bay, and half that distance from Cape Gracias. We reached the sound about ten o'clock in the morning, and stopped for breakfast on a narrow sand-spit, where a few trees on the shore gave shade and fuel. The day was excessively hot, and we waited for the evening before pursuing our voyage. During the afternoon, however, we were joined by Mr. H., who had got wind of the designs of the trader, and attempted to warn us, but found that we had gone. Indignant at his treachery, he had abandoned the brutal captain, and determined to return to the Cape.

He explained to me that our danger had been greater than we had supposed. The old *Sukia* woman possessed more power over the Sambos than king or chief, and her commands were never disputed or neglected. The grandfather of the present king, he said, had been killed by her order, as had also his great aunt; and although the immediate perpetrators of the deed had been executed, yet the king had not dared to bring the dreaded *Sukia* to justice. She had, however, been obliged to leave Cape Gracias, lest, during the visit of some English vessel of war, she should be punished for complicity in the murder of a couple of Englishmen, named Collins and Pollard, who had been slaughtered some years before, while turtling on the cays off the coast. Another reason for her departure had been the advent of a more powerful and less malignant *Sukia* woman, who, he assured me, was gifted with prophecy, and a knowledge of things past and to come. He represented her as young, living in a very mysterious manner, far up the Cape River, among the mountains. None knew who she was, nor whence she came, nor had he seen her more than once, although he had consulted her by proxy on several occasions. I was amused at the gravity with which he recounted instances of her power over disease and her knowledge of events, and could not help thinking, that he had resided so long on the coast as to get infected with the superstitions of the people. There was, however, no mistaking his earnestness, and I consequently abstained from ridiculing his stories. "You shall see and hear for yourself," he added, "and then you will be better able to judge if I am a child to be deceived by the silly juggles of an Indian woman. These people have inherited from their ancestors many mysterious and wonderful powers; and even the inferior order of *Sukias* can defy the poison of snakes, and the effects of fire. Flames and the bullets of guns are impotent against them."

I found H. a man of no inconsiderable intelligence, and he gave me much information about the coast and its inhabitants, and, altogether, before embarking we had become fast friends, and I had accepted an invitation to make his house my home during my stay at the Cape.

I have several times alluded to the filthy *mishla* drink, which is the universal appliance of the Sambos for getting up the "big drunk." I never witnessed the disgusting process of its preparation, but it has been graphically described by Roberts, who was a trader on the coast, and who, twenty years before, had been a witness of the "rise and progress" of a grand debauch at Sandy Bay.

"Preparations were going on for a grand feast and *mishla* drink. For this purpose the whole population was employed—most of them being engaged in collecting pine-apples, plantains, and cassava for their favorite liquor. The expressed juice of the pine-apple alone is a pleasant and agreeable beverage. The *mishla* from the plantain and banana, is also both pleasant and nutritive; that from the cassava and maize is more intoxicating, but its preparation is a process exceedingly disgusting. The root of the cassava, after being peeled and mashed, is boiled to the same consistence as when it is used for food. It is then taken from the fire, and allowed to cool. The pots are now surrounded by all the women, old and young, who, being provided with large calabashes, commence an attack upon the cassava, which they chew to the consistence of a thick paste, and then put their mouthsful into the bowls, until the latter are filled. These are then emptied into a canoe which is drawn up for the purpose, until it is about one third filled. Other cassava is then taken, bruised in a kind of wooden mortar, until it is reduced to the consistence of dough, when it is diluted with cold water, to which is added a quantity of Indian corn, partly boiled and masticated, and then all is poured into the canoe, which is filled with water, and the mixture afterward frequently stirred with a paddle. In the course of a few hours it reaches a high and abominable state of fermentation. The liquor, it may be observed, is more or less esteemed, according to the health, age, and constitution of the masticators. And when the chiefs give a private *mishla* drink, they confine the mastication to their own wives and young girls."

After fermentation, the *mishla* has a cream-like appearance, and is to the highest degree intoxicating. The drinking never ceases, so long as a drop can be squeezed from the festering dregs that remain, after the liquid is exhausted.

Chapter XII.

CAPE GRACIAS Á DIOS, was so called by Columbus, when, after a weary voyage, he gave "Thanks to God" for the happy discovery of this, the extreme north-eastern angle of Central America. Here the great Cape, or Wanks River, finds its way into the sea, forming a large, but shallow harbor. It was a favorite resort of the buccaneers, in the olden time, when the Spanish Main was associated with vague notions of exhaustless wealth, tales of heavy galloons, laden with gold, and the wild adventures of Drake, and Morgan, and Llonois. Here, too, long ago, was wrecked a large slaver, destined for Cuba, and crowded with negroes. They escaped to the shore, mixed with the natives, and, with subsequent additions to their numbers from Jamaica, and from the interior, originated the people known as the "Mosquito Indians." Supported by the pirates, and by the governors of Jamaica, as a means of annoyance to the Spaniards, they gradually extended southward as far as Bluefields, and at one time carried on a war against the Indians, whom they had displaced, for the purpose of obtaining prisoners, to be sold in the islands as slaves.

But with the suppression of this traffic, and in consequence of the encroachments of the semi-civilized Caribs on the north, their settlement at the Cape has gradually declined, until now it does not contain more than two hundred inhabitants. The village is situated on the south-western side of the bay or harbor, not far from its entrance, on the edge of an extensive, sandy savannah.

Between the shore and the village is a belt of thick bush, three or four hundred yards broad, through which are numerous narrow paths, difficult to pass, since the natives are too lazy to cut away the undergrowth and branches which obstruct them. The village itself is mean, dirty, and infested with hungry pigs, and snarling, mangy dogs. The huts are of the rudest description, and most of them unfitted for shelter against the rain. The only houses which had any pretensions to comfort, at the time of my visit, were the "King's house," another belonging to a German named Boucher, and that of my new friend H. The latter was boarded and shingled, and looked quite a palace after my experience of the preceding two months, in Mosquito architecture. Mr. H. made us very comfortable indeed. In addition to the numerous native products of the country, he had a liberal supply of foreign luxuries. As a trader he had, for many years, carried on quite a traffic with the Wanks River Indians, in deer skins, sarsaparilla, and mahogany, and with the Sambos themselves in turtle-shells. And whatever nominal authority may have existed previously at the Cape, it was obvious enough that he was now the *de facto* governor.

Thoroughly domesticated in the country, he had no ambitions beyond it, and had made several, although not very successful, attempts to introduce industry, and improve the condition of the natives. At one time he had had a number of cattle on the savannah—which, although its soil is too poor for cultivation, nevertheless affords abundance of good grass—but the Sambos killed so many for their own use, that he sold the remainder to the trading vessels. He had now undertaken their introduction again, with better success, and had, moreover, some mules and horses. The latter were sorry-looking beasts; since, for want of proper care, the wood-ticks had got in their ears, and caused them not only to lop down, but also, in some instances, entirely to drop off.

The Sambos have a singular custom, unfavorable, certainly, to the raising of cattle, which Mr. H. had not yet entirely succeeded in suppressing. Whenever a native is proved guilty of adultery, the injured party immediately goes out in the savannah and shoots a beeve, without regard to its ownership. The duty of paying for it then devolves upon the adulterer, and constitutes the penalty for his offence!

Nearly all the Sambos at the Cape speak a little English, and I never passed their huts without being saluted "Mornin', sir; give me grog!" In fact their devotion to grog, and general improvident habits, are fast thinning their numbers, and will soon work their utter extermination. Although there are several places near the settlement where all needful supplies might be raised, yet they are chiefly dependent on the Indians of the river for their vegetables.

There is little game on the savannah, but on the strip of land which separates the harbor from the sea, and which is called the island of San Pio, deer are found in abundance. This island is curiously

HUNTING DEER.

diversified with alternate patches of savannah, bush, and marsh, and offers numerous coverts for wild animals. The deer, however, are only hunted by the few whites who live at the Cape, and they have hit upon an easy and novel mode of procuring their supply. The deer are not shy of cattle, and will feed side by side with them in the savannahs. So Mr. H. had trained a favorite cow to obey reins of cord attached to her horns, as a horse does his bit. Starting out, and keeping the cow constantly between himself and the deer, he never has the slightest difficulty in approaching so close to them as to shoot them with a pistol. If there are more than one, the rest do not start off at the discharge, but only prick up their ears in amazement, and thus afford an opportunity for another shot, if desired. I witnessed this labor-saving mode of hunting several times, and found that H. and his cow never failed of their object.

While upon the subject of game, I may mention that San Pio abounds with birds and water-fowl. Among them are two varieties of snipe, beside innumerable curlews, ducks, and teal. The blue and green-winged teal were great favorites of mine, being always in good condition. They were not obtained, however, without the drawback of exposure to the sandflies, which infest the island in uncountable millions. The European residents always have a supply of turtles, which are purchased at prices of from four to eight yards of Osnaberg, equal to from one to two dollars, according to their size. Two kinds of oysters are also obtained here, one called the "bank oyster," corresponding with those which I obtained in Pearl Cay Lagoon, and the little mangrove oysters. The latter are about the size of half a dollar, and attach themselves to the roots of the mangrove-trees. It is a question whether a hungry man, having to open them for himself, might not starve before getting satisfied. A few hundreds, with a couple of Indians to open them, make a good, but moderate, lunch !

The bay and river swarm with fish, of the varieties which I have enumerated as common on the coast. During still weather they are caught with seines, in large quantities. These seines belong to the foreigners, but are drawn by the natives (when they happen to be hungry !), who receive half of the spoil.

Mr. H. was not a little piqued at my incredulity in the *Sukias*, and, faithful to his promise, persuaded one of them to give us an example of her powers. The place was the enclosure in the rear of his own house, and the time evening. The *Sukia* made her appearance alone, carrying a long thick wand of bamboo, and with no dress except the *ule tournou.* She was only inferior to her sister at Sandy Bay, in ugliness, and stalked into the house like a spectre, without uttering a word. H. cut off a piece of calico, and handed it to her as her recompense. She received it in perfect silence, walked into the yard, and folded it carefully on the ground. Meanwhile a fire had been kindled of pine splints and branches, which was now blazing high. Without any hesitation the *Sukia* walked up to it, and stepped in its very centre. The flames darted their forked tongues as high as her waist ; the coals beneath and around her naked feet blackened, and seemed to expire ; while the *tournou* which she wore about her loins, cracked and shriveled with the heat. There she stood, immovable, and apparently as insensible as a statue of iron, until the blaze subsided, when she commenced to walk around the smouldering embers, muttering rapidly to herself, in an unintelligible manner. Suddenly she stopped, and placing her foot on the bamboo staff, broke it in the middle, shaking out, from the section in her hand, a full-grown *tamagasa* snake, which, on the instant coiled itself up, flattened its head, and darted out its tongue, in an attitude of defiance and attack. The *Sukia* extended her hand, and it fastened on her wrist with the quickness of light, where it hung, dangling and writhing its body in knots and coils, while she resumed her mumbling march around the embers. After a while, and with the same abruptness which had marked all of her previous movements, she shook off the serpent, crushed its head in the ground with her heel, and taking up the cloth which had been given to her, stalked away, without having exchanged a word with any one present.

Mr. H. gave me a triumphant look, and asked what now I had to say. "Was there any deception in what I had seen?" I only succeeded in convincing him that I was a perversely obstinate man, by suggesting that the *Sukia* was probably acquainted with some antidote for the venom of the serpent, and that her endurance of the fire was nothing more remarkable than that of the jugglers, "fire kings," and other vagrants at home, who make no pretence of supernatural powers.

"Well," he continued, in a tone of irritated disappointment, "can your jugglers and 'fire kings' tell the past, and predict the future? When you have your inmost thoughts revealed to you, and when the spirits of your dead friends recall to your memory scenes and incidents known only to them, yourself, and God—tell me," and his voice grew deep and earnest, "on what hypothesis do you account for things like these? Yet I can testify to their truth. You may laugh at what you call the vulgar trickery of the old hag who has just left us, but I can take you where even your scoffing tongue will cleave to its roof with awe; where the inmost secrets of your heart shall be unvailed, and where you shall *feel* that you stand face to face with the invisible dead!"

I have never felt it in my heart to ridicule opinions, however absurd, if sincerely entertained; and there was that in the awed manner of my host which convinced me that he was in earnest in what he said. So I dropped the conversation, on his assurance that he would accompany me to visit the strange woman to whom he assigned such mysterious power.

Antonio had been an attentive witness of the tricks of the *Sukia*, and expressed to me the greatest contempt for her pretensions. Such exhibitions, he said, were only fit for idle children, and were not to be confounded with the awful powers of the oracles, through whom the "Lord of Teaching and the spirits of the Holy Men" held communion with mortals. I spoke to him of the mysterious woman, who was greater than all the *Sukias*, and lived among the mountains. "She is of our people," he exclaimed, warmly, "and her name is *Hoxom-Bal*, which means the Mother of the Tigers. It was to seek her that I left the Holy City of the Itzaes, with no guide but my Lord who never lies. And now her soul shall enter into our brothers of the mountains, and they shall be tigers on the tracks of our oppressors!"

The form of the Indian boy had dilated as he spoke; his smooth limbs were knotted by the swelling muscles; his eyes burned, and his low voice became firm, distinct, and ominous. But it was only for an instant; and while I listened to hear the great secret which swelled in his bosom, he stopped short, and, turning suddenly, walked away. But I could see that he pressed his talisman closer to his breast.

The *Sukias* of the coast are usually women, although their powers and authority are sometimes assumed by men. Their preparation for the office involves mortifications as rigorous as the Church ever required of her most abject devotees. For months do the candidates seclude themselves in the forests, avoiding the face of their fellows, and there, without arms or means of defense, contend with hunger, the elements, and wild beasts. It is thus that they seal their compact with the mysterious powers which rule over earth and water, air and fire; and they return to the villages of their people, invested with all the terrors which superstition has ever attached to those who seem to be exempt from the operations of natural laws.

These *Sukias* are the "medicine-men" of the coast, and affect to cure disease; but their directions are usually more extravagant than beneficial. They sometimes order the victim of fever to go to an open sand-beach by the sea, and there, exposed to the burning heat of the vertical sun, await his cure. They have also a savage taste for blood, and the cutting and scarification of the body are among their favorite remedies.

The Mosquitos, I may observe here, have no idea of a supreme beneficent Being; but stand in great awe of an evil spirit which they call *Wulasha*, and of a water-ghost, called *Lewire*. *Wulasha* is supposed to share in all the rewards which the *Sukias* obtain for their services. His half of the stipulated price, however, is shrewdly exacted beforehand, while the payment of the remainder depends very much upon the *Sukia's* success.

Among the customs universal on the coast, is infanticide, in all cases where the child is born with any physical defect. As a consequence, natural deformity of person is unknown. Chastity, as I have several times had occasion to intimate, is not considered a virtue; and the number of a man's wives is only determined by circumstances, polygamy being universal. Physically, the Mosquitos have a large predominance of negro blood; and their habits and superstitions are African rather than American.

They are largely affected with syphilitic affections, resulting from their unrestrained licentious intercourse with the pirates in remote, and with traders (in character but one degree removed from the pirates) in later times. These affections, under the form of the *bulpis*, red, white, and scabbed, have come to be a radical taint, running through the entire population, and so impairing the general constitution as to render it fatally susceptible to all epidemic diseases. This is one of the powerful causes which is contributing to the rapid decrease, and which will soon result in the total extinction of the Sambos.

Their arts are limited to the very narrow range of their wants, and are exceedingly rude. The greatest skill is displayed in their dories, canoes, and pitpans, which are brought down by the Indians of the interior, rudely blocked out, so as to give the purchaser an opportunity of exercising his taste in the finish. Essentially fishers, they are at home in the water, and manage their boats with great dexterity. Their language has some slight affinity with the Carib, but has degenerated into a sort of jargon, in which Indian, English, Spanish, and Jamaica-African are strangely jumbled. They count by twenties, *i. e.*, collective fingers and toes, and make fearful work of it when they "get up in the figures." Thus, to express thirty-seven, they say, "*Iwanaiska-kumi-pura-matawalsip-pura-matlalkabe-pura-kumi*," which literally means, one-twenty-and-ten-and-six-and-one, *i. e.*, 20+1+10+6+1.

They reckon their days by sleeps, their months by moons, and their years by the complement of thirteen moons.

Altogether, the Mosquitos have little in their character to commend. Their besetting vice is drunkenness, which has obliterated all of their better traits. Without religion, with no idea of government, they are capricious, indolent, improvident, treacherous, and given to thieving. All attempts to advance their condition have been melancholy failures, and it is probable they would have disappeared from the earth without remark, had it not suited the purposes of the English government to put them forward as a mask to that encroaching policy which is its always disclaimed, but inseparable and notorious characteristic.

There is a suburb of the village at the Cape, near the river, which is called Pullen-town. Here I was witness of a curious ceremony, a *Seekroe* or Festival of the Dead. This festival occurs on the first anniversary of the death of any important member of a family, and is only participated in by the relatives and friends of the deceased. The prime element, as in every feast, is the *chicha*, of which all hands drink profusely. Both males and females were dressed in a species of cloak, of *ule* bark, fantastically painted, with black and white, while their faces were correspondingly streaked with red and yellow (*anotto*). The music was made by two big droning pipes, played to a low, monotonous vocal accompaniment. The dance consisted in slowly stalking in a circle, for a certain length of time, when the immediate relatives of the dead threw themselves flat on their faces on the ground, calling loudly on the departed, and tearing up the earth with their hands. Then, rising, they resumed their march, only to repeat their prostrations and cries. I could obtain no satisfactory explanation of the practice. "So did our ancestors," was the only reason assigned for its continuance.

We had been at the Cape about a week, when Mr. H. received information that the news of our affair at Quamwatla had reached Sandy Bay, and that the vindictive trader had dispatched a fast-sailing dory by sea to Bluefields, to obtain orders for our "arrest and punishment." This news was brought in the night, by the same Indian whom I had protected from the trader's brutality, and who took this means of evincing his gratitude. I had already frankly explained to Mr. H. the circumstances of our fight, which, he conceded, fully justified all we had done. Still, as the trader might make it a pretext for much annoyance, he approved the plan which I had already formed, for other reasons, to explore the Wanks River, and accompany my Poyer boy to the fastnesses of his tribe, in the untracked wilderness lying between that river and the Bay of Honduras. By taking this course, I would be able again to reach the sea beyond the Sambo jurisdiction, in the district occupied by the Caribs, not far from the old Spanish port of Truxillo. Furthermore, the tame scenery of the lagoons had become unattractive, and I longed for mountains and the noise of rushing waters. The famous *Sukia* woman also lived on one of the lower branches of the river, and in accordance with this plan we could visit her without going greatly out of our way.

In fulfillment of his promise, Mr. H. prepared to accompany us as far as the retreat of the mysterious seeress, and two days afterward, following the lead of his pitpan, we embarked. The harbor connects with the river by a creek at its northern extremity, which is deep enough to admit the passage of canoes. Emerging from this, we came into the great Wanks River, a broad and noble stream, with a very slight current at its low stages, but pouring forth a heavy flood of waters during the rainy season. It has ample capacity for navigation for nearly a hundred miles of its length, but a bad and variable bar at its mouth presents an insurmountable barrier to the entrance of vessels. Very little is known of this river, except that it rises within thirty or forty miles of the Pacific, and that, for the upper half of its course, it flows among high mountains, and is obstructed by falls and shallows.

We made rapid progress during the day, the river more resembling an estuary than a running stream. The banks, for a hundred yards or more back from the water, were thickly lined with bush; but beyond this belt of jungle there was an uninterrupted succession of sandy savannahs. There were no signs of inhabitants, except a few huts, at long intervals, at places where the soil happened to be rich enough to admit of cultivation. We nevertheless met a few Indians coming down with canoes, to be sold at the Cape, who regarded us curiously, and in silence.

Near evening, we encamped at a point where a ridge of the savannah, penetrating the bush, came down boldly to the river, forming an eddy, or cove, which seemed specially intended for a halting-place. Mr. H. had named the bluff "Iguana Point," from the great number of iguanas found there. They abound on the higher parts of the entire coast, but I had seen none so large as those found at this place. It is difficult to imagine uglier reptiles—great, overgrown, corrugated lizards as they are, with their bloated throats, and snaky eyes! They seemed to think us insolent intruders, and waddled off with apparent sullen reluctance, when we approached. But the law of compensations holds good in respect to the iguanas, as in regard to every thing else. If they are the ugliest reptiles in the world, they are, at the same time, among the best to eat. So our men slaughtered three or four of the largest, selecting those which appeared to be fullest of eggs. Up to this time I had not been able to overcome my repugnance sufficiently to taste them; but now, encouraged by H., I made the attempt. The first few mouthfuls went much against the grain; but I found the flesh really so delicate, that before the meal was finished, I succeeded in forgetting my prejudices. The eggs are especially delicious, surpassing even those of the turtle. It may be said, to the credit of the ugly iguana, that in respect of his own food, he is as delicate as the humming-bird, or the squirrel, living chiefly upon flowers and blossoms of trees. He is frequently to be seen on the branches of large trees, overhanging the water, whence he looks down with curious gravity upon the passing voyager. His principal enemies are serpents, who, however, frequently get worsted in their attacks, for the iguana has sharp teeth, and powerful jaws. Of the smaller varieties, there are some of the liveliest green. Hundreds of these may be seen on the snags and fallen trunks that line the shores of the rivers. They will watch the canoe as it approaches, then suddenly dart off to the shore, literally walking the water, so rapidly that they almost appear like a green arrow skipping past. They are called, in the language of the natives, by the generic name, *kakamuk.*

In strolling a little distance from our camp, before supper, I saw a waddling animal, which I at first took for an iguana. A moment after, I perceived my mistake. It appeared to be doing its best to run away, but so clumsily that, instead of shooting it, I hurried forward, and headed off its course. In attempting to pass me, it came so near that I stopped it with my foot. In an instant it literally rolled itself up in a ball, looking for all the world like a large sea-shell, or rather like one of those curious, cheese-like, coralline productions, known among sailors as sea-eggs. I then saw it was an armadillo, that little mailed adventurer of the forest, who, like the opossum, shams death when "cornered," or driven in "a tight place." I rolled him over, and grasping him by his stumpy tail, carried him into camp. He proved to be of the variety known as the "three-banded armadillo," cream-colored, and covered with hexagonal scales. I afterward saw several other larger varieties, with eight and nine bands. The flesh of the armadillo is white, juicy, and tender, and is esteemed one of the greatest of luxuries.

Chapter XIII.

AT noon, on the second day of our departure from Cape Gracias, we came to a considerable stream, named Bocay, which enters the river Wanks from the south-west. It was on the banks of this river, some ten or fifteen miles above its mouth, that the famed *Sukia* woman resided. We directed our boats up the stream, the water of which was clear, and flowed with a rapid current. We were not long in passing through the belt of savannah which flanks the Cape River, on both sides, for fifty miles above its mouth. Beyond this came dense primitive forests of gigantic trees, among which the mahogany was conspicuous. The banks, too, became high and firm, occasionally presenting rocky promontories, around which the water swept in dark eddies. Altogether, it was evident that we had entered the mountain region of the continent, and were at the foot of one of the great dependent ranges of the primitive chain of the Cordilleras.

In places, the river was compressed among high hills, with scarped, rocky faces, where the current was rapid and powerful, and only overcome by vigorous efforts at the paddles. These were succeeded by beautiful intervals of level ground, inviting localities for the establishments of man. We passed two or three sweet and sheltered nooks, in which were small clearings, and the picturesque huts of the Indians. Excepting an occasional palm-tree, or isolated cluster of plantains, clinging to the shore where their germs had been lodged by the water, there was nothing tropical in the aspect of nature, unless, perhaps, the greater size of the forest-trees, and the variety of parasitic plants which they supported.

Our progress against the current was comparatively slow and laborious, and it was late in the evening when the glittering of fires on the bank, and the barking of dogs, announced to us the proximity of the Indian village of Bocay, to which we were bound. We reached it in due time, and were received quite ceremoniously by the old men of the place, who seemed to be perfectly aware of our coming. This struck me at the time as due to the foresight of Mr. H., but I afterward learned that he had given the Indians no intimation of our proposed visit.

A vacant hut was assigned to us, and we commenced to arrange our hammocks and prepare our supper. Our meal was scarcely finished, when there was a sudden movement among the Indians, who clustered like bees around our door, and a passage for some one approaching was rapidly opened. A moment afterward, an old woman came forward, and, stopping in the low doorway, regarded us in silence. In bearing and dress she differed much from the rest of the people. Around her forehead she wore a broad band of cotton, in which were braided the most brilliant feathers of birds. This band confined her hair, which hung down her back, like a vail, nearly to the ground. From her waist depended a kilt of tiger-skins, and she wore sandals of the same on her feet. Around each wrist and ankle she had broad feather bands, like that which encircled her forehead.

Her eyes soon rested upon Antonio, who, on the instant of her approach, had discontinued his work, and advanced to the door. They exchanged a glance as if of recognition, and spoke a few hurried and, to us, unintelligible words, when the old woman turned suddenly, and walked away. I looked inquiringly at the youthful Indian, whose eyes glowed again with that mysterious intelligence which I had so often remarked.

He came hastily to my side, and whispered in Spanish, "The Mother of the Tigers is waiting!" Then, with nervous steps, he moved toward the door. I beckoned to H., and followed. The Indians opened to the right and left, and we passed out, scarcely able to keep pace with the rapid steps of the Indian boy. On he went, as if familiar with the place, past the open huts, and into the dark forest. I now saw that he followed a light, not like that of a flame, but of a burning coal, which looked close at one moment, and distant the next. The path, though narrow, was smooth, and ascended rapidly. For half an hour we kept on at the same quick pace, when the trees began to separate, and I could see that we were emerging from the dark forest into a comparatively open space, in which the graceful plumes of the palm-trees appeared, traced lightly against the starry sky. Here the guiding fire seemed to halt, and, coming up, we found the same old woman who had visited us in the village, and who now carried a burning brand as a direction to our steps. She made a sign of silence, and moved on slowly, and with apparent caution. A few minutes' walk brought us to what, in the dim light, appeared to be a building of stone, and soon after to another and larger one. I saw that they were partly ruined, for the stars in the horizon were visible through the open doorways. Our guide passed these without stopping, and led us to the threshold of a small cane-built hut, which stood beyond the ruin. The door was open, and the light from within shone out on the smoothly beaten ground in front, in a broad unwavering column. We entered; but for the moment I was almost blinded by a blaze of light proceeding from torches of pine-wood, planted in each corner. I was startled also by an angry growl, and the sudden apparition of some wild animal at our feet. I shrank back with a feeling of alarm, which was not diminished when, upon recovering my powers of vision, I saw directly in front of us, as if guardian of the dwelling, a large tiger, its fierce eyes fixed upon us, and slowly sweeping the ground with its long tail, as if preparing to spring at our throats.

It, however, stopped the way only for a moment. A single word and gesture from the old woman drove it into a corner of the hut, where it crouched down in quiet. I glanced around, but excepting a single rude Indian drum, placed in the centre of the smooth, earthen floor, and a few blocks of stone planted along the walls for seats, there were no other articles, either of use or ornament, in the hut. But at one extremity of the low apartment, seated upon an outspread tiger-skin, was a woman, whose figure and manner at once marked her out as the extraordinary *Sukia* whom we had come so far to visit. She was young, certainly not over twenty, tall, and perfectly formed, and wore a tiger-skin in the same manner as the old woman who had acted as her messenger, but the band around her forehead, and her armlets and anklets, were of gold.

She rose when we entered, and, with a faint smile of recognition to H., spoke a few words of welcome. I had expected to see a bold pretender to supernatural powers, whose first efforts would be directed to work upon the imaginations of her visitors, and was surprised to find that the "Mother of the Tigers" was after all only a shy and timid Indian girl. Her looks, at first, were troubled, and she glanced into our eyes inquiringly ; but suddenly turning her gaze toward the open door, she uttered an exclamation of mingled surprise and joy, and in an instant after she stood by the side of Antonio. They gazed at each other in silence, then exchanged a rapid signal, and a single word, when she turned away, and Antonio retired into a corner, where he remained fixed as a statue, regarding every movement with the closest attention.

"THE MOTHER OF THE TIGERS."

No sooner had the *Sukia* resumed her seat, than she clasped her forehead in her open palms, and gazed intently upon the ground before her. Never have I seen the face of a human being which wore a more earnest expression. For five minutes, perhaps, the silence was unbroken, when a sudden sound, as of the snapping of the string of a violin, directed our attention to the rude drum that stood in the centre of the hut. This sound was followed by a series of crackling noises, like the discharges of electric sparks. They seemed to occur irregularly at first, but as I listened, I discovered that they had a harmonious relationship, as if in accompaniment to some simple melody. The vibrations of the drum were distinctly visible, and they seemed to give it a circular motion over the ground, from left to right. The sounds stopped as suddenly as they had commenced, and the *Sukia,* lifting her head, said solemnly, "The spirits of your fathers have come to the mountain! I know them not; you must speak to them."

* * * * * * * *

I hesitate to recount what I that night witnessed in the rude hut of the *Sukia,* lest my testimony should expose both my narrative and myself to ridicule, and unjust imputations. Were it my purpose to elaborate an impressive story, it would be easy to call in the aid of an imposing machinery, and invest the communications which were that night made to us with a portentous significance. But this would be as foreign to truth as repugnant to my own feelings; for whatever tone of lightness may run through this account of my adventures in the wilderness, those who know me will bear witness to my respect for those things which are in their nature sacred, or connected with the more mysterious elements of our existence. I can only say, that except the somewhat melo-dramatic manner in which we had been conducted up the mountain by the messenger of the *Sukia,* and the incident of the tamed tiger, nothing occurred during our visit which appeared to have been designed for effect, or which was visibly out of the ordinary course of things. It is true, I was somewhat puzzled, I will not say impressed, with the perfect understanding, or relationship, which seemed to exist between the *Sukia* and Antonio. This relationship, however, was fully explained in the sequel. Among the ruling and the priestly classes of the semi-civilized nations of America, there has always existed a mysterious bond, or secret organization, which all the disasters to which they have been subjected, have not destroyed. It is to its present existence that we may attribute those simultaneous movements of the aborigines of Mexico, Central America, and Peru, which have, more than once, threatened the complete subversion of the Spanish power.

* * * * * * * *

It was past midnight when, with a new and deeper insight into the mysteries of our present and future existence, and a fuller and loftier appreciation of the great realities which are to follow upon the advent of every soul into the universe, and of which earth is scarcely the initiation, that H. and myself left the sanctuary of the *Sukia*. The moon had risen, and now silvered every object with its steady light, revealing to us that we stood upon a narrow terrace of the mountain, facing the east, and commanding a vast panorama of forest and savannah, bounded only by the distant sea. Immediately in front of the hut from which we had emerged, stood one of the ruined structures to which I have already alluded. By the clear light of the moon I could perceive that it was built of large stones, laid with the greatest regularity, and sculptured all over with strange figures, having a close resemblance, if not an absolute identity, with those which have become familiarized to us by the pencil of Catherwood.

THE SANCTUARY OF THE SUKIA.

It appeared originally to have been of two stories, but the upper walls had fallen, and the ground was encumbered with the rubbish, over which vines were trailing, as if to vail the crumbling ruins from the gaze of men. As we moved away, and at a considerable distance from the ruins, we observed a large erect stone, rudely sculptured in the outline of a human figure. Its face was turned to the East, as if to catch the first rays of the morning, and the light of the moon fell full upon it. To my surprise, its features were the exact counterparts of those which appeared on Antonio's talisman. There was no mistaking the rigid yet not ungentle expression of the "Lord who never lies."

Silently we followed the guide, who had conducted us up the mountain, into the narrow path which led to the village. She indicated to us the direction we were to pursue with her hand, and left us without a word. I was so absorbed in my own reflections that it was not until we had reached our temporary quarters that I missed Antonio. He had remained behind. But when I awoke next morning he had returned, and was busily preparing for our departure. "It is well with our brothers of the mountains!" was his prompt response to my look of inquiry. From that day forward his absorbing idea seemed to be to return as speedily as posible to his people. It was long afterward that I discovered the deep significance of the visit of the youthful chieftain of the Itzaes to the Indian seeress of the River Bocay. Since then the Spaniard, though fenced round with bayonets, has often shuddered when he has heard the cry of the tiger in the stillness of the night, betraying the approach of those injured men, whose relentless arms, nerved by the recollections of three centuries of oppression, now threaten the utter extermination of the race of the conquerors!

Our passage down the Bocay was rapid compared with the ascent, and at noon we had reached the great river. My course now lay in one direction, and that of Mr. H. in another, but we were loth to separate, and he finally agreed to accompany us to our first stopping-place, and, passing the night with us there, return next day to the Cape. It was scarcely four o'clock when we reached the designated point, chiefly remarkable as marking the termination of the savannahs. Beyond here the banks of the river became elevated, rising in hills and high mountains, densely covered with a gigantic primeval forest. Our Indian companions speedily supplied us with an abundance of fish, with which the river seemed to swarm. And as for vegetables—wherever the banks of the river are low there is a profusion of bananas and plantains, growing from bulbs, which have been brought down from the interior, and deposited by the river in its overflows.

Mr. H. had once ascended the river to its source, in the elevated mining district of New Segovia, the extreme north-western department of Nicaragua. The ascent had occupied him twenty days. In many places, he said, the channel is completely interrupted by falls and impassable rapids, around which it was necessary to drag the canoes. In other places the river is compressed between vertical walls of rock, and the water runs with such force that it required many attempts and the most vigorous exertions to get the boats through.

He represented that New Segovia has a considerable population of civilized Indians, whose principal occupation is the washing of gold, which is found in all of the upper waters. Their mode of life he described as affording a curious illustration of the influence of the Catholic priests, who are scattered here and there, and who exercise almost unbounded influence over the simple natives. The nature of their relationship, as well as their own manners, were so well illustrated by an incident which befell him during his visit there, that I shall attempt to relate it, as nearly as possible in his own words. The reader must bear in mind that the recital was made in a fragmentary manner, in the intervals of vigorous puffing at a huge cigar, and that I have taken the liberty of commencing at the beginning of the story, and not at the end.

A Tale of Wanks River.

"On our nineteenth evening from the Cape," said H., "after a fatiguing day of alternate poling and paddling, we reached Pantasma, the extreme frontier Segovian settlement on the river. As we drew up to the bank, thankful for the prospect of shelter and rest which the village held out, we were surprised to hear the music of drums and pipes, and, for a moment, were under the pleasing impression that the people had, in some way, got information of our approach, and had taken this mode of giving us a welcome. However, we soon saw that the musicians were in attendance on a white man, whose garb had a strange mixture of civilized and savage fashions. He regarded us curiously for a few moments, and then, giving the nearest musicians each a vigorous kick, he ran down to the water, and bestowed upon all of us an equally hearty embrace! Propounding a dozen inquiries in a breath, he announced himself an Englishman 'in a d—l of a fix,' whose immediate and overshadowing ambition was, that all hands should go straight to his hut and have something to drink! Our first impression was decidedly that the man was mad; but we were undeceived when we got to his house, which we found profusely supplied with food, and where we were not long in making ourselves thoroughly at home. Perhaps what we drank had something to do with it, but certainly we nearly died with laughter in listening to our host's recital of his adventures in Central America, and especially of the way in which he had got to Pantasma, and came to have an escort of musicians.

"His name, he said, was Harry F——. He was the son of a London merchant, who was well to do in the world. As usual with sons of such papas, he had gone to school when younger, and entered his father's establishment when old enough, where, as the probable successor of the principal, he was, in his own estimation at least, an important personage, and, altogether, above work. He nevertheless affected a great liking for the packing department, for the reason that it connected with a vault, in which he had established a smoking-room, where he spent the day in devising plans of amusement for the night, in company with chosen spirits and choice Havanas.

"When he had reached his majority, his father thought it prudent to detach him from his associations, by giving him a little experience in the severities of the world. Having several friends in Belize, he fitted him out with an adventure, costing some twenty-five hundred dollars, and consisting of nearly every useless article that could be found, which, by its glitter and gaud, it was supposed, would attract the easily-dazzled eyes of the people of the tropics. He duly arrived at Belize, full of bright anticipations. One of his cherished schemes was to sell his jewelry in the towns of the interior, at four hundred per cent. profit, and after paying expenses and losses, to return at once to London, with five thousand dollars clear profit! So he went to Guatemala, and spread out his tempting wares. But he met with poor success, and at the end of two years, having gone on from bad to worse, he at last found himself in the Indian town where we discovered him—a Catholic Mission, under a Reverend Padre, who had been educated at Leon, and had passed most of his simple life, being now over threescore and ten, among the simple Indians, whom he governed. When Harry first arrived, he proceeded to the nearest hut, where the usual hospitality of room to hang his hammock was accorded him, while his valise was installed in a corner—said valise containing the remnants of the venture from

London, now dwindled down to a very small compass indeed. Of his success in trading, Harry spoke very frankly: 'The hardest lot of worthless articles I ever saw; some that I could not even give away; and those which I sold, I had to trust to people so poor that they never paid me! So I let one man pick out all he had a mind to, for one thousand dollars in cash; and that paid my expenses in Guatemala, until I got tired of the place, and started off down here.'

"After swinging his hammock in his new quarters, Harry made the tour of the village, and called on the padre, who was delighted to see him, as padres always are, took him to his church, which was as large as a city parlor, and then gave him a good dinner of fish and turtle. Harry had not had so sumptuous a meal for many a day; and when the good father brought forth a joint of bamboo, which held nearly a gallon, and drew from it a supply of tolerable rum, he felt that he had fallen into the hands of a good Samaritan. So long as this hospitality lasted, he sought no change. In the fullness of his gratitude, he made visits to all the huts in the village, and overwhelmed the inmates with presents of articles which he had not been able to give away in other places. In return, they gave him part of a morning's fishing, or part of a turtle, and thus kept him in provisions. But times changed after a few days; his friend the padre ceased to bring forth the bamboo joint, and at the same time commenced to exhort him to repentance, and to the acceptance of the true church. His host, too, declined to catch any more fish than were consumed by his interesting wife and three naked children.

"Harry smoked long and intensely over the subject. He might make a 'raise' on a pair of pantaloons, but then, 'when that was gone?' It was the first time in his life that he had been obliged seriously to reflect how he should be able to get his next meal. He tried oranges, bananas, and pineapples, but still he was hungry. As to fishing, he had never caught a fish in his life, and a turtle would be perfectly safe under his feet. His case became desperate. Such cases require desperate remedies, and Harry went to the padre, to consult with him as to the best mode of reaching Leon, distant some two hundred miles, beyond the mountains.

"It was a lucky moment for a visit to the reverend father, since, in return for some hides, sarsaparilla, and balsam, sent by him to his correspondent, the padre at Choluteca, a large town on the Pacific, he had received, among other luxuries, a reënforcement of bamboo joints. These had already added to his good humor, and given to his fat corporation and ruddy face an unusual glow. He gave Harry a warm greeting, and pointing to the broached joint, told him to help himself, which he did without reserve. Harry, in his best, though very bad Spanish, stated his case, and the holy father listened and replied. The next morning our hero awoke, and was rather surprised to find himself yet at the padre's house, where he had slept in a hammock. An empty bamboo joint was beside him, and he had a glimmering idea of a compact with the padre, through which he was to be extricated from his present uncomfortable position, and reach Leon in a most acceptable manner. But how this was to be done had escaped him; he had only a faint recollection that the padre had insisted upon initiating him into some mystery or other, and that in the fullness of heart he had assented, to the great joy of the priest, who, on the spot had given him a hearty embrace, and commenced learning him how to make the sign of the cross. The worthy padre awoke with rather different sensations, for he felt exalted with the thought that he, a poor priest over a miserable Indian community for forty years, should finally be able to rescue the soul of a heretic from the arch enemy. He was thankful that his eloquence had enabled him to attach an immortal being to the true church—a white one at that, who was of more value than a whole community of savages. It was a miracle, he was satisfied, of his patron saint, Leocadia! So without loss of time he proceeded with the work of redemption. Harry proved an apt disciple; and after making up a lot of cigars from the tobacco-pouch of the padre, the latter proceeded to explain to him what he required in the premises. Harry's mouth opened, and his cigar fell unheeded to the ground, when the padre announced his intention to administer to him the rite of baptism without delay.

"By the time he had finished his explanation, Harry's mind was made up ; as there were no lookers on whom he cared for, he would let the padre have his way, or, as he afterward expressed it, 'put him through.'

"For several days the padre and himself worked hard. He went carefully over the various responses and prayers, as they were dictated to him, made the sign of the cross in due form and proper place, and, by the assistance of the bamboo joint, was, on the second day pronounced in a hopeful state, and told that the afternoon following should witness the final act of his salvation. The sun was declining, when Harry, habited in his best, proceeded to the padre's house. He was rather surprised at meeting so many people, for he had not been consulted in any of the arrangements, and was not aware that every native in the vicinity had been notified of the ceremony in which he was to take so important a part. All had come, men, women, and children, dressed in very scanty, but very clean white cotton garments. They opened a passage for him to enter the padre's house, whom he found arrayed in his priestly vestments. He was informed that all were about proceeding to his house to escort him to the church, but that, being on the spot, the procession would form at once. Harry submitted without question to the padre's directions, had a quiet interview with the bamboo joint, and was ready. The procession was headed by four alcaldes, of different villages, each with his official baton, a tall, gold-headed staff. Next came the music, consisting of three performers on rude clarionets, made of long joints of cane, and three performers on drums, each made of a large calabash with a monkey-skin drawn over it. Next came Harry and the worthy padre, and then the people of the village, and the 'invited guests,' six deep, and a hundred all told. When our hero took his place in the procession, the padre threw over his shoulders a poncho, six feet long, gaudily decorated with the tails of macaws, bright feathers from strange birds, and strings of small river-shells, which rattled at every step; and thus they started. First they went to Harry's own hut, and, as they doubled that, and took their route toward the church, he could see the last of the procession leaving the vicinity of the padre's house. After the manner of their processions on high religious festivals, they came singing and dancing, and altogether appearing very happy. Harry was glad in his heart that no white man was looking on, and had to laugh inwardly at the fuss that was made over him. In due time they arrived at the church, and the usual ceremonies of baptism were gone through with, succeeded by a dance, on the grass, to say nothing of a liberal dispensation from the padre's bamboo joints. The padre dismissed the assembly very early, and retired, never having had so glorious or so fatiguing a day within his memory, and he was the oldest inhabitant!

"Harry wended his way to his hammock, made a cigar, thought over the events of the day, and wondered whether the church was now bound to find him fish and the et ceteras; but, before any conclusion could be come at in his mind, he fell asleep. Awaking in the morning, he was accosted at his door by several neighbors, who asked him to accept the presents they had brought, which he did of course, without knowing that it is always the custom to send something to every villager whenever he happens to have a christening, a marriage, or a death in his family. This being a very great occasion, every body had been liberal and generous withal, and in a short space he found himself supplied with provisions for a long time, more fish than he could eat in months, turtles, chickens, pigs, eggs, piles of fruit of all kinds, yams, wild animals, in fact every thing that was edible. Sending a large part of his presents as an offering to the church, Harry returned to his hammock and cigar, while his hostess commenced cooking with an agreeable alacrity.

"Late in the afternoon he started for the padre's house, but had hardly emerged from his hut when he was somewhat surprised to find himself joined by the musicians of the village, the clarionet taking precedence, and the drum filing in, both playing the usual no-tune to the best of their ability. And thus it happened for weeks afterward, for thus did the padre seek to do honor to the new disciple of the faith.

"It was on one of these formal promenades," continued H., "that we made our appearance at

Pantasma, to Harry's exceeding astonishment, and great joy. We ridiculed him for his emphatic dismissal of his musical friends, but he was too much delighted to be captious, and sent straightway for the padre, who brought with him a bamboo-joint, wherewith we made merry, even to the going down of the sun. We all went to sleep while the worthy priest was reading to us the certificate of Harry's baptism, which he had carefully engrossed on five closely-written pages."

And what, I inquired, became of the convert?

"Oh! he returned with us; and that old Port which you tasted at the Cape is one of the many evidences which I have received of his grateful recollection, since he has returned to London to the inheritance of his fathers."

Chapter XIV

FOR three days after our parting with H., we kept on our course up the Great Cape river. The current increased as we advanced, and large rocks of quartz and granite began to appear in the channel. The valley of the river also contracted to such a degree as to deserve no better name than that of a gorge. Sometimes we found ourselves, for miles together, shut in between high mountains, whose rugged and verdureless tops rose to mid-heaven, interposing impassable barriers to the vapor-charged clouds which the north-east trade-winds pile up against their eastern declivities, where they are precipitated in almost unceasing rains. Night and storm overtook us in one of these gigantic mountain clefts. The thunder rolled along the granite peaks, and the lightning burned adown their riven sides, and were flashed back by the dark waters of the angry river. The dweller in northern latitudes can poorly comprehend any description which may be given of a tropical storm. To say that the thunder is incessant, does not adequately convey to the mind the terror of these prolonged peals which seem to originate in the horizon, roll upward to the zenith, louder and louder, until, silent for a moment, they burst upon the earth in blinding flame, and a concentrated crash, which makes the very mountains reel to their foundations. Not from one direction alone, but from every quarter of the compass, the elements seem to gather to the fierce encounter, and the thunder booms, and the lightning blazes from a hundred rifts in the inky sky. So intense and searing is the electric flame, that for hours after heavy storms I have had spasmodic attacks of blindness, accompanied with intense pain of the eyeballs. I found that my Indian companions were equally affected, and that to avoid evil consequences they always bound their handkerchiefs, dipped in water, over their eyes, while the storm continued. The Indians, I may here mention, have many prejudices on the subject of electricity, as well as in regard to the effect of the rays of the moon. They will not sleep with their faces exposed to its light, nor catch fish on the nights when it is above the horizon. My companions, at such times, always selected the densest shade for our encampment. They affirmed that the effect of exposure would be the distortion of the features, and the immediate mortification of such wounds and bruises as might be reached by the moonlight. I afterward found that the mahogany-cutters on the north coast never felled their trees at certain periods of the moon, for the reason, as they asserted, that the timber was then not only more liable to check or split, but also more exposed to rot. They have the same notion with the Indians as to the effect of the moonlight on men and animals, and support it by the fact that animals, left to themselves, always seek shelter from the moon, when selecting their nightly resting-places.

We had now ascended the river, five full days from the Cape, having, according to my computation, advanced one hundred and twenty miles. The Poyer was perfectly acquainted with the stream, which he had several times descended with the people of his village, in their semi-annual visits to the coast. In these visits, he told me, they took down liquid amber, a few deer-skins, a little anotto, and sarsaparilla, bringing back iron barbs for their arrows, knives, machetes, and a few articles of ornament.

On the night of the fifth day, we encamped at the mouth of the Tirolas, a considerable stream, which enters the Wanks from the north, and up which we, next morning, took our course. Our advance was now slow and laborious, owing to the rapidity of the current, and the numerous rocks and fallen trees which obstructed the channel. The river wound among hills, which increased in altitude as we penetrated farther inland, until I discovered that we were approaching the great mountain range, which traverses the country from south-west to north-east, constituting the "divide," or water-shed, as I afterward found, between the valley of the Cape River and the streams which flow northward into the Bay of Honduras. Hour by hour we came nearer to this great barrier, which presented to us a steep and apparently inaccessible front. I was rather appalled when my Poyer told me that the village of his people lay beyond this range, over which we would be obliged to climb in order to reach it. However, there was now no alternative left but to go ahead, so I gave myself no further concern, although I could not help wondering how we were to clamber up the dizzy steeps which appeared more and more abrupt as we approached them.

It was on the second evening after leaving the great river, that we reached the head of canoe navigation on the Tirolas, at a point where two bright streams, tumbling over their rocky beds, united in a placid pool of clear water, at the very feet of the mountains. It was a spot of surpassing beauty. The pool was, perhaps, a hundred yards broad, and, in places, twenty or thirty feet deep, yet so clear that every pebble at the bottom, and every fish which sported in its crystal depths, were distinctly visible to the eye. Upon one side rose huge gray rocks of granite, draped over with vines, and shadowed by large and wide-spreading trees, whose branches, crowded with the wax-like leaves and

EMBARCADERO ON THE TIROLAS.

flowers of innumerable air-plants, cast dark, broad shadows on the water. Upon the other side was a smooth, sandy beach, completely sheltered from the sun by large trees, beneath which were drawn up a number of canoes, carefully protected from the weather by rude sheds of cahoon leaves. These canoes belonged to the Poyer Indians, and are used by them in their voyages to the Cape. A little lower down the stream were clusters of palm-trees, and large patches of bananas and plantains, which seemed to have been carefully nurtured by the Indians in their visits to this picturesque "embarcadero."

The slant rays of the evening sun fell upon one half of the pool, where the little ripples chased each other sparkling to the shore, while upon the other part, the rocks and forest cast their cool, dark shadows. And as our canoe shot in upon its transparent bosom, I could not help joining in my Poyer boy's shout of joy. Even "El Moro" fluttered his bright wings, and screamed in sympathetic glee. A few vigorous strokes of the paddles, and our canoe drove up half its length on the sandy shore, the sharp pebbles grating pleasantly beneath its keel. For the present, at least, I had done with lagoons and rivers, and a new excitement awaited me among the giddy steeps and untracked solitudes of the mountains. Farewell now to the cramped canoe, and the eternal succession of low and tangled banks ; and ho, for the free limb and the expanding chest of the son of the forest !

With glad alacrity, my companions and myself set to work to form our encampment, on the clean dry sand. Then came Antonio, laden with the golden clusters of the plantain, while the spear of the Poyer darted down in the clear waters of the pool with unfailing skill. The rousing fire, the murmur of the mountain-torrents, and the distant cry of the fierce black tiger, the satisfied sense of having safely accomplished an arduous undertaking, high anticipations of new adventures, and the consciousness of being the first white man who had ever trusted himself in these unknown fastnesses—all these, joined to the contagious joy of my faithful companions, combined to give the keenest edge and zest to that night's enjoyment. In my darkest hours, its recollection comes over my soul like a beam of sunlight through the rifts of a clouded sky—"a joy forever." Blessed memory, which enables us to live over again the delights of the past, and gives an eternal solace to the cheerful mind!

That night I made a formal present of the canoe and its appurtenances to my Poyer boy, and we selected such articles as were indispensable to us, leaving the rest to be sent for by the Indians when we should reach the village. My purpose was to commence our march at dawn on the following day. But in the morning I arose with one of my feet so swollen and painful that I could neither put on my boot nor walk, except with great difficulty. The cause was, outwardly, very trifling. During the previous day the water in the Tirolas had been so shallow that it frequently became necessary to get out of the canoe and lighten it, in order to pass the various rapids. I had therefore taken off my boots, and gone into the water with my naked feet. I remember stepping on a rolling stone, slipping off, and bruising my ankle. The hurt was, however, so slight, that I did not give it a second thought. But, from this trifling cause, my foot and ankle were now swollen to nearly double their natural size, and the prosecution of my journey, for the time being, was rendered impossible. Under the tropics, serious consequences often follow from these slight causes. I have known tetanus to result from a little wound, of the size of a pea, made by extracting the bag of a *nigua* or *chigoe*, which had burrowed in the foot!

The skill of my companions was at once put in requisition. They made a poultice of ripe plantains baked in the ashes, and mixed with cocoa-nut oil, which was applied hot to the affected parts. This done, our canoe was hauled up, and an extempore roof built over it, to protect me from the weather, in case it should happen to change for the worse. I passed a fretful night, the pain being very great, and the swelling extending higher and higher, until it had reached the knee. The applications had no perceptible effect. Under these circumstances, I determined to send my Poyer to his village for assistance. He represented it as distant five days, but that it could be reached, by forced marches, in four. He objected to leave me, but on the second day, my foot being no better, he obeyed my positive orders, and started, taking with him only a little dried meat, his spear, and his bow.

Antonio now redoubled his attentions, and I certainly stood in need of them. The pain kept me from slumber, and I became irritable and feverish.

But no mother could have been more constant, more patient, or more wakeful to every want than that faithful Indian boy. He exhausted his simple remedies, and still the limb became worse, and the unwilling conviction seemed to be forced on his mind, that the case was beyond his reach. When, in the intervals of the pain, he thought me slumbering, I often saw him consult his talisman with undisguised anxiety. He however, always seemed to feel reassured by it, and to become more cheerful.

On the third day a suppuration appeared at the ankle, and the pain and swelling diminished; and on the succeeding morning I probed the wound, and, to my surprise, removed a small splinter of stone, which had been the cause of all my affliction. From that moment my improvement was rapid, and I was soon able to move about without difficulty.

I amused myself much with fishing in the pool, in which there were large numbers of an active kind of fish, varying from ten to sixteen inches in length, of reddish color, and voracious appetites. Toward evening, when the flies settled down near the surface, they rose like the trout, and kept the pool boiling with their swift leaping after their prey. I improved my limited experience in fly-fishing at home, to devise impromptu insects, and astonished Antonio with that, to him, novel device in the piscatory art. These fish, with an occasional wild turkey, the latter generally tough and insipid, constituted about our only food. Ducks, curlews, and snipe, so common in the vicinity of the lagoons, were here unknown, and we listened in vain for the cry of the *chachalaca.* There were, however, numerous birds of song, and of bright plumage, but not fit for food. I saw some owls; and now and then a large hawk would settle down sullenly on the trees which overhung the pool. Gray-squirrels also occasionally rustled the branches above our heads, but the foliage was so dense that I was only successful in obtaining a single specimen. Once a squadron of monkeys came trooping through the tree-tops to rob the plantain-grove, but a charge of buckshot, which brought two of them to the ground, was effectual in deterring them from a second visit. They were of a small variety, body black, face white, and "whiskered like a pard." Antonio cooked one of them in the sand, but he looked so much like a singed baby which I once saw taken out of the ruins of a fire in Ann-street, that I could not bring myself to taste him. So my Indian had an undisputed monopoly of the monkey.

But the most exciting incident, connected with our stay on the banks of the Tirolas, was one which I can never recall without going into a fit of laughter—although, at the time, I did not regard it as remarkably amusing. Among the wild animals most common in Central America, is the *peccary*, sometimes called "Mexican hog," but best known by the Spanish name of *Savalino.* There is another animal, something similar to the *peccary*, supposed to be the common hog run wild, called *Javalino* by the Spaniards, and *Waree* by the Mosquitos. If not indigenous, the latter certainly have multiplied to an enormous extent, since they swarm all over the more thickly-wooded portions of the country. They closely resemble the wild-boar of Europe, and, although less in size, seem to be equally ferocious. They go in droves, and are not at all particular as to their food, eating ravenously snakes and reptiles of all kinds. They have also a rational relish for fruits, and especially for plantains and bananas, and would prove a real scourge to the plantations, were they always able to break down the stalks supporting the fruit. Unable to do this, they nevertheless pay regular visits to the plantations, in the hope of finding a tree blown down, and of feasting on the fallen clusters.

With these intimations as to their character and habits, the reader will be better qualified to appreciate the incident alluded to. It was a pleasant afternoon, and I had strolled off with my gun, in the direction of the plantain-patch, stopping occasionally to listen to the clear, flute-like notes of some unseen bird, or to watch a brilliant lizard, as it flashed across the gray stones. Thus sauntering carelessly along, my attention was suddenly arrested by a peculiar noise, as if of some animal, or rather of many animals engaged in eating. I stopped, and peered in every direction to discover the cause, when finally my eyes rested upon what I at once took to be a pig of most tempting proportions. He was moving slowly, with his nose to the ground, as if in search of food. Without withdrawing my gaze, I carefully raised my gun, and fired. It was loaded with buck-shot, and although the animal fell, he rose again immediately, and began to make off. Of course I hurried after him, with the view of finishing my work with my knife—but I had not taken ten steps, when it appeared to me as if every stick, stone, and bush had been converted into a pig! Hogs rose on all sides, with bristling backs, and tusks of appalling length. I comprehended my danger in an instant, and had barely time to leap into the forks of a low, scraggy tree, before they were at its foot. I shall never forget the malicious look of their little bead-like eyes, as they raved around my roosting-place, and snapped ineffectually at my heels. Although I felt pretty secure, I discreetly clambered higher, and, fixing myself firmly in my seat, revenged myself by firing a charge of bird-shot in the face of the savagest of my assailants. This insult only excited the brutes the more, and they ground their teeth, and frothed around the tree in a perfect paroxysm of porcine rage.

THE WAREE.

I next loaded both barrels of my gun with ball, and deliberately shot two others through their heads, killing them on the spot, vainly imagining that thereby I should disperse the herd. But never was man more mistaken. The survivors nosed around their dead companions for a moment, and then renewed their vicious contemplations of my position. Some squatted themselves upon their hams, as much as to say that they intended to wait for me, and were nowise in a hurry! So I loaded up again, and slaughtered two more of the largest and most spiteful. But, even then, there were no signs of retreat; on the contrary, it seemed to me as if reënforcements sprang out of the ground, and that my besiegers grew every moment more numerous!

How long this might have lasted, I am unprepared to say, had not Antonio, alarmed at my rapid firing, hastened to my rescue. No sooner did my assailants catch sight of his swarthy figure than they made after him with a vehement rush. He avoided them by leaping upon a rock, and then commenced a most extraordinary and murderous contest. Never did a battalion of veteran soldiers charge upon an enemy, with more steadiness than those wild pigs upon the Indian. He was armed with only a lance, but every blow brought down a porker. Half alarmed lest they should finally overmatch him, I cheered his exploits, and kept up a brisk fire by way of a diversion in his favor. I am ashamed to say how many of those pigs we killed; it is, perhaps, enough to add, that it was long after dark before the beasts made up their minds to leave us uneaten. And it was with a decided sensation of relief that we heard them moving off, until their low grunt was lost in the distance.

At one time, the odds were certainly against us,

and it seemed not improbable that the artist and his adventures might both come to a pitiful and far from a poetical end. But fortune favored, and my faithful gun now hangs over my table in boar-tusk brackets, triumphal trophies from that bloody field! Instead of being eaten, we ate, wherein consists a difference; but I was ever after wary of the *waree!*

True to his promise, on the evening of the tenth day, my Poyer boy bounded into our encampment, with a loud shout of joy. His friends were behind, and he said would reach us in the following afternoon. There were five of them, sober, silent men, who made their encampment apart from us, and whom I vainly endeavored to engage in conversation. They displayed great aptness in packing our various articles in net-work sacks, which they carried on their backs, supported by bands passing around their foreheads. They wore no clothes except the *tournou,* unless sandals of tapir-hide, and a narrow-brimmed hat, braided of palm-bark, fall within that denomination. Besides his sack, each man carried a peculiar kind of *machete,* short and curved like a pruning-hook; only one or two had bows.

It was with real regret that I left our encampment beside the bright pool, and abandoned my old and now familiar canoe, in the sides of which, like a true Yankee, I had carved my name, and the dates of my adventures. I turned to look back more than once, as we filed away, beneath the trees, in the trail leading to the mountains. The Indians led the way, while Antonio and myself brought up the rear. "El Moro," perched upon the tallest pack, shrieked and fluttered his wings, occasionally scrambling down to take a mischievous bite at the ear of his Indian carrier. Whenever he was successful in accomplishing this feat, he became superlatively happy and gleeful. In default of other amusement, he sometimes suspended himself from the netting by a single claw, like a dead bird, with drooping wings and dangling head, and then suddenly scrambled back again to his perch, with triumphant screams. He was a rare rollicking bird, that same Moro!

For the first day our course followed a line nearly parallel with the base of the mountains, through a thick and tangled forest. We crossed innumerable small and rapid streams of the clearest water, sparkling over beds of variously-colored quartz pebbles—for we were now skirting one of the great ranges of primitive rocks, which form the nucleus of the continent. My long confinement in the canoe had contributed to disqualify me for active exertions, and long before night I became much fagged, and would fain have gone into camp. But the Indians traveled so tranquilly under their loads, that I was loth to discover to them my lack of endurance, and so kept on without complaint. In the afternoon our path began to ascend, and we gradually emerged from the thick and tangled woods into a comparatively open forest, which, in turn, gave place to groves of scattered pines and oaks, among which we encamped for the night.

From our elevated position I could overlook the wilderness which we had traversed during the day. It was at that season of the year when the *erythrina* puts on its scarlet robe of blossoms, and the ceiba clothes itself in flames, in splendid relief to the prevailing green. It seemed as if Nature held high holiday among these primeval solitudes, and arrayed herself only to wanton in the sense of her own beauty. But while vegetation was thus lavishly luxuriant in the valley, behind us the mountains rose, stern, steep, and bare. Vainly the dark pines, clinging to their sides, sought to vail their flinty frown. Wherever a little shelf of the rocks supported a scanty bed of soil, there the mountain grasses, and the sensitive-plant with its amaranthine flower, took root, like kindly thoughts in the heart of the hard and worldly man. From the gnarled oaks, and even from the unfading pines, hung long festoons of gray moss, which swayed sadly in the wind. And when the night came on, and I lay down beside the fire, beneath their shade, they seemed to murmur in a low and mournful voice to the passing breeze, which, laden with the perfume of the valley, rose with downy wings to bear its tributary incense to the skies.

Morning broke, but dark and gloomily, and although we resumed our march, directing our course diagonally up the face of the mountain, we were obliged to stop before noon, and seek shelter under a mass of projecting rocks, from a cold, drizzly rain, which now began to fall steadily, with every promise of merging in a protracted temporal. The clouds ran low, and drifted around and below us, in heavy, cheerless volumes, shutting from view every object except the pines and stunted oaks, in their gray, monastic robes, now saturated and heavy from the damp. Stowing our few valuables securely under the rocks, we lighted a fire, now acceptable not less for its heat than its companionship. Its cheerful flame, and the sparkle of its embers, revived my drooping spirits, and helped to reconcile me to the imprisonment which the temporal would be sure to entail. I can readily understand how fire commended itself to the primitive man as an emblem of purity and power, and became the symbol of spirit and those invisible essences which pervade the universe. God robed himself in flame on Sinai; in tongues of flame the Spirit descended upon the disciples at Jerusalem; an eternal fire burned upon the altars of the virginal Vesta, and in the Persian Pyrothea; to fire was committed the sacrifice of propitiation, and by its ordeal was innocence and purity made manifest. Among the American Indians it was held in especial reverence. The Delawares and the Iroquois had festivals in its honor, and regarded it as the first parent of the Indian nations. The Cherokees paid their devotions to the "great, beneficent, supreme, holy Spirit of Fire," whose home was in the heavens, but who dwelt also on earth, in the hearts of "the unpolluted people." And even the rude Indians who huddled with me beneath the protecting rocks in the heart of the wilderness, never commenced their simple meals without first throwing a small portion of their food in the fire, as an offering to the protecting Spirit of Life, of which it is the genial symbol.

The temporal lasted for three days, during which time it rained almost incessantly, and it was withal so cold, that a large and constant fire was necessary to our comfort. At the end of that time the clouds began to lift, and the sun broke through the rifts, and speedily dispersed the watery legions. But the rocks were slippery with the wet, and the earth, wherever it was found among the rocks, was sodden and unstable, rendering our advance alike disagreeable and dangerous. We remained, therefore, until the morning of the fourth day, when we resumed our march.

FOR a day and a half we continued to ascend, now skirting dizzy precipices, and next stealing along cautiously beneath beetling rocks, which hung heavily on the brow of the mountain. The features of the great valley which we had left were no longer distinguishable. What we had regarded as mountains there, now shrunk into simple undulations, like folds in some silken robe, thrown loosely on the ground. There was no longer a foothold for the pines, and their places were supplied by low bushes, thrusting their roots deep in the clefts, and clinging like vines to the faces of the rocks.

Finally, to my great joy, we reached the crest of the mountain. Upon the north, however, it fell away in a series of broad steps or terraces, lower and lower, until, in the dim distance, it subsided in the vast alluvial plains bordering on the Bay of Honduras, the waters of which could be distinguished, like a silver rim, on the edge of the horizon.

The air, on these high plateaus, was chill, and only the hardy mountain-grasses and the various forms of cactus found root in their thin and sterile soil. The latter were numerous and singular. Some appeared above the earth, simple, fluted globes, radiating with spines, and having in their centre a little tuft of crimson flowers. Others were mere articulated prisms, tangled in clumps, and also bristling with prickles. But the variety, known in Mexico as the *nopal*, was most abundant, and grew of tree-like proportions.

Few as were these forms of vegetable life, animals and birds were fewer still. An occasional deer contemplated us at a distance, and a little animal, similar to the prairie-dog of the West, tumbled hurriedly into his hole as we approached his solitary covert. In places, the disintegrated quartz rock appeared above the surface for wide distances, reflecting back the rays of the sun, which seemed to pour down with unwonted and blinding brilliancy, from a cloudless sky. I could scarcely comprehend the sudden change from the region of the lagoons, where the overladen earth sweltered beneath forests teeming with life, and the air was oppressed with the cloying odors of myriads of flowers, and this stern region, ribbed with rock, where Nature herself seemed paralyzed, and silence held an eternal reign.

It was a singular spectacle, that little troop of ours, as it hurried rapidly across these mountain wastes, or huddled closely together, when night came on, around a scanty fire, made of wood which the Poyer boy, with wise prevision, had deposited there, on his return to the Tirolas. As we descended from terrace to terrace, we came again into the region of pines and oaks, which, in their turn, gave place to forests of other varieties of trees, interrupted by strips of open or savannah lands. We early struck a little stream, which, I observed, we followed constantly. It proved to be the branch of the great river Patuca, upon which the Poyer village is situated, and bore the musical name of Guallambre. At night, when we encamped, the Poyer boy took a calabash, and, motioning to me to follow, led the way down the stream to a little sand-bar. Scooping up some of the sand in his bowl, and then filling it with water, he whirled it rapidly, so that a feathery stream of mingled sand and water flew constantly over its edge. He continued this operation until the sand was nearly exhausted, and then filled the bowl again. After repeating this process several times, he grew more careful, balancing the bowl skillfully, and stopping occasionally to pick out the pebbles, which, owing to their weight, had not been carried over by the water.

I understood at once that this was the primitive

mode of washing gold, and was, therefore, not greatly surprised when, after the process was complete, the Poyer showed me a little deposit of gold, in grains, at the bottom of the calabash, equal to about a fourth of an ounce in weight. He then told me that all the streams, flowing down the mountains toward the north, carried gold in their sands, and that the latter were frequently washed by his people, to obtain the means of purchasing such articles of civilized manufacture as they might need from the Spaniards of Olancho, and the traders who visited the coast.*

On the eighth day from our encampment on the Tirolas, after a laborious march among heavily-wooded hills, following, for most of the distance, the bed of the Guallambre, now swollen to a considerable stream, we reached the Poyer village. I say village, for such it was, in fact, although composed of but a single house! This was a substantial structure, forty paces in length, and ten broad, supported on stout posts, and heavily thatched with palm-leaves. The front and ends were open, but

* The whole district of country lying on the north flank of the mountains which bound the valley of the Rio Wanks, in the same direction, enjoys a wide celebrity for its rich deposits of gold. There is hardly a stream of which the sands do not yield a liberal proportion of that precious metal. Yet, strange to say, the washing is confined almost exclusively to the Indians, who seek to obtain no more than is just sufficient to supply their limited wants. Among the reduced, or, as they are called, christianized Indians, in the valley of Olancho, the women only wash the gold for a few hours on Sunday morning. With the supply thus obtained, they proceed to the towns, attend mass, and make their petty purchases, devoting the rest of the week to the fullest enjoyment of the *dolce far niente.*

along the back extended a series of little apartments, separated from each other by partitions of the outer shells of the cabbage-palm, which, when split and pressed flat, make good substitutes for boards. These were the dormitories, or private apartments of the mated or married occupants, and of the girls. The places for the boys were on elevated platforms, beneath the roof. A row of stones, set firmly in the ground, defined the outline of the building. Within them the earth was elevated a foot or more, to preserve it dry and unaffected by the rains. The position was admirably chosen, on a kind of step or shelf of a considerable hill, which rose behind, clothed with dense verdure, while in front it subsided rapidly to the stream, here tumbling noisily among the rocks, and yonder circling, bubble-sprinkled, in dark pools, beneath the trees. The ground around was beaten smooth and hard, and numbers of tamed curassows stalked to and fro, gravely elevating and depressing their crests ; while within the building, and on its roof, numerous parrots and macaws waddled after each other, or exercised their voices in loud and discordant cries. There were also a few pigs and ducks, all appearing to be as much at home beneath the roof, as were the naked Indian babies, with whom they mingled on terms of perfect equality.

My boy had gone ahead, and had returned to meet us in company with two old men, who were the lawgivers of the establishment, and who reverentially touched my knee with their foreheads, by

POYER VILLAGE ON THE GUALLAMBRE.

way of salutation. They said but a single word, which I suppose was one of welcome, and then led the way silently to the house. At one end a space had been recently fenced off, containing two new crickeries, within which my various articles were deposited, and which were at once indicated to me as my special apartment.

All the proceedings had been conducted so rapidly, that I was fairly installed in my novel quarters before I was aware of it. Our arrival had evidently been anticipated, for almost immediately the women brought us hot rolls of a species of bread made of ground cassava, baked in the ashes, with the addition of some stewed flesh of the *waree*, so tender and savory that it would have commended itself to a far more fastidious appetite than mine. I made a prodigious meal, to the palpable satisfaction of my faithful Poyer, who kept every calabash heaped up with food.

As I have said, the Indians of Central America differ widely from their fiercer brethren of our country, not less in their modes of life than in all their social and civil relations. This Poyer community afforded an example of a purely patriarchal organization, in which the authority of paternity and of age was recognized in the fullest degree. Every evening the old men, each taking a lighted brand, gathered within a small circle of stones, at one corner of the house, and there deliberated upon the affairs of the community, and settled its proceedings for the following day. In these conferences neither the women nor young men were permitted to take part. All the labor of the community was performed in common, and all shared equally in the results. In one or two of the recesses which I have described, were some ancient and helpless crones, who were treated with all the care and tenderness of children. The whole establishment, according to the best of my count, consisted of about one hundred and forty persons, young and old, of whom thirty-five were full-grown men.

In figure the Poyers or Payas are identical with the Towkas and Woolwas, except more muscular—the consequence, probably, of their cooler climate and severer labor. The women were less shy, perhaps from their more social mode of living. In common with those of the coast, they go naked to the waist, whence depends a skirt of striped cotton cloth, reaching to the knees. Their hair is invariably parted in front, and held in place by a cotton band, bound tightly around the forehead. They were always occupied. Some, squatting on the ground, spun the native cotton, of which all the Indians raise small quantities, while others wove it into cloth. Both processes were rude but ingenious. The spindle consists of a small ball of heavy wood, through which passes a thin shaft, the whole resembling an overgrown top, the lower end resting in a calabash, to prevent it from toppling over. Some of the cotton is attached to this spindle, which is twirled between the thumb and forefinger. While it is in motion the thread is carefully drawn out from a pile of cotton in the lap of the spinner. When it stops the thread is wound on the spindle, and the same process repeated. The process of weaving was certainly a simple one, but after several unsatisfactory attempts to describe it, I am obliged to confess my inability to do so, in an intelligible manner.

But a principal occupation of the women was the grinding of maize for tortillas, and of preparing the cassava. For these purposes there were a number of flat stones elevated on blocks, which were called by the Mexican name of *metlatl.* These were somewhat concave on the upper surface, in which fitted a stone roller, worked by hand. With this the maize was speedily ground to a fine consistence; the paste was then made into small cakes, which were baked rapidly on broad earthen platters, supported over brisk fires. The cakes require to be eaten when crisp and hot, in order to be relished; for when cold they become heavy and tasteless. Upon these stones they also crushed the stalks of the indigenous sugar-cane to extract the juice, which, mixed with powdered wild-cacao, is allowed to ferment, constituting an agreeable and exhilirating beverage, called *ulung.*

Every morning all the girls went down to the stream to bathe, which they did without any overstrained affectation of modesty; but the mothers and old women always sought a spot secluded from the general gaze. It was only when thus engaged that the girls were at all playful. They dashed the water in each others' faces, and sought to drag each other under the surface, in the deep pools, where they swam about as mermaids are supposed to do, and as if the water was their native element. At all other times they were as distant and demure as the daintiest damsels in all New England.

The Poyers are certainly a provident people. Although there were no signs of plantations in the vicinity of their establishments, yet, at various points in the neighborhood, where there occurred patches of rich interval land, were small fields of sugar-cane, plantains, squashes, maize, yucas, and cassava, all protected by fences, and attended with the utmost care. From every beam of the house depended bunches of plantains and bananas, huge yams, and dried flesh of various kinds, but chiefly that of the *waree*, while closely packed, on platforms under the roof, were a few bales of sarsaparilla, which I found they were accustomed to carry down to the coast for purposes of barter.

The Poyers or Payas, as I have intimated, are eminently agriculturists, and although they sometimes follow the chase, it is not as a principal means of support. Nor is it followed from any fantastic notion of excitement or adventure, but in a direct and downright manner, which is the very reverse of what is called "sport." I had an example of this in their mode of fishing, which quite astonished all my previous notions on that subject, and which evinced to me furthermore, that fishes, although cold-blooded, are not exempt from having their heads turned, provided they are approached in a proper manner.

My Poyer boy, who was unwearying in his devices to entertain and interest me, one day conceived a brilliant idea, which he hastened to communicate to the old men, who held a sober *monexico*, or council upon it, and resolved that there should be made a grand demonstration upon the fish, for the double purpose of amusing the stranger, and of replenishing the supplies. The resolution, taken at night, was carried into execution in the morning. While a portion of the men proceeded down the stream to construct a temporary wier of boughs, others collected a large quantity of a species of vine called *bequipe*, which is common in the woods, has a rank growth, is full of juice, and emits a pungent odor. These vines were cut in sections, crushed between stones, and placed in large earthen pots, left to steep, over a slow fire.

I watched all the operations with curious interest. About the middle of the afternoon they were completed; the pots containing the decoctions were duly shouldered, and we all started up the stream. At the distance of perhaps a quarter of a mile, we met a number of men wading down the channel, and beating the water with long poles, by way of concentrating the fish in the direction of the wiers. Here the pots were simultaneously emptied in the stream, which the contents tinged of a brownish hue. Up to this moment, the various preparations had greatly puzzled me, but now I discovered that the purpose of the decoction was to poison, or rather to intoxicate the fish, which it did effectively; for, as we proceeded down the stream, numbers rose struggling to the surface, vainly endeavoring to stem the current, which swept them toward the wiers.

At every step they became more numerous, until the whole stream was thronged with them. Some were quite stupefied, and drifted along helplessly, while others made spasmodic efforts to resist the potent influence of the *bequipe*. But, sooner or later, they too drifted down, with a faint wagging of their tails, which seemed to express that they fairly "gave it up."

The wier had been built at the foot of a considerable pool, which was literally covered with the stupefied fishes. There were many varieties of them, and the Indians stationed at that point were already engaged in picking out the largest and best, tossing the others over the wier, to recover their senses at their leisure, in the clear water below. As soon as the fish were thrown ashore, they were taken charge of by the women, who cleaned them on the spot, and with wonderful dexterity. They were afterward taken to the house, rubbed with salt, and smoke-dried over fires, after the manner which I have already described, as practiced by the Sambos at Pearl Cay Lagoon.

It would naturally be supposed that a decoction so powerful as to affect the water of a large stream, would also damage the fish, and unfit them for food. But such is not the case. The effect seems to be precisely that of temporary intoxication, and the fish, if left in the water, would soon recover from its influence.

Time passed pleasantly among the hospitable Poyers, and I was treated with such ceremonious deference and respect, that I began to think that a far worse fortune might befall me, than that of becoming a member of this peaceful and prosperous community, on the banks of the Guallambre. In fact, I finally detected myself speculating upon the possibility of promoting one of the dark Naiads, whom I every morning watched sporting in the river, to the occupancy of the vacant crickery in my apartment. And then the fact that there were two crickeries—was not that intended as a delicate suggestion on the part of the Poyers, whose ideas of hospitality might be less circumscribed than my own? The thought that they might imagine me dull of apprehension, and slow to improve upon a hint, grew upon me with every new and nearer contemplation of the Naiads, and I began seriously to think of submitting a formal proposition on the subject, to the *monexico.* But men's fates often hinge upon trifling circumstances, and had I not detected a deepening shadow of anxiety on the face of Antonio, I might have become a patriarch in Poyerdom! Who knows?

Early after our arrival at the Poyer village, I was surprised to observe Antonio in close consultation with the old men, in the nightly *monexico.* They seemed to be deeply interested in his communications, and I imagined that they became daily more thoughtful. But now, whatever purpose Antonio might have had in view, it appeared to have been accomplished.

So, one evening, I called him aside, and announced that I was ready to depart. He grasped my hand, pressed it to his heart, and said, in a tone of emotion—"The voice of the tiger is loud in the mountain, and the sons of the Holy Men are waiting by the lake of the Itzaes!"

I comprehended the latent meaning of these poetical words, for I had already seen enough of Antonio to discover that his absence from Yucatan was in some way connected with a concerted movement of the aborigines, and that now some crisis was approaching which drew him irresistibly toward his native land. Resolved not to be instrumental in delaying him for an hour unnecessarily, and half repenting that I had detained him so long—for his attachment and gratitude were too real to permit him to abandon me in the wilderness—I at once communicated my intention of leaving to the old men. They took it under serious deliberation, which resulted in their dispatching some men before daybreak, on the following morning, to prepare a canoe for our descent of the Patuca. The canoes, I found, were not kept on the Guallambre, for two reasons: first, that its course is circuitous, and second, and principally, because it runs through the settlements of the Spaniards of Olancho, with whom the Indians avoid all relations which are not absolutely necessary. Their boats were therefore kept half a day's journey distant, beyond a chain of high hills, on a large tributary of the Patuca, called Amacwass.

I verily believe I would have been a welcome guest among my Poyer friends, so long as I might have chosen to remain ; yet they did not urge me to stay, but hastened to help me off, as if my intimations were to be regarded as commands.

During the day a large quantity of provisions were dispatched to the boat, and at night the *monexico* selected two men, and my old companion the Poyer boy, to accompany us to the coast. We took our departure early in the morning, while it was yet dark, without creating the slightest disturbance in the establishment. Only the old men, who had come out to meet us two weeks before, now went ahead with large brands of fire, to light the way ; but, when the day broke, they again touched their foreheads to my knee, and returned, leaving us to prosecute our journey alone.

We reached the Amacwass in the afternoon, and found a boat, twice as large as the canoe in which we had navigated the lagoons, all prepared for instant departure. A space near the middle was covered with a thatch of palm branches, to protect me from the sun, and altogether it promised a degree of comfort and convenience to which I had been a stranger, in my previous voyagings.

We embarked at once, and dropped rapidly down with the current, the Indians only using their paddles to direct the boat, and keep it clear of the rocks which obstructed the channel. The water was wonderfully clear, every where revealing the bottom with the greatest distinctness. The banks were covered with a heavy forest, in which the eye was often arrested by the stately forms of the mahogany-tree, with its massive foliage, rising high above the general level; or by the still taller and more graceful plumes of the palmetto-royal. Vegetation seemed to have a more vigorous, but less redundant life, than on the Mosquito Shore; that is to say, it assumed more compact and more decided forms, occasioned, probably, by the comparative absence of jungle, not less than by peculiarities of soil.

There was something exhilarating in our rapid course; and the voice of the waters, here murmuring over a pebbly bottom, and yonder breaking hoarsely over the obstructing rocks, reminded me of my distant New England home, and recalled the happy hours which I had spent in the sole companionship of its merry mountain streams. It was, after all, by the standard of my youthful experiences, that I measured my present enjoyments; and it was rare indeed, even in my most cheerful moods, that the comparison was favorable to the latter. The senses blunted by years, and the memory crowded with events, fails to appreciate so keenly or record so deeply, the experiences of middle life, and pure happiness, after all, dwells chiefly in the remembrance of the distant past.

As soon as the shadows of evening began to settle

over the narrow valley of the Amacwass, we halted, and made our camp, maintaining throughout the night a great fire, not less for its cheerful influences than for protection against the fierce black tigers, or pumas, which abound on this flank of the mountains. We heard their screams, now near, now distant, to which the monkeys responded with alarmed and anxious cries, so like those of human beings in distress, as more than once to startle me from my slumbers. These caricatures on humanity seemed to be more numerous here than further down the coast, and we often saw large troops of them in the overhanging trees, where they gravely contemplated us as we drifted by. Occasionally one, more adventurous than the rest, would slide down a dependent limb or vine, scold at us vehemently for a moment, and then scramble back again hurriedly, as if alarmed at his own audacity.

On the second day the current of the Amacwass became more gentle, and just before night we shot out of its waters into the large and comparatively majestic Patuca. Our course down this stream was not so rapid. In places the current was so slight that it became necessary to use our paddles; while elsewhere the greatest caution was requisite to guide our boat safely over the numerous *chiflones* or rapids by which it was interrupted. But these, though difficult, and in some instances dangerous, sunk into insignificance when compared with what is called *El Portal del Infierno*, or the "Gateway of Hell." My Poyer boy had several times alluded to it, as infinitely more to be dreaded than any of the passes which we had yet encountered, and as one which would be likely to excite my alarm.

We reached it on the day after we had entered the Patuca. As we advanced, the hills began to approach each other, and high rocks shut in the river upon both sides. Huge detached masses also rose in the middle of the stream, around which the water whirled and eddied in deep, dark gulfs, sucking down the frayed and shattered trunks of trees, from which the branches had long before been torn by rude contact with the rocks, only to reject them again from their depths, far below. The velocity of our boat increased, and I became apprehensive in view of the rushing current and rocky shores; nor was the feeling diminished, when the men commenced to lash the various articles contained in the boat by thongs to its sides, since that precaution implied a possibility of our being overset. Antonio urged me to strip, which I did, in preparation for the worst contingency. Meanwhile the stream narrowed more and more, and the rocks towered higher and higher above our heads. The water no longer dashed and chafed against the shores, but, dark and glassy, shot through the narrow gorge with a low hissing sound, more fearful than its previous turbulence. I involuntarily held my breath, grasping firmly the sides of the boat, and watching anxiously the dark forms of the Indians, as, silently, and with impassible features, they guided the frail slab upon which our lives depended. On, on we swept, between cliffs so lofty and beetling as to shut out the sun, and involve us in twilight obscurity. I looked up, and, at a dizzy height, could only trace a narrow strip of sky, like the cleft in the roof of some deep cavern. A shudder ran through every limb, and I could well understand why this terrible pass had been named the "Mouth of Hell!" He must have been a bold man who ventured first within its horrid jaws!

"GATEWAY OF HELL."

I drew a long breath of relief when the chasm began to widen, and the current to diminish in violence. But it was probably then that we were in the greatest danger, for the bed of the stream was full of angular rocks which had been swept out from the *cañon*, to be heaped up here in wild disorder. A misdirected stroke of a single paddle would have thrown our frail boat upon them, and dashed it into a thousand pieces.

Before night, however, we had entirely passed

the rapids, and were drifting quietly over the smooth, deep reaches of the river—the bubbles on its surface, and the flecks of white foam clinging to its banks, alone indicating the commotion which raged above.

There are many legends connected with the "Portal del Infierno." Within it the Indians imagine there dwells a powerful spirit, who is sometimes seen darting through its gloomiest recess, in the form of a large bird. That night, each of the Poyers poured a portion of his allowance of *chicha* in the stream, as a thank-offering to the spirit of the river. This, and the offerings made to fire, were the only religious rites which I witnessed while in their country; but it is not thence to be inferred that they are without religious forms, for it is precisely these that they are most careful to conceal from the observation of the stranger.

As we proceeded down the river, and entered the alluvions of the coast, both the stream and its banks underwent an entire change. The latter became comparatively low, and frequently, for long distances, were wholly covered with feathery palms, unrelieved by any other varieties of trees. Snags and stranded logs obstructed the channel, and sand-bars appeared here and there, upon which the hideous alligators stretched themselves in the sun, in conscious security. Occasionally, we observed swells or ridges of savannah land, like those on the Mosquito Shore, supporting pines and acacias. But the general character of the country was that of a broad alluvion, in places so low as to be overflowed during floods—rich in soil, and adapted to the cultivation of all the tropical staples.

On the seventh day from the Poyer village, we reached a point where the river divides, forming a delta, the principal channel leading off to the sea direct, and the other conducting to a large lagoon, called *Brus* by the Spaniards, where the Caribs of the coast have their establishments. We took the latter, and the Indians plied their paddles with increased energy, as if anxious to bring our tedious voyage to a close.

ALTHOUGH we had previously moored our boat with the approach of darkness, yet this night the Indians kept on their course. The river was now wide and still, and the banks low and tropical. With the fading light of day, the sea-breeze set in, fresh and pungent, from the ocean. Fire-flies sparkled like stars along the shore, and only the night-hawk, swooping down after its prey, startled the ear of night with its rushing pinions.

The night advanced, and the steady dip of the paddles soothed me into a slumber, from which I was only roused by the noise of drums and the sound of revelry. I leaped up suddenly, with some vague recollections of the orgies at Sandy Bay, which, however, were soon dispelled, and I found that we had already passed Brus Lagoon, and were now close to its northern shore, where the Carib town is situated. There were many lights and fires, and shouts and laughter rang out from the various groups which were gathered around them. I perceived at once that some kind of a festival was going on, and had some hesitation in venturing on shore. But I was reassured by the conduct of the Indians, who paddled the boat up to the beach, with the utmost confidence. Before it touched the sand, however, we were hailed by some one on the shore, in a language which I did not understand. A moment after, the hail was repeated in another dialect, to which my Poyer boy replied, with some kind of explanation. "Advance, friend!" was the prompt response of the challenger, who stepped into the water, and lent a hand to drag up the canoe.

I scrambled forward, and leaped ashore, when I was immediately addressed by the same voice which had hailed us, with, "Very welcome to Brus!" My first impression was, that I had fallen in with Europeans, but I soon saw that my new friend was a pure Indian. He was dressed in white pantaloons and jacket, and wore a sash around his waist, and, altogether, looked like a good fellow. He at once invited me to his house, explaining, as we went along, that the village was in the midst of a festival, held annually, on the occasion of the return of the mahogany-cutters from the various works, both on this coast and in the vicinity of Belize. The next day, he said, they expected a large reënforcement of their numbers, and that then the festivities would be at their height.

Meantime, we had reached the house of our new friend, whose impromptu hospitality I made no hesitation in accepting. It was empty; for all hands were occupied with the festival. Our host stirred up the embers of a fire, which were smouldering beneath a little roof in front of the hut, and hastened away to call his family.

While I awaited his return, I smiled to think what a free and easy way I had contracted since leaving Jamaica, of making myself at home under all circumstances, and with all sorts of people. No letters of introduction, given with hesitation, and received with doubt. And then, the happy excitement of an even chance whether one's welcome may come in the form of a bullet or a breakfast! These things will do to tell my friend Sly, I soliloquized, and fell into a revery, which was only broken by the return of my host, accompanied by one of his wives —a very pretty and well-dressed Carib woman, her hair neatly braided on the top of her head, and stuck full of flowers. Although it was now past midnight, she insisted on preparing something for us to eat, and then returned to participate in the dances and rejoicings which were going on in the centre of the village.

I would have accompanied my host there also, had it not been for an incident which, for that night at least, banished my idle curiosity. While occupied in arranging my personal baggage in our new quarters, I had observed my Poyer companion standing apart, and regarding me with an earnest and thoughtful expression. I was several times on the point of speaking to him, and as often had my attention diverted by other circumstances. Finally, however, I turned to seek him, but he was gone. I inquired of Antonio what had become of him, but he could give me no information ; and, a little concerned himself, he started for the scene of the revelry, under the impression that he might have been attracted thither. He returned with a hasty step, and reported that neither the Poyer or his companions were to be found. We hurried to the shore, where we had left the boat, but that also was gone. The reader may, perhaps, smile when I say that I strained my eyes to penetrate the darkness, if only to catch one glimpse of my Poyer boy ; and that I wept when I turned back to the village. And when, on the following day, as I unrolled my scanty wardrobe, a section of bamboo-cane, heavy with gold-dust, rolled upon the floor, I felt not only that I had lost a friend, but that beneath the swarthy breast of that untutored Indian boy there beat a heart capable of the most delicate generosity. Be sure, my faithful friend, far away in your mountain home, that your present shall never be dishonored ! Washed from the virginal sands, and wrought into the symbol of our holy faith, it rests above a heart as constant as thine own ; and, inscribed with the single word "FIDELITY," it shall descend to my children, as an evidence that Faith and Friendship are heavenly flowers, perennial in every clime !

The Caribs (who pronounce their own name *Caribees*), those Dyacks of the Antilles, had always been associated in my mind with every thing that was savage in character and habits, and I was astonished to find that they had really considerable pretensions to civilization. It should be observed, however, that they are here an intruded people, and that, first and last, they have had a large association with the whites. They now occupy the coast from the neighborhood of the port of Truxillo to Carataska Lagoon, whence they have gradually expelled the Sambos or Mosquitos. Their original seat was San Vincent, one of what are called the Leeward Islands, whence they were deported in a body, by the English, in 1798, and landed upon the then unoccupied island of Roatan, in the Bay of Honduras. Their position there was an unsatisfactory one, and they eagerly accepted the invitation of the Spanish authorities to remove to the mainland.

Positions were assigned them in the vicinity of Truxillo, whence they have spread rapidly to the eastward. All along the coast, generally near the mouths of the various rivers with which it is fringed, they have their establishments or towns. These are never large, but always neat, and well supplied with provisions, especially vegetables, which are cultivated with great care, and of the highest perfection. They grow rice, cassava, sugar-cane, a little cotton, plantains, squashes, oranges, mangoes, and every variety of indigenous fruits, besides an abundance of hogs, ducks, turkeys, and fowls, of all of which they export considerable quantities to Truxillo, and even to Belize, a distance of several hundred miles.

The physical differences which existed among them at San Vincent are still marked. Most are pure Indians, not large, but muscular, with a ruddy skin, and long, straight hair. These were called the Red or Yellow Caribs. Another portion are very dark, with curly hair, and betraying unmistakably a large infusion of negro blood, and are called the Black Caribs. They are taller than the Red Caribs, and well-proportioned. They contrast with the latter, also, in respect of character, being more vehement and mercurial. The pure Caribs are constant, industrious, quiet, and orderly. They all profess the Catholic religion, although observing very few of its rites, except during their visits to the Spanish towns, where all their children are scrupulously taken to be baptized.

I was agreeably astonished when I awoke on the morning after our arrival at Brus, to find a cup of coffee, well served in a china cup, awaiting my attentions. And when I got up, I was still further surprised to observe a table spread with a snow-white cloth, in the principal apartment of the house, where my host welcomed me, with a genuine "good morning." I expressed my surprise at his acquaintance with the English, which seemed to flatter him, and he ran through the same salutation in Spanish, Creole-French, Carib, and Mosquito. Whereupon I told him he was a "perambulating polyglot," which he did n't understand, although he affected to laugh at the remark.

I had now an opportunity to make my observations on the village of Brus and its people. The town is situated on a narrow, sandy tongue of land, lying between the sea and the lagoon. This strip of land supports a magnificent forest of cocoa-palms, relieved only by a few trees of gigantic size and dense foliage, which, I suppose, must be akin to the banyan-tree of India, inasmuch as they send down numerous stems or trunks, which take root in the ground, and support the widely-spreading branches. The establishment of my host, including his house and the huts of his various wives, were all built beneath a single tree, which had thirty-five distinct trunks, besides the central or parent stem. A belt of miscellaneous trees is also left seaward, to break the force of the north wind, which would otherwise be sure to destroy the palms. But the underbrush had all been carefully removed, so that both the sea and the lagoon were visible from all parts of the village. The design of their removal was the excellent one of affording a free circulation of air; a piece of sanitary wisdom which was supported by the additional precaution of building the huts open only to the sea-breeze, and closed against the miasmatic winds which blow occasionally from the land side.

Nothing could be more beautiful than the palm-grove, with its graceful natural columns and ever-green arches, beneath which rose the picturesque huts of the village. These were all well-built, walled, floored, and partitioned, with cabbage-palm boards, and roofed with the branches of the same tree. Episodically, I may repeat what has probably often been observed before, that the palm, in its varieties, is a marvel of economic usefulness to dwellers under the tropics. Not only does it present him with forms of enchanting beauty, but it affords him food, drink, and shelter. One variety yields him excellent substitutes for bread and yeast; another sugar and wine; a third oil and vinegar; a fourth milk and wax; a fifth resin and fruit; a sixth medicines and utensils; a seventh weapons, cordage, hats, and clothing; and an eighth habitations and furniture!

The plantations of the village, except a few clusters of banana-trees and sugar-canes, on the edge of the lagoon, were situated on the islands of the latter, or on its southern shore. Those on the islands were most luxuriant, for the principal reason that they are fully protected from the wild beasts, which occasionally commit extensive depredations on the maize, rice, and cassava fields. One of the islands nearest the village, on which my hostesses had their plantations, I visited frequently during my stay. It was a delicious spot, covered with a most luxuriant growth of fruits and vegetables. I could well understand why it had been selected by the English for their settlement, when they sought to establish themselves on the coast, during the great war with Spain. A partially-obliterated trench and breast-work, a few iron guns half-buried in the soil, at the most elevated portion of the island, and one or two large iron cauldrons, probably designed to be used in sugar-works, were now the only traces of their ancient establishments.

The lagoon abounds in fish and water-fowl, and there are some savannahs, at a considerable distance up the Patuca, and on other streams flowing into the lagoon, which are thronged with deer. But it would seem that these are only occasionally hunted by the Caribs, and then chiefly for their skins, of which large numbers are exported.

As I have said, we arrived in Brus during the annual carnival, which follows on the return of those members of the community who have been absent in the mahogany-works. It is in these works that the able-bodied Caribs find their principal employment. They hire for from ten to twelve dollars per month, and rations, receiving one half of their pay in goods, and the other half in money. As a consequence, they have among them a great variety of articles of European manufacture, selected with a most fantastic taste. A Carib dandy delights in a closely-fitting pantaloons, supported by a scarlet sash, a jaunty hat, encircled by a broad band of gold lace, a profuse neck-cloth, and a sword, or purple umbrella. It is in some such garb that he returns from the mahogany-works, to delight the eyes and affect the sensibilities of the Carib girls; nor does he fail to stuff his pockets with gay beads, and ear-rings and bracelets of hoop-like dimensions, richly gilt and glowing with colored glass, wherewith to follow up any favorable impression which may be produced by his own resplendent person. He then affects to have forgotten his Carib tongue, and finds himself constantly running into more familiar English, after the immemorial practice of great and finished travelers. He scorns the native *chicha* for the first day, but overcomes his prejudice, and gets glorious upon it the next. In fact, he enacts an unconscious satire upon the follies of a class, whose vanity would never enable them to discover the remotest possible parallelism between themselves and the Caribs of Honduras!

During the day several large boats arrived at Brus from Limas and Roman, both of which are mahogany stations. They all carried the Hondurus flag at the topmast, and bore down on the shore with their utmost speed, only striking their sails when on the edge of the breakers, when the occupants would all leap overboard, and thus float their boats to the shore. Here, under the shade of the trees, all the inhabitants of the village were gathered. They shouted and beat drums, and fired muskets, by way of welcome to their friends, who responded with the whole power of their lungs. Here, too, expectant wives, affectionate sisters, and anxious mothers, spread out tables, loaded with food, fruits, bottles of rum, and jars of *chicha,* wherewith to regale husband, brother, or son, on the instant of his arrival. It was amusing to witness the rivalry of the various wives of the same anxiously-expected husband, in their efforts to outvie each other in the arrangement of their respective tables, and the variety of eatables and drinkables which they supported. They were all particularly ambitious in their display of glass-ware, and some of them had a profusion of gay, and, in some instances, costly decanters and tumblers. One yellow dame, with her shoulders loaded with beads and but half-concealed by a silken scarf of brightest crimson, was complacent and happy in the exclusive possession of a plated wine-server, which supported three delicately-cut bottles of as many different colors, and filled with an equal variety of liquors.

Every body drank with every body on the occasion of every body's arrival, a process which, it may be suspected, might, by frequent repetition, come to develop a large liberality of feeling. At noon, it exhibited itself in a profuse and energetic shaking of hands, and toward night in embraces more prolonged and unctious than pleasant or endurable to one receiving his initiation in the practice. So I was fain to retire early from the shore, although enjoying highly the excitement, in which I could not fail to have that kind of sympathy which every manifestation of genuine feeling is sure to inspire. Even Antonio, whose impassible brow had latterly become anxious and thoughtful, partook of the general exhilaration, and wore a smiling face.

I was treated with great consideration by the entire population, who all seemed alike consequential and happy, when an opportunity was afforded to them of shaking me by the hand, and inquiring, "How do you do?"

As I have intimated, the Caribs, like the Mosquitos, practice polygamy; but the wives have each a distinct establishment, and require a fair and equal participation in all of the favors of their husband. If he make one a present, he is obliged to honor all the others in like manner; and they are all equally ready to make common cause against him, in case of infidelity, or too wide an exhibition of gallantry. The division of duties and responsibilities is rather extraordinary. When a Carib takes a wife, he is obliged to build her a house and clear her a plantation. But, this done, she must thenceforth take care of herself and her offspring; and if she desire the assistance of her husband in planting, she is obliged to pay him, at the rate of two dollars per week, for his services. And although the husband generally accompanies his wives in their trading excursions to Truxillo and elsewhere, he carries no loads, and takes no part in the barter. As a consequence, nearly all the labor of the villages is performed by the women; the men thinking it rather beneath them, and far from manly, to engage in other occupation than mahogany-cutting and the building of boats, in which art they are very expert, using the axe, saw, and adze with great skill. Altogether, the Caribs are kind, industrious, provident, honest, and faithful, and must ultimately constitute one of the most important aids to the development of the country. They are brave, and some companies, which have been in the service of the government, have distinguished themselves in the field, not less for their subordination than for their valor and powers of endurance. They are usually temperate, and it is rare to see one of them drunk, except during the continuance of some festival, of which they have several in the course of the year.

I remained but a few days at Brus, and availed myself of the departure of a large *creer*, or Carib boat, bound for Roatan, to take passage for that island. I could not prevail upon my host to accept any thing in return for his hospitality, except "El Moro," for whom one of his children had conceived a strong liking, which the bird was far from reciprocating. Mischievous Moro! The last I saw of him was while waddling stealthily across the floor, to get a bite at the toes of his admirer!

Our course from Brus lay, first, to the island of Gunaja, distinguished historically as the one whence Columbus first descried the mainland of America. Our sole purpose there was to carry a demijohn of brandy to a solitary Scotchman, living upon one of the cays which surround it, to whom it had been sent by some friend in Belize. It had been intrusted to the Carib owner of the boat, who went thus out of his way to fulfill his commission, without recompense or the hope of reward. One would suppose that a demijohn of brandy was a dangerous article to intrust to the exclusive custody of Indians; but those who know the Caribs best have most faith in their integrity.

The Bay of Honduras is remarkable for its general placidity, and the extreme purity of its waters. It has a large number of coral cays and reefs on its western border, which almost encircle the peninsula of Yucatan, as with a belt. The fine islands of Roatan and Guanaja are belted in like manner, but there are several openings in the rocky barriers which surround them, through which vessels may enter the protected waters within.

APPROACH TO GUANAJA.

The wind was fresh and fair, the sky serene, and the sea was bright and sparkling in the sunlight. We swept on swiftly and gayly, the pine-clad mountains of Guanaja rising slowly and smilingly above the horizon. By-and-by the palm-trees on the surrounding cays became visible, their plumes appearing to spring from the clear waters, and to rise and fall with the motion of our boat. As we approached nearer to them, we could make out the cays themselves, supporting masses of emerald verdure, within a silvery ring of sand. Between them and the island, with its wealth of forest, the sea was of the loveliest blue, and placid as a "painted ocean." But, before we reached their fairy-like shores, the wind died away, and our sail drooped from the mast. We were partly under the lee of the land, and the surface of the sea soon became

"———charmed in a calm so still
That not a ripple ruffled its smooth face."

And as we drifted on, our boat yielding to the gentle swells, I amused myself in looking over the side, and contemplating the forms of marine life which the transparent water revealed to our gaze. The bottom was distinctly visible, studded with the wonderful products of the coral polypus, here spreading out like fans, there taking the forms of flattened globes radiating with spines, and yonder shooting up in branching, antler-like stems. Dark patches of jelly-like sponge, the white shells of myriads of conchs, and occasionally a large fish, whose pulsating gills alone gave sign of life—all these contributed to lend variety and interest to those glimpses of the bottom of the sea. It was to me a new revelation of Nature, and as I gazed, and gazed, the musical song of the "dainty Ariel" rang its bell-like cadences in my ears ;

"Full fathoms five thy father lies;
Of his bones are corals made;

Those are pearls that were his eyes;
Nothing of him that doth fade,
But doth suffer a sea-change
Into something rich and strange!"

Our men stretched themselves in the bottom of the boat, waiting, as they said, for the evening breeze. But the evening breeze came not, and they were finally obliged to paddle the boat to the nearest cay—a coral gem indeed, with its clustering palms, drooping gracefully over the sea, as if, Narcissus-like, contemplating their own beauty in its mirror-like surface.

The moon was in her first quarter, and as she rose above the placid sea, revealing the island in its isolation and beauty, jeweled round with cays, I seated myself apart, on the sand of the shore, and drank in the beauty of the scene. Gradually my thoughts recurred to the past, and I could hardly realize that but little more than five months had elapsed since I had held an unwitting conference with the demon, in my little studio in White-street. And yet what an age of excitement and adventure had been crowded in that brief space! I felt that I had entered upon a new world of ideas and impressions, and wondered to think that I had lived so long immured in the dull, unsympathizing heart of the crowded city. It was with a pang of regret that I now found myself drifting upon civilization again. A few days would bring me to Belize, where I knew Antonio would leave me, to return to the fastnesses of his people. Where then should I go?

These reflections saddened me, and the unwilling conviction was forced upon my mind that I must soon be roused from my long, delicious dream, perhaps never again to court its enchantments with success. I gazed upon the moonlit waters, and listened to the gentle chime of the waves upon the sand, and almost regretted that I had been admitted within the grand arcanum of Nature, to adore her unvailed beauties, since they were now to be shut out from me forever, by the restraints, the unmeaning forms, the follies and vices of artificial life! A heavy weight of melancholy settled on my heart, and I bowed my head on my knees, and—shall I own it?—wept!

It was then that Antonio approached me, silently as when he stole to my side on the fearful night of our shipwreck, and quietly laid his hand on my shoulder. I knew who it was, but I said nothing, for I hesitated to betray my emotion.

He respected my silence, and waited until my momentary weakness had passed away, when I raised my head, and met his full and earnest gaze. His face again glowed with that mysterious intelligence which I had remarked on several previous occasions; but now his lips were unsealed, and he said:—

"This is a good place, my brother, to tell you the secret of my heart; for on that dark island slumber the bones of our fathers. It was there that my powerful ancestor, Baalam Votan, led the white-robed holy men, when they fled from the regions of the rising sun. It was there that our people raised a temple to the Imperial Tiger, whose descendant I am—for am I not Baalam,* and is not this the Heart of the People ?"

This exclamation was made with energy, and, for a moment, he was silent, and gazed earnestly upon his cherished talisman.

When he resumed, it was in a less exalted strain. He told me of the ancient greatness of his people, when the race of Baalam Votan reigned over the Peninsula of Yucatan, and sent the missionaries of their religion to redeem the savage nations which surrounded them, even to the country of the Huastecas, on the river of Panuco. It was then, he said, that the Lord of Life smiled on the earth ; then the ears of maize were many times larger than now, the trees were loaded with unfailing supplies of fruit, and bloomed with perennial flowers ; the cotton grew of many colors ; and, although men died, their spirits walked the earth, and held familiar converse with the children of the Itzaes.

Never have I heard a voice more intense and fervid than that of the Indian boy, as he described the traditionary golden age of his people. I listened with breathless interest, and thought it was thus that the prophets of old must have spoken, when

* *Baalam*, in the language of Yucatan, signifies *Tiger*, and *Votan* is understood to denote *Heart*. The Maya tradition is, that Baalam Votan, the Tiger-Heart, led the fathers of the Mayas to Yucatan, from a distant country. He is conspicuously figured in the ruined temples around the Lake of Itza, as well as at Çhichen and Palenque.

the people deemed them inspired of heaven. But when he came to recount the wrongs of his nation, and the destruction of the kingdom of his fathers, I could scarcely believe that the hoarse voice, and words but half-articulated from excess of passion, proceeded from the same lips. It was a fearful sight to witness the convulsive energy of that Indian boy, whose knotted muscles, and the veins swelling almost to bursting on his forehead, half-induced me to fear that he had been stricken with madness.

But soon he became calm again, and told me how the slumbering spirit of his people had become roused, and how wide-spread and terrible was the revenge which they were meditating upon their oppressors. A few years before, his father had gathered the descendants of the ancient Caziques amid the ruins at Chichen-Itza, and there they had sworn, by the Heart of Baalam Votan, to restore the rule of the Holy Men, and expel the Spaniards from the Peninsula. It was then, that the sacred relic which he wore on his breast had been dug up from the hiding-place where it had lain for centuries, to lend the sanctity and power of the traditionary Votan to his chosen successor. But the movement had been premature ; and although the excited, but poorly-armed Indians performed prodigies of valor, and carried their victories to the very walls of Merida, yet there they received a sudden, and, as it seemed, a final check, in the death of Chichen-Pat, their cherished leader. He fell at the head of his followers, who rescued only the talisman of Votan, called the "Heart of the People," and then fled in dismay to their fastnesses in the wilderness. But the spirit which had been evoked was not subdued. Another convocation was held, and the only son of their late leader was invested with the symbol of authority. A scheme of insurrection was devised, which was intended to include, not only the Indians of Yucatan and of Central America, but even those of Mexico and Peru, in one grand and terrible uprising against the Spanish dominion.

To this end messengers were sent in every direction; and the proud cavalier at Bogota or Mexico, spurring his horse, with arrogant mien, past the strange Indian, who shrank aside at his approach, or stood with head uncovered in his presence, little thought what torrents of hate were dammed up in that swarthy breast, or what wide-laid schemes of vengeance were revolving beneath that impassible brow! The emissaries toiled through wildernesses and deep marshes, over high mountains and dangerous rivers, enduring hunger and fatigue, and the extremes of heat and cold, to fulfill their respective missions. Even the daughters of the Holy Men, like the seeress of the river Bocay, ventured afar from the homes of their people, and among distant and alien tribes, became the propagandists of the meditated Revenge!

* * * * * * *

The night had worn on, and the crescent moon rested on the verge of the horizon. I had heard the great secret of the Indian boy; his bitter recital of past wrongs and failures, and his hopes of future triumph. I now knew that the angel of blood was indeed abroad, and that, in his own figurative language, "The voice of the Tiger was loud in the mountain!"

FAREWELL TO THE MOSQUITO SHORE!

I was silent and thoughtful when he had finished; but when, after a long pause, he asked, "Will my brother go with me to the lake of the Itzaes?" I grasped his hand and swore, by a name holier than that of Votan, to justify a friendship so unwavering by a faith as boundless as his own. And when I left the outposts of civilization, and plunged into the untracked wilderness, with no other friend or guide, never did a suspicion or a doubt darken for an instant my confidence, or impair my faith in the loyal heart of ANTONIO CHUL—once the mild-eyed Indian boy, but now the dreaded chieftain and victorious leader of the unrelenting Itzaes of Yucatan!

Time only can determine what will be the final result of the contest which is now waging upon the soil of that beautiful, but already half-desolated peninsula. Almost every arrival brings us the news of increased boldness, and new successes on the part of the Indians ; and, it now seems, as if the great drama of the conquest were to be closed by the destruction of the race of the conquerors ! Terribly the frown darkens on the front of Nemesis !

"The voice of the Tiger is loud in the mountain !"

APPENDIX.

A.

HISTORICAL SKETCH OF THE MOSQUITO SHORE.

The general physical characteristics, and the climate and productions of the Mosquito Shore, have probably been sufficiently indicated in the foregoing rapid narrative. Nevertheless, to supply any deficiencies which may exist in these respects, as well as to illustrate the history of this coast, to which recent political events have given some degree of interest, I have here brought together a variety of facts derived from original sources, or such as are not easily accessible to the general reader.

The designation "Mosquito Shore" can only properly be understood in a geographical sense, as applying to that portion of the eastern coast of Central America lying between Cape Gracias à Dios and Bluefields Lagoon, or between the twelfth and fifteenth degrees of north latitude, a distance ot about two hundred miles. The attempts which have been made to apply this name to a greater extent of shore, have had their origin in strictly political considerations.

This coast was discovered by Columbus, in his fourth voyage, in 1502. He sailed along its entire length, stopping at various points, to investigate the country, and ascertain the character of its inhabitants. He gave it the name *Cariay*, and it was accurately characterized by one of his companions, Porras, as "*una tierra muy baja*," a very low land. Columbus himself, in his letter to the Spanish sovereigns, describes the inhabitants as fishers, and "as great sorcerers, very terrible." His son, Fernando Columbus, is more explicit. He says, they were "almost negroes in color, bestial, going naked; in all respects very rude, eating human flesh, and devouring their fish raw, as they happened to catch them." The language of the chroniclers warrant us in believing that these descriptions applied only to the Indians of the sea-coast, and that those of the interior, whose language then was different, were a distinct people.

The great incentive to Spanish enterprise in America, and which led to the rapid conquest and settlement of the continent, was the acquisition of the precious metals. But little of these was to be found on the Mosquito Shore, and, as a consequence, the tide of Spanish adventure swept by, heedless of the miserable savages who sought a precarious subsistence among its lagoons and forests. It is true, a grant of the entire coast, from Cape Gracias to the Gulf of Darien, was made to Diego de Nicuessa, for purposes of colonization, within ten years after its discovery, but the expedition which he fitted out to carry it into effect, was wrecked at the mouth of the Cape, or Wanks river, which, in consequence bore, for many years, the name of *Rio de los Perdidos.*

From that time forward, the attention of Spain was too much absorbed with the other parts of her immense empire in America, to enable her to devote much care to this comparatively unattractive shore. Her missionaries, inspired with religious zeal, nevertheless penetrated among its people, and feeble attempts were made to found establishments at Cape Gracias, and probably at other points on the coast. But the resources of the country were too few to sustain the latter, and the Indians themselves too debased and savage to comprehend the instructions of the former.

The coast, therefore, remained in its primitive condition, until the advent of the buccaneers in the sea of the Antilles, which was about the middle of the seventeenth century. Its intricate bays and unknown rivers, furnished admirable places of refuge and concealment, for the small and swift vessels in which they roved the seas. They made permanent stations at Cape Gracias and Bluefields, from which they darted out like hawks on the galleons that sailed from Nombre de Dios and Carthagena, laden with the riches of Peru. Indeed Bluefields, the present seat of Mosquito royalty, derives its name from *Bleevelt*, a noted Dutch pirate, who had his rendezvous in the bay of the same name.

The establishment at Cape Gracias, however, seems to have been not only the principal one on this coast, but in the whole Caribbean Sea. It is mentioned in nearly every chapter of the narratives, which the pirates have left us, of their wild and bloody adventures. Here they met to divide their spoil, and to decide upon new expeditions. The relations which they maintained with the natives are well described by old Jo. Esquemeling, a Dutch pirate, who wrote about 1670 :—

"We directed our course toward Gracias à Dios, for thither resort many pirates who have friendly correspondence with the Indians there. The custom is, that when any pirates arrive, every one has the liberty to buy himself an Indian woman, at the price of a knife, an old axe, wood-bill or hatchet. By this contract the woman is obliged to stay with the pirate all the time he remains there. She serves him, meanwhile, with victuals of all sorts that the country affords. The pirate has also liberty to go and hunt and fish where he pleases. Through this frequent converse with the pirates, the Indians sometimes go to sea with them for whole years, so that many of them can speak English." (*Buccaneers of America, London*, 1704, p. 165.)

He also adds that they were extremely indolent, "wandering up and down, without knowing or caring so much as to keep their bodies from the rain, except by a few palm-leaves," with "no other clothes than an apron tied around their middle," and armed with spears "pointed with the teeth of crocodiles," and living chiefly on bananas, wild fruits and fish.

We have a later account of them by De Lussan, another member of the fraternity of freebooters:

"The Cape has long been inhabited by *mulasters* [mulattos] and negroes, both men and women, who have greatly multiplied since a Spanish ship, bound from Guinea, freighted with their fathers, was lost here. Those who escaped from the wreck were courteously received by the *Mousticks* [Spanish *Moscos*, English *Mosquitos*] who live hereabout. These Indians assigned their guests a place to grub up, and intermixed with them.

"The ancient *Mousticks* live ten or a dozen leagues to the windward, at a place called *Sanibey* [Sandy Bay]. They are very slothful, and neither plant or sow but very little; their wives performing all the labor. As for their clothing, it is neither larger or more sumptuous than that of the *mulasters* of the Cape. There are but few among them who have a fixed abode, most of them being vagabonds, and wandering along the river side, with no other shelter than the *latarien-leaf* [palm-leaf], which they manage so that when the wind drives the rain on one side, they turn their leaf against it, behind which they lie. When they are inclined to sleep, they dig a hole in the sand, in which they put themselves." (*De Lussan's Narrative, London*, 1704, p. 177.)

The negroes wrecked from the Spanish slave-ship were

augmented in number by the *cimarones*, or runaway slaves of the Spanish settlements in the interior; and, intermingling with the Indians, originated the mongrel race which now predominates on the Mosquito Shore. Still later, when the English planters from Jamaica attempted to establish themselves on the coast, they brought their slaves with them, who also contributed to increase the negro element. What are called Mosquito Indians, therefore, are a mixed race, combining the blood of negroes, Indians, pirates, and Jamaica traders.

Many of the pirates were Englishmen, and all had relations more or less intimate with the early governors of Jamaica, who often shared their profits, in return for such indulgences as they were able to afford. Indeed, it is alleged that they were often partners in the enterprises of the buccaneers. But when the protracted wars with Spain, which favored this state of things, were brought to a close, it became no longer prudent to connive at freebooting; and, as a kind of intelligence had sprung up with the Mosquito Shore, they conceived the idea of obtaining possession of it, on behalf of the British crown. Various plans to this end, drawn up by various individuals, were at this period presented to the royal government, and by them, it would seem, referred to the governors of Jamaica.

But the governors of that island had already taken the initiative. As early as 1687 one of the Mosquito chiefs had been taken to Jamaica, for the purpose of having him place his country under the protection of England. Sir Hans Sloane has left an account of how, having escaped from his keepers, "he pulled off the European clothes his friends had put on, and climbed to the top of a tree!"

It seems, nevertheless, that he received "a cocked hat, and

a ridiculous piece of writing," which, according to Jeffreys, was a commission as king, "given by his Grace, the Duke of Albemarle, under the seal of the island!"

It was not, however, until 1740, that an attempt was made to obtain a cession of the coast, from the extraordinary monarch thus created by the Duke of Albemarle. In that year Governor Trelawney wrote to the Duke of Newcastle, suggesting the expediency of rousing the Mosquito Indians against the Spaniards, with whom the English were at war, and purposing an absolute occupation of their country. He represented that there were about one hundred Englishmen there, "*mostly such as could live nowhere else*," who might be brought together, reënforced, and, by the help of the Mosquitos, finally induce the other Indians to revolt, "and thus spread the insurrection from one part to another, till it should become general over the Indies, and drive the Spaniards entirely out."

In pursuance of this scheme, Governor Trelawney commissioned one Robert Hodgson, to proceed to the Mosquito Shore, fully provided with every thing necessary to enable him to tamper with the Indians. The manner in which he executed his instructions is naïvely told by Hodgson himself, in a letter addressed to the Governor. The following extracts are from the original letter, now in the possession or Colonel Peter Force, of Washington.

SANDY BAY, April 8th, 1740.

"May it please Your Excellency,—

"I arrived at St. Andrews on the 4th of March, and sailed for Sandy Bay on the 8th, where I arrived on the 11th, but was prevented by a Norther from going ashore till the 13th.

"King Edward being informed of my arrival, sent me word that he would see me next day, which he did, attended by several of his captains. I read to him Your Excellency's letter, and my own commission, and when I had explained them by an interpreter, I told them my errand, and recommended to them to seek all opportunities of cultivating friendship and union with the neighboring Indian nations, and especially such as were under subjection to the Spaniards, and of helping them to recover their freedom. They approved every thing I said, and appointed the 16th to meet the Governor, John Briton, and his captains at the same place, to hear what I had further to say.

"On the 16th they all came, except Admiral Dilly and Colonel Morgan, who were, like General Hobby and his captains, at too great a distance to be sent for, but their presence not being material, I proceeded to explain to them that, as they had long acknowledged themselves subjects of Great Britain, the Governor of Jamaica had sent me to take possession of their country in His Majesty's name—then asked if they had any thing to object. They answered, they had nothing to say against it, but were very glad I had come for that purpose; so I immediately set up the standard, and reducing what I had said into articles, I asked them both jointly and separately, if they approved, and would abide by them. They unanimously declared they would. I had them then read over again, in solemn manner, under the colors, and, at the end of every article fired a gun, and concluded by cutting up a turf, and promising to defend their country, and procure for them all assistance from England in my power.

"The formality with which all this was done seems to have had a good effect upon them.

"The articles I enclose, and hope Your Excellency will excuse so much ceremony; for, as I had no certain information whether the country was ever taken possession of before, or ever claimed otherwise than by sending them down commissions, I thought the more voluntary and clear the cession was the better. * * * The king is very young, I believe not twenty, and is not much observed; but were he to be in England or Jamaica a while, *'tis thought he would make a hopeful monarch enough.*

"On the 18th the king, with his captains, came of their own accord to consult about a proper plan to attack [the Spaniards], but hearing that Captain Jumper was expected from the other side of the Cape, and neither the Governor, Admiral Dilly, nor Colonel Morgan being present, I thought it best to defer it till they were summoned. The king brought his mother, and the captains their wives. I entertained them as usual, but there always comes such a train *that I should have had three or four, instead of one puncheon of rum.*" * * *

Hodgson then goes on to describe the appearance of one Andrew Stewart, a pirate, to whom the Indians had made a promise of assistance, from which he endeavored to dissuade them, in order to accompany him; but the Indians finally agreed to attack the river Cocelijo to oblige Stewart, and San Juan de Veragua to oblige Hodgson. He continues:—

* * * "They intoxicate themselves with a liquor made of honey, pine-apple, and cassava, and, if they avoid quarrels, which often happen, they are sure to have fine promiscuous doings among the girls. The old women, I am told, have the liberty of chewing the cassava, before it is put in, that they may have a chance in the general rape as well as the young ones.

"I fell into one of their drunken-bouts by accident yesterday, when I found Admiral Dilly and Colonel Morgan retailing my advice to them to little effect, for most of them were too drunk to mind it, and so hideously painted that I quickly left them to avoid being daubed all over, which is the compliment they usually pay visitors on such occasions.

* * * "Their resentment of adultery has lost its edge too much among them, which I have no doubt they are obliged to us for, as also for the breach of promise in their bargains. * * * They will loll in their hammocks until they are almost starved, then start up, and go a turtling in a pet; and if they have not immediate success, and their happens to be many boats together, they form a design upon some Spanish or Indian town. * * * *

"The country is fine, and produces good cotton, better than Jamaica. * * * Those Indians, on this side, do not appear so averse to government as I supposed, and those on the other are tractable enough. * * * I don't take their number to be so many as the author of the project makes them out.

(Signed) "ROBERT HODGSON."

In a subsequent letter, from Chiriqui Lagoon, dated June 21, 1740, Hodgson gives a further account of his expedition, and asks for some blank commissions for Mosquito admirals and generals, and also implores the Governor to send him out some men as a guard; for, he says, "my life is in more danger from these Indians than from the Spaniards."

Previously to this mission of Hodgson, viz., on the 28th of October, the Spanish Embassador in London had made complaints that the incursions of the Zambos and Indians of the Mosquito Shore, on the adjacent Spanish settlements, were "at the instigation and under the protection of the English of Jamaica, who have a commerce with them, and give them in exchange for the captive Indians whom they purchase for slaves, firearms, powder, shot, and other goods, contrary to the natural rights of these people."

The "cession" of the Mosquito Shore, thus procured by Hodgson, was followed up by occupation. Several Jamaica planters established themselves there, and Hodgson shortly afterward received the appointment of "Superintendent of the Mosquito Shore."

In 1744 an order was issued in Council, dispatching a certain number of troops from Jamaica to the Mosquito Shore, and in 1748 another order for sending a supply of ordnance to the "new settlements" established there. In fact, everything indicated the purpose of a permanent occupation of the country. The Spaniards remonstrated, and in 1750–51 threatened a forcible expulsion of the English, whereupon Trelawney instructed Hodgson to represent to them, that "the object of keeping a superintendent among the Indians was to restrain them in their hostilities against the Spaniards!" For a time the Spaniards were deceived, and even went so far as to confer on Hodgson the title of Colonel, for the services which he professed to render to them. They, however, finally discovered his duplicity, and made arrangements to carry out their threat.

This not only alarmed the settlers, but also Governor Knowles, who had succeeded Trelawney in Jamaica. He opened a correspondence with the Captain-General of Guatemala for the cessation of hostilities, till he could hear from England, whither he wrote that the whole Mosquito affair was "*a job*," and that if Hodgson were not checked or recalled, "he would involve the nation in difficulties," and that the "Indians were so perplexed that they did not know what part to take." A little later the Indians themselves took up arms against the English, being discontented with the treatment which they had received.

These things did not escape the notice of Spain, and had their influence in bringing about the troubles which were ended by the treaty of Paris, in 1763, by which Great Britain agreed to demolish all the fortifications which she had erected, not only on the Mosquito Shore, but in all "other places in the territory of Spain, in that part of the world." This treaty, nevertheless, did not have the effect of entirely terminating English intrigue and aggression on the Mosquito Shore and elsewhere, and its provisions were consequently revived, and made more explicit and stringent by the subsequent treaty of 1783. This treaty provided that all the "English settlements on the Spanish continent" should be abandoned; but, on the pretext that "the Mosquito Shore was not part of the *Spanish* continent, but of the *American* continent," the English managed to evade its provisions, and to keep up their connection with that coast, as before. This piece of duplicity led to severe reclamations on the part or

Spain, which were only settled by the supplementary treaty of 1786, which stipulated that

> "His Britannic Majesty's subjects, and other colonists who have enjoyed the protection of England, shall evacuate the country of the Mosquitos, as well as the continent in general, and the islands adjacent without exception," etc. And that "If there should still remain any persons so daring as to presume, by entering into the interior country, to obstruct the evacuation agreed upon, His Britannic Majesty, so far from affording them any succor or protection, will disavow them in the most solemn manner," etc., etc.

The English, nevertheless, under authority of another article of this treaty, were allowed to cut logwood, within a certain accurately-defined territory on the coast of Yucatan, now known as "Belize," or "British Honduras." But they were strictly forbidden to make permanent establishments, erect fortifications, or organize any form of government; nor was the permission thus accorded to be construed as in any way derogating from the "sovereign territorial rights of the King of Spain." Yet from this simple permission to cut wood, thus hedged round with solemn treaty stipulations, Great Britain, by a series of encroachments and aggressions has come to arrogate absolute sovereignty, not only over Belize and a wide expanse of adjacent territory, but also over the large islands of Roatan, Guanaja, etc., in the Bay of Honduras, which have been organized as colonies of the British crown!

From 1786 forward, Great Britain ceased to hold any open relations with the Mosquito Indians, until the decline of the power of Spain, and the loss of her American possessions. In the interval, the governors of the provinces of Central America had made various establishments on the Mosquito Shore, at Cape Gracias, and at Bluefields, and had erected a fort for the protection of the harbor of San Juan, at the mouth of the river of the same name.

But when the country passed into the hands of the comparatively feeble states of Central America, whom it was supposed could offer no effectual resistance to aggression, the English revived their schemes of aggrandisement on the Mosquito Shore. And while these states were occupied with the questions incident to their new political organization, agents were dispatched to the coast, from Jamaica and Belize, to tamper again with the Indians, and to induce them to reject the authority of the republics which had succeeded to the rights of Spain. In this they seem to have been, to a certain degree, successful. Neither rum, nor commissions as kings, admirals, generals, and governors, were wanting, to operate upon the weakness of the savages. "A regalia," says Macgregor, "consisting of a silver-gilt crown, a sword, and sceptre of moderate value," were sent out to lend dignity and grandeur to the restored dynasty of Mosquito! A savage chief, or head-man, who suited the purposes of the Jamaican Warwicks, was pitched upon, taken to Belize, and formally "crowned." But he turned out badly. In the language of Macgregor, in his Report to the British Parliament, "he combined the bad qualities of the European and Creole, with the vicious propensities of the Sambo, and the capriciousness of the Indian." He was killed in a drunken brawl, in 1824, and was succeeded by his half-brother, Robert. But it was soon found that Robert was in the Spanish interest, and he was accordingly set aside, by the British agents, who took into favor a Sambo, named "George Frederick." But he, too, proved to be an indifferent tool, and either died, or was dropped, for another Sambo, who was called by the high-sounding name of "*Robert Charles Frederick*," and who promised to answer every purpose.

His "coronation" was effected at Belize, on the 23d of April, 1825, upon which solemn occasion a number of so-called chiefs were got together, under the seductive promise of a "big drunk." The ceremonies which took place have been described by a British subject, who was an eye-witness of the proceedings. His picture needs no heightening to make it irresistibly ludicrous!

"On the previous evening cards of invitation were sent to the different merchants, requesting their attendance at the court-house early in the morning. At this place the king, dressed in a British major's uniform, made his appearance; and his chiefs similarly clothed, but with sailors' trowsers, were ranged around the room. A more motley group can hardly be imagined. Here an epaulette decorated a herculean shoulder, tempting its dignified owner to view his less favored neighbor with triumphant glances. There a wanting button displayed a greasy olive skin under the uniform of a captain of infantry. At one side a cautious noble might be seen, carefully braced up to the chin, like a modern dandy, defying the most *penetrating* eye to *prove* him shirtless; while the mathematical movements of a fourth, panting under such tight habiliments, expressed the fear and trembling with which he awaited some awful accident.

"The order of procession being arranged, the cavalcade moved toward the church; his Mosquito Majesty on horseback, supported on the right and left by the two senior British officers of the settlement, and his chiefs following on foot two by two. On its arrival his Majesty was placed in a chair, near the altar, and the English coronation service was read by the chaplain to the colony, who, on this occasion, performed the part of the Archbishop of Canterbury. When he arrived at this part, 'And all the people said, let the King live forever, long live the King, God save the King!' the vessels of the port, according to a previous signal, fired a salute, and the chiefs rising, cried out, 'Long live King Robert!'

"His Majesty seemed chiefly occupied in admiring his finery, and, after his anointing, expressed his gratification by repeatedly thrusting his hands through his thick, bushy hair, and applying his finger, to his nose—in this expressive manner indicating his delight at this part of the service.

"Before, however, his chiefs could swear allegiance to their monarch, it was necessary that they should profess Christianity; and, accordingly, with shame be it recorded, they were baptized 'in the name of the Father, Son, and Holy Ghost!' They displayed total ignorance of the meaning of this ceremony; and when asked to give their names, took the titles of Lord Rodney, Lord Nelson, or some other celebrated officer, and seemed grievously disappointed when told that they could only be baptized by simple Christian names.

"After this solemn mockery was concluded, the whole assembly adjourned to a large school-room to eat the coronation dinner, when these poor creatures all got intoxicated with rum! A suitable conclusion to a farce, as blasphemous and wicked as ever disgraced a Christian country." (*Dunn's Central America*, pp. 26, 27.—1828.)

After having been thus invested with the Mosquito purple, "King Robert Charles Frederick" was conducted back to the Mosquito Shore, and turned loose to await the further development of British designs. After the unctious ceremonies at Belize, he seems to have taken the proceeding in earnest, and to have deluded himself with the belief that he was really a king! In this character, and moved thereto by the suggestions of divers scheming traders, and the powerful incentives of gay cottons and rum, he proceeded, of his sovereign will and pleasure, to make grants to the aforesaid traders, of large portions of his alleged dominions. These grants were not only so extensive as to cover the entire shore, but conveyed the absolute sovereignty over them to the various grantees—Rennick, Shepherd, Haly, and others.

When these proceedings came to the ears of the Governor of Jamaica, and the Superintendent of Belize, who had created "His Mosquito Majesty" for their own use and purposes, they created great alarm. Says Macgregor, "it appears that these grants were made without the knowledge of the British agent, who had usually been residing on the coast, *to keep up the connection with England*." He adds that "upon their coming to the knowledge of the British government, they were very properly disallowed."

Not only were they disallowed, but a vessel of war was sent to the coast to catch "Robert Charles Frederick," and take him to Belize, where he would be unable to do more mischief. This was done, but "His Majesty" could not endure the restraints of civilization—he pined away, and died. But before this lamentable catastrophe took place, he was induced to affix "his mark" to a document styled "a Will," in which it was provided that the affairs of his kingdom should be administered by Colonel McDonald, the Superintendent of Belize, as Regent, during the minority of his heir; that McDonald should be guardian of his children; and, with reference to the spiritual wants of his beloved subjects, "the United Church of England and Ireland should be the established religion of the Mosquito nation forever!" Sainted Robert!

Upon the death of "Robert Charles Frederick," his son, "George William Clarence," the present incumbent of the Mosquito throne, was duly proclaimed "King" by the Regent McDonald, and his colleagues. His first act, under their direction, was the revocation of all the grants which his father had made to the traders, on the ground that the royal Robert Charles was drunk when he made them, and that they had been given without a consideration. An agent was then appointed to take charge of this tender scion of royalty, at Bluefields, where the latter still remains, in complete subjection to his masters, who direct all his acts, or rather compel his endorsement of their own. From 1841 up to 1848 the proceedings of the English agents, in developing their policy in respect to the Mosquito Shore, and in preparing the way for its final aggregation to the British crown, rise beyond the scope of sober history or serious recital, and could only be properly illustrated by the appropriate pens of Charivari, or of Punch.

All these proceedings were firmly and earnestly protested against by the Central American States, who, however, received no satisfactory replies to their remonstrances. They were, furthermore, too much occupied with their own interior dissensions to undertake any effectual resistance to the aggressions of the English agents. In this emergency they addressed an appeal to the civilized nations of Europe, and a particular and fervent one to the United States, for its interference in behalf of their clear territorial rights and sovereignty.

Before time was afforded for action on these appeals, the termination of the war with Mexico, and the purchase of California by the United States, precipitated the course of English intrigue and encroachment on the Mosquito Shore. The British government was not slow to perceive that the acquisition of California would give to the long-cherished project of establishing a ship-canal between the Atlantic and Pacific Oceans, a new, practical, and immediate importance, and rightly foresaw that it would soon come to attract a large share of public attention in the United States. Orders were at once issued for the seizure of the Port of San Juan de Nicaragua, the only possible eastern terminus for a canal by way of the river San Juan, and the Nicaraguan lakes. This port had always been in the undisputed occupation both of Spain and Nicaragua; not a single Mosquito Indian had ever dwelt there, or within fifty miles of it, in any direction, yet, under pretext that it constituted "part of the proper dominions of his Mosquito Majesty, of whom Great Britain was the lawful protector," two British vessels-of-war entered the harbor in the month of January, 1848, tore down the Nicaraguan flag, raised that of "Mosquito," turned out the Nicaraguan officers, and filled their places with Englishmen. This done, they sailed away; but no sooner did the intelligence of the event reach the interior, than the Nicaraguan government sent down a small force, expelled the intruders, and resumed possession. The British forces, considerably augmented, thereupon returned. The Nicaraguans, unable to oppose them, retired up the river, and erected some rude fortifications on its banks. They were followed by an English detachment, and finally routed, with great loss. Hostilities were further prosecuted, until the Nicaraguans, powerless against the forces of Great Britain, consented to an armistice, which provided that they should not disturb San Juan, or attempt to reoccupy the port, pending the negotiations which, it was foreseen, would follow upon the seizure. All attempts to induce them to relinquish their claims of sovereignty over the port, were, however, unsuccessful.

By this high-handed act, committed in time of profound peace, Lord Palmerston, who had directed it, fondly hoped to secure for Great Britain the control of the then-supposed only feasible means of communication between the seas. He had grasped, as he thought, the key of the Central American Isthmus. English officers were at once installed in San Juan, and a "Consul General" appointed to reside there, with the most absolute dictatorial powers, supported by what was called a "police force," from Jamaica, and the almost constant presence of a British vessel of war in the harbor.

This act was shortly followed by the attempted seizure of

the Island of Tigre, and the Gulf of Fonseca, the supposed western terminus of the proposed canal, on the Pacific. This attempt was thwarted by American diplomacy in that quarter.

The results of American interference are too recent and well-known to need recapitulation. An American company obtained the privileges of a transit through Nicaragua, and it was not long before American steamers began to run to San Juan. A large number of American citizens established themselves at the port, where they soon succeeded in suffocating British influence. They took the direction of affairs in their own hands, adopted a constitution, and organized a regular and stable government, pending the final settlement of the various questions concerning Central America, then in course of negotiation between the United States and Great Britain. In this condition the place remained, well-ordered, and affording the fullest protection to person and property, until the month of June of last year, when, under a misrepresentation of facts, and the grossest perversions of truth, inspired by unscrupulous personal hostility, the United States government was induced to issue such orders in respect to it, to a naval officer of more zeal and ambition of notoriety than either wisdom or discretion, as resulted in its bombardment and total destruction. Since this act, which has met the unanimous reprehension of the country, the town has been partly rebuilt and re-occupied, and now maintains an extraordinary and most anomalous condition, which can not long endure without resulting in serious complications. The United States insists, and justly, that it pertains to Nicaragua, and that all authority which may be exercised there, not derived from that State, is an usurpation; while, on the other hand, without insisting on the sovereignty of Mosquito, Great Britain denies it to Nicaragua, and prohibits her from attempting to exercise jurisdiction over it. Meantime San Juan and its people are left helplessly in a political Limbo, suffering witnesses of their inability to serve two masters. The obvious, and probably the only peaceable solution of this complication, is the voluntary establishment of San Juan as a free port by Nicaragua, under the joint protection of England and the United States.

Since 1849, nearly the whole interest of the "Mosquito question" has been centered in San Juan. It is true, Messrs. Webster and Crampton agreed upon a *projet*, defining the limits of Mosquito jurisdiction, and establishing a *de facto* Sambo monarchy on the coast, recognized, if not guaranteed, both by the United States and Great Britain. But the *projet* found no favor in this country, and was, moreover, indignantly rejected by Nicaragua. How far subsequent negotiations have tended to bring affairs to a settlement, remains to be disclosed.

It is nevertheless certain that, while Nicaragua has fretted, the United States blustered, and Great Britain silently and sullenly relaxed her gripe, as circumstances have rendered it necessary, the "Kingdom of Mosquito" has undergone no change, but has kept on the even tenor of its way—a happy illustration of the conservative and peaceful tendencies of well-established monarchical institutions! Under all the complications of the modern time, the royal Clarence, the hospitable Drummer, and the bibulous Slam, ignorant of the exalted place which they occupy in the instructions, and dispatches, and notes of conference, wherewith the Slams and Drummers of other lands do gravely amuse themselves, still cherish the well-being of their beloved and fellow-subjects, who, in turn, hunt, and fish, and cultivate the "big drunk" as of yore! Σ.

B.

VARIOUS NOTES ON THE TOPOGRAPHY, SOIL, CLIMATE, AND NATIVES OF THE MOSQUITO SHORE.

THE subjoined extracts, from various published works and memoirs of acknowledged authenticity, and from original documents, exhibit the condition of the people of the Mosquito Shore, their habits and modes of life, from the year 1700 up to the present time. It will be seen that few if any changes have taken place for the better, in this long period of a hundred and fifty years.

1710.

From Dampier's "Voyage around the World," London, 1717, p. 7–11.

"The Mosquito Indians are but a small nation or family, and not a hundred men of them in number, inhabiting on the main, on the north side, near Cape Gracias à Dios. * * They are coveted by the privateers as hunters. * * They have no form of government among them, but take the Governor of Jamaica to be one of the greatest princes in the world."

1757.

Extracts from "Some account of the Mosquito Territory, written in 1757, *while that country was in the possession of the British, by Col. Robert Hodgson, formerly His Majesty's Commander-in-Chief, Superintendent, and Agent on the Mosquito Shore.*

This Colonel Hodgson was son of the Captain Hodgson who was sent to the Mosquito Coast, in 1740, by

Governor Trelawney. He states that the population of the shore, at the time of his writing (1757), exclusive of aborigines was: "Whites 154, Mestizoes and Mulattoes 170, Indian and Negro slaves 800—total 1124." He observes that the "whites are without laws," but, nevertheless, living with great regularity; and that, if the number of white children is small, "it may be imputed to most of the women having lived with so much freedom formerly." He then proceeds to give a very clear and accurate account of the country, its products, and people, as follows:—

"The face of the country is various. The sea-coast, from Cape Cameron to Bluefields, is low and level, but the land rises gradually up any of the large, fair rivers with which it abounds, and whose regular flowery banks form beautiful avenues, and about twenty miles up is high enough for any purpose. But the lowland is full of swamps. Near the coast are several large lagoons, whose length, for the most part, is parallel thereto, and are so joined to each other by narrow necks of water, that half this distance may be gone inland, upon smooth water; in the flood times this may be called a range of islands, lying close in with the main, but the land is not much overflowed. To the westward and southward of the above capes, the land is high, almost to the sea-side, the hills rising gently like the swell of the sea. The greater part of the higher land is covered with large woods; but the lowland consists chiefly of large, level lawns, or savannahs, as they are called, with scarce a tree, and some of them very extensive. The whole country is remarkably well watered by many fine rivers, which have a long course; by innumerable smaller ones, and by creeks and lagoons; but all the rivers have the inconvenience of shoal bars at their mouths. The soil of the high woody land is the best, and is every where excellent; being either a deep black mould, or rich brick clay. What low woody ground is interspersed among the lawns is not so good; but the inhabitants who hitherto have chosen it for their plantations, have found that it will produce what they want very well. The savannah lands are the worst; the soil is light sand mixed with some rich mould, but might be greatly improved and made very useful. At present they are used for pasturage. The swamps or marshes are very rich soil; and if the wood which grows on them were cut down, they would either dry up, or, with a little more pains, might be drained."—P. 21.

"Indigo grows all about the country, of the same kind with that of the province of Guatemala, which is esteemed the best in the world.

"Cotton grows every where, in the worst land; the staple is remarkably good. There are three species of that kind which is manufactured, one of which is a light reddish brown, and looks like silk."—P. 23.

"Sugar, of which the little that is planted grows remarkably well in this country, which is much better adapted for it than any of the islands, on account of the great convenience of streams of water for such works and for carriage; the country not being subject to severe droughts, and free from hurricanes."—P. 29.

"The climate is very sensibly cooler than that of Jamaica, and very healthy, on which account people from that island sometimes come hither. Indeed, the disorders in both are of the same nature; but here they are not near so frequent or so violent as in that island. During the north winds the season may, with propriety, be called winter.

"The wind most common is the sea-breeze, or *trade-wind*. It blows fresh in June and July, but very moderate in April,

May, August, and September, particularly in April, and from the middle of August to the latter part of September. But from that time to the end of October, a westerly wind prevails along the coast to the westward of Cape Gracias, and a southerly one along the coast to the south of it; after which, to the end of February, at the full and change of the moon, strong north winds may be expected, veering round from east to west, and continuing about a week, yet is scarce ever so strong as to prevent vessels from beating to windward, and, if they choose it, getting in to Bonacca. * * * The land wind blows seven leagues off to sea, although sometimes very weak. * * * The month of March is very uncertain. The seasons are much the same as in other parts of the continent. In the rainy season, scarce a day passes without a heavy shower; the first commonly begins in June, and lasts about six weeks, in which time the rivers rise considerably, and are very rapid. The second begins about the middle of October, and lasts about two months. When they are over, the vegetation is surprisingly quick, and there is the further advantage of frequent, intermediate, gentle showers. * * * The harbors on this coast do not answer the occasion there would be for them. On the bar of Brewer's Lagoon there is seven feet water; often more on that of Black River. On those of Carataska and Warina Sound, nine feet; Great River and Pearl Cay, eight feet. * * *

"The natives or Mosquito people are of two breeds, one the original Indians, and the other a mixture of those and negroes, called Sambos. The latter originated from the cargoes of two Dutch ships filled with negroes, which were cast away on the coast, where, after several battles, the negroes had wives and ground given to them; since which they have greatly multiplied, and there is now no distinction between them in their rights and customs."—P. 40.

"Though they are to all intents and purposes one people, yet they are not so properly a single state as three united, each of which is independent of the others.

"I. Those who inhabit the southern extremity till Bragman's, and are mostly the *original Indians*; their head-man is called *Governor*.

"II. Those who extend to about Little Black River, and are mostly Sambos; their chief is called *King*.

"III. Those westward, who are Indians and Sambos mixed; their head-man is called *General*.

"The power of these three head-men is nearly equal, with a small difference in favor of the king, who is a little supported by the whites for the sake of his name. But none of these chiefs have much more than a negative voice, and never do any thing without consulting a council of old men. "* * * *The king has his commission or patent for being called so from the Governor of Jamaica.* And all the other chief people have commissions (admirals and captains) from His Majesty's Superintendent; and, upon the strength of these, always assume much more authority than they could without. However, it is at best such that it may be more properly said, that their directions are followed, than their orders obeyed; for even the young men are above serving the king, and will tell him that they are as free as he is, so that if he had not a few slaves of other Indians, he would be obliged to do all his own work."—P. 49.

Hodgson next speaks of the ravages of small-pox and drunkenness among them, and concludes:

"* * * Hence, the number of Mosquito people, in their present way of life, probably never exceeded *ten or eleven* *thousand.* * * * From the best computation, they are not above *seven thousand souls.*"

1787.

George Chalmers, Secretary of Board of Trade. From MSS. Notes for use of Board.

"The present number of the Mosquito Indians is unknown. It happened among them, probably, as among the North American Indians, that they declined in numbers and degenerated in spirit in proportion nearly as the white people settled among them. The Mosquitos, like the Caribs of San Domingo, consist of three distinct races: the aborigines, the descendants of certain African negroes who were formerly wrecked on the coast, and a generation containing the blood of both. If the Spaniards earnestly desired to destroy them, they could not, I think, make a very vigorous resistance. They are chiefly defended by the rivers, morasses, and woods of the country, and, perhaps, still more by the diseases incident to the climate."

1818.

From Roberts' Narrative of Voyages and Excursions on the East Coast of Central America.

"In the Mosquito Shore, a plurality of mistresses is considered no disgrace. It is no uncommon circumstance for a British subject to have one or more of these native women at different parts of the coast. They have acquired great influence through them.

"I have never known a marriage celebrated among them; these engagements are mere tacit agreements, sometimes broken by mutual consent. The children here and at Bluefields are in general baptized by the captains of trading vessels from Jamaica, who, on their annual visit to the coast, perform this ceremony, with any thing but reverence, on all who have been born during their absence; and many of them are indebted to these men for more than baptism. In proof of this, I could enumerate more than a dozen acknowledged children of two of these captains, who seem to have adopted, without scruple, the Indian idea of polygamy to its fullest extent. By this licentious and immoral conduct, they have, however, so identified themselves with the natives, as to obtain a sort of monopoly of the sale of goods. They have also insinuated themselves into the good graces of some of the leading men, so that their arrival is hailed with joy by all classes, as the season of festivity, revelry, christening, and licentiousness!"

1828.

From "Report of the Commissioners of Legal Inquiry in the case of the Indians of Honduras," ordered by the House of Commons "to be printed," July 10, 1828.

"The Mosquito Indians are a barbarous and cruel people, in the lowest state of civilization, and under the most abject subjection to their kings or chiefs. They are hostile to all the other Indian nations, who are a mild, timid, and peaceful race, and who appear to live under patriarchal governments. * * * Differences so striking between nations of the same continent, and divided by no inaccessible barriers, have given rise to a conjecture, confirmed by concurrent tradition, that the Mosquitos had a distinct origin. This tradition states, that a ship loaded with negro men from Africa was, at a very remote period, wrecked on the Mosquito shore; that these negroes seized upon the male inhabitants of the sea-coasts, massacred them, and then, by intermixture with the Indian women, altered the race and habits of the nation. This tradition is confirmed by the physical appearance of the Mosquitos, who indicate this mixture between the Indian and negro."

1836.

James Woods, for some time a resident on the Mosquito Shore.

In the year 1836, one James Woods, a native of Ipswich, England, went out to Central America, under the auspices of a "Colonization Company." On his return, he published an account of his adventures, to serve as a warning against other companies. He resided awhile at Cape Gracias, in charge of a store of provisions, rum, etc. He says:

"The rum was a dangerous thing in the store, for the Indians will kill a man for a glass of rum; and there were only five Europeans at the Cape. I had a demijohn of brandy for the Indian king, but he was gone up the river. He and his brother were taken from the Mosquito shore when young, and carried to the island of Jamaica, where they were taught to read and write the English language. After staying there a number of years, they were brought back to the shore. One was made king, the other a general, and although brought up in a civilized state, yet they returned to the wild and savage condition in which their people live, getting drunk, and giving themselves up to the most disgusting habits. No sooner had the king heard that I had a demijohn of brandy for him, than he set out to return home. He went to the house of a Frenchman, named Bouchet, who came down to the beach and told me his majesty wanted to see me. I went to the house, where the king was lying on a bed, rather unwell. I made my compliments to him, and asked him how he did. He told me he was very poorly, and wanted a gallon of brandy, which I accordingly got for him. He asked me to drink, and stay and dine with him, which I did. He told me that he loved me. I replied, 'You love the brandy better;' but I turned it off with a laugh, or he would have been offended with me. He staid for two or three days, and then left for Bluefields. * * * These Indians far exceed all the Indians I have ever met with in lying, thieving, and every thing that is disgusting. They are given up to idolatry, and lead an indolent life." After giving details of their ignorance and barbarism, he adds: "They are also great drunkards, and are never easy except when they are drunk." And of the English settlers and traders, he says: "They are almost as bad as the natives, and live in almost as disgusting a manner."

The *Athenæum* contains the following letter from *Squier* Bard, relating to some charges of plagiarism which had been preferred:

New York, Nov. 18, 1855.

A Correspondent of the *Athenæum* of the 20th ult. (Oct.), Mr. Dudley Costello, has called public attention to what he imagines to be a plagiarism in my little work, "Waikna," from a tale written by him, and entitled "Beware of the Chocolate of Chiapa." Opinions may differ as to whether there exists any substantial resemblance between the incident recounted in "Waikna," and that given in Mr. Costello's tale. But whatever of similarity there may be is entirely accidental, as I never saw the tale in question. Furthermore, Mr. Costello's incident is purely imaginary while any doubts in reference to the adventure described in "Waikna" may easily be dispelled by the testimony of the Mr. H. of the narrative,—who is Mr. Stanislaus Haly, at present, I believe, Her Britannic Majesty's Consular Agent at Cape Gracias. The whole matter is really of very little consequence; and the explanation which I have given cannot probably be of the slightest interest to any one, except to Mr. Costello; and to him only as affording another illustration of the saying that "truth is stranger than fiction."

I am, &c. SAML. A. BARD.

C.

BRIEF VOCABULARY OF THE MOSQUITO LANGUAGE.

In language, the Mosquitos differ wholly from the neighboring Indians, so that they are unable to communicate with them, except through interpreters. This fact, not less than their different character and habits of life, go to show that they are of a radically different stock. From their long intercourse with the English, they have adopted many English words, which are nevertheless pronounced in a manner which renders them nearly unintelligible. Their own language, however, is not deficient in euphony, although defective in grammatical powers. It has no article, definite or indefinite; but the numeral adjective *kumi* (one), is used whenever the idea of number is prominent. The adjectives follow the noun, as do also the numerals. All nouns are understood to be masculine, unless qualified by the word *mairen* (woman or female). The pronouns are twelve in number, but have neither gender nor number, both of which must be inferred from the connections in which they are used. The verbs have mood, tense, and person, but are wanting in number.

English.	Mosquito.
Man,	waikna.
Woman,	mairen.
Father,	aize.

Mother,	yapte.
Boy,	tukta.
Girl,	kiki.
Husband,	maia.
Wife,	maia-mairen.
Head,	lel.
Hand,	mita.
Mouth,	bila.
Foot,	mena.
Blood,	tala.
House,	watla.
Thing,	dera.
Dory,	duerka-taira.
Paddle,	kuahi.
Arrow,	trisba.
Harpoon,	waisku, silak.
Gun,	rokbus.
Sea,	kabo.
River,	awala.
Water,	li.
Food,	plun.
Cassava,	yaura.
Bread,	tane.
Maize,	aya.
Fish,	inska.
Iguana,	kakamuk.
Stone,	walpa.
Sky,	kasbrika.
Sun,	lapta.
Moon,	kati.
Star,	silma.
Wind,	pasa.

Thunder,	alwane.
Earthquake,	niknik.
Island,	daukwara.
Chief,	wita.
Paint,	orowa.
Curassow,	kusu.
Dog,	yul.
Monkey,	ruskika, waklin.
Ox,	bip, (beef?)
Deer,	sula.
Alligator,	tura.
Manitus,	palpa.
Forest,	untara.
Savannah,	twi.
Cotton,	wamuk.
Palm-tree,	hatak.
Mahogany,	yulu.
Cocoas,	duswa.
I,	yung.
Thou,	man.
He,	wetin.
This,	baha.
That,	naha.
Other,	wala.
To drink,	diaia.
To eat,	piaia.
To run,	plapia.
To paddle,	kaubia.
To laugh,	kikia.
To speak,	aisaia.
To hear,	walaia.
To sleep,	yapaia.

1,	kumi.
2,	wal.
3,	niupa.
4 (2+2,)	walwal.
5,	matasip.
6,	matlalkabe.
7 (6+1),	matlalkabe puri kumi.
8 (6+2),	matlalkabe puri wal.
9 (6+3),	matlalkabe puri niupa.
10 (5×2),	matawalsip.
11 (5×2+1),	matawalsip pura kumi.
20 (20×1),	iwanaiska kumi.
21 (20×1+1),	iwanaiska kumi pura kumi.
30 (20×1+10),	iwanaiska kumi pura matawalsip.
37 (20×1+10+6+1),	iwanaiska kumi pura matawalsip pura matlalkabe pura kumi.
40 (20×2),	iwanaiska wal.
100 (20×5),	iwanaiska matsip.

THE END.

www.ingramcontent.com/pod-product-compliance
Lightning Source LLC
LaVergne TN
LVHW010144110826
845151LV00002B/423

* 9 7 8 1 4 2 5 5 3 8 1 6 3 *